RESURGENT INDIA

RESURGENT INDIA

Edited by

Prabhat Jha

Ocean Books Pvt. Ltd.

ISO 9001:2015 Publishers

Published by
Ocean Books (P) Ltd.
4/19 Asaf Ali Road,
New Delhi-110 002 (INDIA)
e-mail: info@oceanbooks.in

ISBN 978-81-8430-201-1
RESURGENT INDIA
Edited by Shri Prabhat Jha

Edition
2025

Price
₹ 800.00 (Rupees Eight Hundred only)

Printed at
Narula Printers, Delhi

India will move Forward

'RESURGENT INDIA' is the flight of our imagination. It encompasses the elements of science, sacrifice, god, religion, spirituality and knowledge and it can institutionalise a human being into god from within the common citizens and society. Nation pervades our soul, mind and heart. We have always kept this sense alive. We have neither lost sight of our culture nor shut ourselves to new ideas. This collection has the vision of a Bharat singed with the sensitive spirit of *Antyodaya*, moving up and fast.

Acharya Narendra Dev had defined culture as the cultivation of heart and soul. This is a perennial process. It can neither be missed nor can it be halted. On the one hand, there is the *Saadhna* of man's labour, his vision and inner consciousness and, on the other, he has to suffer the pain and pleasure of life and has to be face to face with the composite environment. Whether be the cultivation of the land or of the human mind, it ushers in harmony and coordination between man and man in the world. It is a vow to remain always constructive in approach, thinking and action.

The picture of the society can not be framed by ignoring the human being and his mind. Equality, collectivism, and coordination are the special characteristics which turn a person into a human being. Without an element of humanity in his heart, no one can be a human being.

Today's situation in the country give rise to many questions which continue to be raised every now and then but lead us nowhere near to a solution. The country is passing through the same phase which it, more or less, went through immediately after independence. We inherited the problem of potable drinking water, education, health and hygiene from our British rulers and we continue to suffer the same today. We have failed to provide these essential amenities to the people so far.

If we look for reasons, our policies turn out to be the only culprit. It is not that no effort was ever made. The reality is that efforts were made but not seriously with a sense of honesty. Whatever has been done was upset by the dragon of ever-rising population. Consequently, the results of our efforts have got eclipsed.

We have to hang our head in shame when in kavi sammelans our country is painted in the following words:

> ***"kal numayish mein mila tha chithde pehne hue,***
> ***maine poochha naam to bola ki Hindustan hai".***

(Yesterday, I found a person in tatters, when asked, he said my name is Hindustan.)

This harrowing picture of the country makes us sit up and think about an alternative. To our regret, in the six decades of our independence we have so far failed to develop a frame work that could emerge as an alternative towards finding a solution of our problems. We took many vows but never cared for the alternatives. Instant solution of a trouble can result in a political way out, but it can never usher in a permanent social solution. What India needs today is not a political patch work, but social resolution of our troubles.

A citizen is much superior and higher than a vote. We celebrated our independence and republic days every year, but did never have a true monitoring and evaluation of the working of our republic. The statistics on paper took us to heights we never conquered. In the process it was the country that suffered. There was erosion of social relations too. Those who were our own continued to fall apart and those who were never ours could never be our own.

We were not what we have become today. What we are today will not be the same tomorrow. It is human nature to keep moving for the better. Before we take our first step in any direction, we have to think first and it is only after that that we take the next step. Now is the time to think, act and move fast. We did a lot of thinking but we lagged behind when it came to action. Today we have to frame a line of action that renders us free from our multi-faceted problems.

We are so much lacking in sense of nationalism that sometimes it looks as if the country is not ours and we are not of the country. Cooling off in our warmth of feelings of love for the country is a bad omen. To us our country is our mother. For us, even our rivers, our hills, the cow, the sacred Ganges are our mothers. We exist only as long as our country lives.

The country surrounded by numerous problems all over is a matter of grave concern for people here, there and everywhere. The scene is very depressing. We have reports of deaths because of lack of water, because of hunger, shortage of night shelters in freezing cold with nothing to put on. Lakhs of children are suffering from malnutrition. There is hell of a life around flowing sewers, slums on the two sides of railway tracks, children begging, helpless patients dying in the corridors of hospitals. The agricultural fields are parched, the ponds and tanks have dried up. Cows and cowsheds are disappearing. There is endless migration from villages as a result of which the population of cities and towns is swelling enormously. Industries and handicrafts are shutting down. Sarva Shiksha Abhiyan campaign is in doldrums. Efforts are being made to sell the Father of the Nation's name. Relations are getting weakened; the institution of family is getting disrupted and there is threat from our own blood relations. Clouds of mistrust are hovering over the whole society. There is foul play with the Constitution for political and electoral purposes. People are moving away from sense of nationalism. There is over emphasis on rights, and duties are being ignored. Bharat has been hurt with attacks on culture and Indian-ness. People's faith is shaking. There is threatening intrusion and encroachments on borders and the Bharat Mata is crying amidst threats from within and outside. The problems that surfaced at the time of independence still continue to torment us, be it the Article 370, or getting areas under illegal occupation by Pakistan liberated, or the problems in North-East, or of national language, national song and national religion. The controversies have not abated. There is danger to the very existence of the holy Ganges. The Yamuna is almost dried up. River Saraswati has disappeared. Democracy is suffering from the pangs of dynasticism.

We are first in poverty and at the top in corruption. 70 per cent of population cannot afford to spend more than Rs. 20-25 per day on its living. We have not been able to get rid of our social evils. The gulf of disparities is fast widening. Sense of equality and of affection is on the wane. Social harmony and collectivism are getting ignored. All these points are vying for an answer.

We are Bharatiya because there is Bharat. It is, therefore, necessary that the sense of nationalism, sense of duty should always be supreme in our minds.

Nirmanon ki katha sankshipta hamari hai.
jo ab tak ho jana tha uski tayyari hai.

(The story of our nation building is very short what should have been done by now is still being planned.)

We are still struggling to achieve what we should have attained much earlier. What we see on the surface of reality is the opposite of what is there on paper. We discover that we have not moved forward but pushed back. There is nothing unusual in the problems of hunger, want, health, hygiene, water supply and education. But what is unusual is that our efforts have not borne fruit because these had not been honest and sincere. We erred when we thought that our fight for freedom is the last struggle we have to wage and nothing would be left to do thereafter. This made our steps stagger. We wanted to attain our goal but reached somewhere else.

It is true that the government does not possess a magical wand to solve the problems facing the nation overnight, with one stroke. The root cause of our problems is the education system, lack of national sense and of maturity in thought. We need to raise a generation that gives priority to performance of duty over stressing for rights. We have to inject inspiration to infuse the sense of nationalism and sense of belongingness to the nation. The government defaulted here. It should have been done much earlier. This blunder of a few moments is costing the nation so heavily and it has to suffer for centuries together. We are citizens of a nation whose Father, wearing a *langoti,* was strong enough to push the mighty British out of this sacred land. Our non-violence is more deadly than the stroke of violence. India is a nation of sentiments. Unfortunately, its people are hard put to beg for crumbs of food. We have everything, yet we continue to be orphans. Politicians only indulged in politics and had no vision or policy to solve the problems of the nation. The intentions of the rulers too were not sincere and that is why they could not get support from others. We have been able to locate water on the moon but the throats of those in the country are still dry.

The quest for a Resurgent India should be a continuous and perennial process. It is the very first step for any programme of action.

We need to instil a sense of faith instead of doubt. It is a message of the spirit of *Antyodaya*. It spreads out the fragrance of collectivism, coordination, morality and steadfastness. It is a ray of hope. It holds a mirror to man's conduct, behaviour and nature. Everybody does not possess this quality.

India has the capability to present an alternative system to the world. The message of *Vasudhaiv Kutumbakam* (The whole world is one family) originated from this land only. *Satyamev Jayate* (Truth will prevail) also echoed from this very sacred land of ours. Faith in the concept of *Dharmachakra Pravartnaye* is visible only in India and nowhere else.

Nature has been very benevolent to us; it gave us everything, but not for its exploitation. A tree never pleads: don't cut me. But it does plead a number of times: plant another tree. We forgot to plant trees and we cut so many that the whole environment got affected. This is the fault of man. We have to move forward by making nature flourish. To create a new Bharat, we have not only to discuss the ways and means, but also to act on what comes out of our deliberations.

The 'Resurgent India' which is in your hand is the result of collective efforts. Resurgent India is not the only one. In preparing it, constructive efforts of many practitioners of word, worhsippers of Saraswati and those saints who are engaged in taking Bharat Mata to the highest level have been employed.

It is not the last form of Resurgent India but we have just moved two steps in that directions. Resurgent India will always keep waiting for you as it has to move towards solutions. It has to find new ways towards solutions. Only those can move in this direction who have sense of duty and those who are alert towards national duty. I am very glad in handing over this effort to you.

—PRABHAT JHA

(MP and BJP National Vice-President)

Contents

Liberhan Commission Report

A compilation of Howlers, Tragedy of Errors

—**Arun Jaitley**

If I do be more realistic as to what the Liberhan Commission Report is, as is apparent from the ATR, it is a report which is devoid of any credibility, it is a report which is an exercise in futility, it is a report which almost all the major media in this country has referred to as a dud report, a report which the ATR itself indicates is an unimplementable document! But, if I go into each of the 999 pages of this report along with its annexures, factually, I cannot help but saying that this report is a slur on a fact finding process in the last seventeen years.

- The first question which comes to light is: Why did it take seventeen years for a Commission to come to a recommendation which is being referred to as a dud recommendation?
- Was this opportunity being used by the gentleman who headed the Commission only to perpetuate self-employment?

There are probably indications coming from a former Cabinet Secretary, who dealt with him, to the effect that this was true. I do not want to go much into the leakage of the document. But the manner of its leak is almost as dubious as the contents of this Report. The Home Minister has categorically stated that neither he nor any of his officers leaked the Report. In fact, he was so cautious, he said that the only copy they had was in the lock and key. That is why perhaps the ATR was very difficult to make because the report was in the lock and key. When the leak took place I mentioned there was one other copy available perhaps with the Commission itself. After I read the Report, I must correct myself. I think it was not one but two copies available outside the Home Ministry. One was, perhaps, with the Chairman of the Commission, and the second as is apparent from the contents of its Report with the defacto author of the Report. When I say de facto author, I think if the Law Minister, Shri Veerappa Moily, takes a leaf out of this Report and one of his proposed law reforms to expedite pendancy of arrears in the Legal Justice system, it would be judgement out-sourcing and this is what the Report seems to have done, and the intrinsic evidence of who wrote the report is in the report itself.

The ATR itself indicates that it is an unimplementable document except for saying 'agreed', 'noted' or 'agreed with some political observations of the judge', all that the ATR says, is: The Communal Violence (Prevention, Control and Rehabilitation of Victims) Bill be legislated. A Bill on which the Central Legislature may perhaps have no legislative jurisdiction and then it further says that some matters will be referred to the UPSC and some matters will be referred to the Election Commission. The author appears to be somebody else. We are all familiar, perhaps, more with the language a judge writes. The first training of a judge is never to enter the political ticket. He looks at the evidence, he looks at the issue which he has to decide, and he links the evidence with the issue and comes to a conclusion. He does not go into political disputes. He does not start commenting on ideologies as to which ideology is good and which is bad. If a judge does that, it becomes a Commission which is not fact finding but a Commission with an ideology, and in this case, just let us read what the Commission says in the last paragraph of its Report on page 999. I am not only referring to the various political statements he has made. My friends in the Left will be very pleased that the draft person of the Report took some inspiration from Karl Marx and said, 'Religion is the opium of the masses.'

After the Commission went on for hundreds of sittings and for 17 years, the judge and the advocate assisting the judge, according to the *Hindustan Times*, has leaked out documents with his name mentioned in which he says that the IB Report is available with the Commission prior to 6th of December, 1992. So, the Judge and the earlier advocate, Mr Gupta, probably had differences. The Commission goes on to pass strictures against Mr. Gupta saying that he betrayed his trust. So, after the evidence was recorded, the entire arguments have been heard. This judge, whose familiarity with the Queen's language was somewhat inadequate, needed a draftsman. So, he gets another gentleman only for the purpose of helping him to draft the Report.

Now, what does the Report need to be done? Somebody has to go through the evidence, somebody has to get the ideas what is the direction of your findings, he has to correct and put the language in place and then he has to find who is guilty and who is not guilty. So, he is saying in the last paragraph of the Report, "Lastly, I am thankful to Harpreet Singh Giani, who has whole-heartedly spent days and nights over the last one year..." -- after the hearings were completed -- "...in helping me..." - to do what -- "...to analyse the evidence, coming to conclusions... editing the report... modifying language...adding to and modifying the ideas...to clear the mess created by predecessors."

So, Mr Giani did all these things. Mr. Giani analysed the evidence, he came to the conclusions, he gave the ideas, he modified the Report, he added to the language and the judge did the rest! As I said, if this is possible and the Government, in all seriousness, can say, 'we accept such a document", I think, judicial outsourcing may, perhaps, be one of the reforms that Shri Veerappa Moily should consider. He is attempting to bring down the arrears. Perhaps, that may speed up our trials and judgement writing.

This is how this document was prepared. The core question — Dr. Abhishek Singhvi was right when he said it - was who demolished this structure and what is the evidence against those people? What is the evidence against those people? Was there a conspiracy or was it a spontaneous reaction of a small group? It was possible on evidence to come to any of the findings, but the finding had to be based on the evidence and the material which was laid before the judge or the Commission. The Commission is to give a finding on evidence. The Commission is not to give a political opinion. The Commission is a truth investigator; a Commission is not a political pundit. I am afraid, this Judge, besides having outsourced the writing of this Report, and either he or outsourcer or the Home Ministry or anybody leaked it out, ignored the entire evidence which was placed before him and then came to a finding which was completely consistent with what was stated in the Report.

Since Dr Singhvi says that this is the 'highway.' Let us deal with this 'highway.' I can go through each one of the pages which he has mentioned. For the benefit of some of the learned friends I mention the page. There were a large number of lawyers and parties who appeared on behalf of certain Muslim organisations. The judge records at page 15, No evidence was led or information provided to the Commission with respect the conspiracy or pre-planning or the joint common enterprise by any of these counsels." So, the persons — representatives of the Muslim organisations — who are naturally aggrieved came up and said, "We have no evidence to prove any conspiracy." Then, he comes to others. At page 775 he says, "No documentary or direct evidence is not possible in a conspiracy of this manner nor unimpeachable or firm evidence of some actions of planning of demolition is available." So, I have no evidence of any planning which is available.

On page 782 the Home Secretary, Mr Godbole appears as a witness. Mr. Godbole stated that there was no information of planning and, as such, it could not be inferred that there was a conspiracy of the Congress and the BJP for demolition. This could not be accepted on the face of it, particularly, in the absence of any specific circumstances leading to such an inference.

Then come the entire Intelligence agencies of this country and everybody else who had to give materials. So, at page 992, he says, "Neither the Police nor the investigative team of the Commission, that is, neither the CBI — CBI was the police in this case — nor the investigative team of the Commission, despite the prolonged process was able to identify any witness nor produce any witness, not a single witness, who could identify any of the demolishers or lead to any other evidence against suspects. Suspects were not even identified. Even after the unprecedented publicity throughout the long spell of inquiry, nobody came forward to advance the case or identify the persons who physically carried out the demolition or the ones who plotted the demolition."

He then goes on to say at page 724, while indicting the RSS he says, "you planned it, but you kept the political leaders out of your knowledge." And, then, he says, "In totality, it becomes obvious that some leaders were consciously kept out of the operational area or planning in order to protect them and preserve their secular credentials for later political use." On the political leadership he says on page 994, "The Commission observes that important leaders of political parties — icons of movements, organisers of the movement—continuously issued statements from time to time in relation to the conspiracy of demolition, but no affidavit was filed before the Commission by any of them."

The Police led no evidence who demolished or an evidence of who plotted. The Muslim organisations which are aggrieved have no evidence. No evidence is led by any political person, not a single man is identified and you wait, merrily, for 17 years and then come to a finding that, well, yes, it could not have happened without the knowledge of X, Y and Z.

Your ideology which started in 1925 is like this. The RSS started in 1925. Your ideology inherently promotes it. Therefore, you are the person who must be accused of this. I have no evidence, not a shred of evidence against you, but I have a political opinion against you; that is why I ask myself this question. Was he a truth investigator or was he a political pundit? For some of these Commissions, heads are chosen. On important matters, you have inquiries whose precedents are cited for generations — The Vivian Bose Inquiry, the Justice Das Inquiry - these were all inquiries held in the 50s where you picked up the most illustrious sitting judge of the Supreme Court and asked him to inquire.

When Britain was shaken by the Profumo scandal, they asked Lord Denning to investigate and head a Commission. Here when the incident takes place, Congress government chooses a junior judge of the Punjab High Court. How do their eyes fall on him? There is a popular saying or a belief with all our appointment processes of judges at the Bar, when they say that there are two kinds of judges. There are those who know the law and there are those who know the Law Minister. And, I am quite clear that this judge fell in the second category, and, that is how a junior Judge of the Punjab High Court was chosen.

A Commission of Inquiry headed by a retired judge gives a Report. It has large ramifications. If you give somebody the authority to make sweeping allegations against people, then, perhaps, all the facts would also have to be gone into. A report must be a document which carries credibility. It cannot be a document which becomes the subject matter of an endless controversy. It cannot be a document which becomes un-implementable. It cannot be a document which becomes a national embarrassment. The difficulty is that you pick up a puny judge who uses 17 years to perpetrate a self-employment and then, the character of the Report almost appears to be an application for a future employment! If these are the kinds of reports these Commissions are going to give, I am afraid the credibility of the entire institution will go down. That is why, we read in newspapers, 'Judges and former judges now commenting whether judges should at all be heading such Commissions, which are to be used for entering the political thicket rather than only going into judicially determinable matters.

What does this Report say? It is probably an outsourced document – it is not like, as Dr. Singhvi says, there is one trivial error here or there; if a judge has heard the evidence and the judge is writing the Report, every fact he says will be connected to the document. I turn page after page. I was reading page 282. Who is the leader of the Ayodhya Movement against whom they tried to find evidence but could not find? It was Prof RS Sharma and Prof DN Jha, two well-known Leftist historians, who appeared on the negotiating side of the Babri Masjid Action Committee. Who is the 'kar sevak'? You are embarrassed only by the name of Mr Jagadambika Pal. So, who is the 'kar sevak'? It is Col. BS Zaidi of the Babri Masjid Action Committee. It is at page 271. Page 270 says, "Persons or leaders or Sadhus and Saints who participated in the Movement." The word 'Movement' is continuously used throughout the Report as the Ayodhya Movement. He mentions here the DGP, Intelligence. See page 69, it is elementary. You ask a primary school child what is the date of birth of Mahatma Gandhi and what is the date of his assassination, he will give it to you correctly. He gives the date of Gandhi's assassination wrong. See page 562. After spending 17 years in doing a research on the RSS and BJP as to who was the founder of the RSS, he says it was Veer Savarkar and Hedgewar only succeeded him.

He erred on basic facts and it leads to my suspicion. These are not all facts which came in the course of a hearing. Just turn to page 566. He wanted to damn the BJP. So, he said that BJP's ideology is like the Muslim League's ideology of Jinnah. That is the argument he wanted to build. So, to build up this argument, he needed a fact. At page 566, para 85.14, and this is important, he comes to a finding. He says, "Deen Dayal Upadhyaya by his conduct agreed with MA Jinnah's theory that Hindus and Muslims were two separate nations." Then, he allegedly quotes Deen Dayal Upadhyaya's saying and the quote is, "The problem of India is not inter-caste, it is international. If peace is to reign here, the major communities must be given their own separate chunks of land. It is nothing but a mere dream to imagine that Hindus and Muslims can stay together in India as members of a composite nationality. The Muslims are not a minority community, they are a nation. They must have their own independent land and their own State." When we read this, we were all surprised how could Deen Dayalji have said this? We started researching the source of this quote and found out that he picked up the quotation of Mohammad Ali Jinnah put it in the mouth of Deen Dayal Upadhyaya and said that look the views of Deen Dayal Upadhyaya and Jinnah are the same. Government wants the whole country to treat this Report with any sense of seriousness. He picks up Jinnah's quotation, puts it into Deen Dayalji's mouth and said that look their views appear to be similar. Then he suddenly realises that it is not his quote. No judge who hears the case, who hears the evidence and then on the basis of that evidence gives findings on facts, will ever come to a conclusion of this kind.

At ten places he says that 'there is no evidence of conspiracy' and then says, "I think, this couldn't have happened without conspiracy.' He has a huge bias against the whole idea of a Ram Temple at Ayodhya. He has a huge bias against social justice and the Mandal Commission. I would like the Home Minister to read these two paragraphs at page 556. No judge who writes on judicially determinable matters would give a political discourse of this kind. "Our leadership must step forth and with more equal responsibility and put a lid on the mischievous element in the society bent upon exploiting the factors referred to above, for their individual aggrandisement through repression, misguidance, acquiring power through mass means and improper reliance on philosophies such as Hindutva, Mandal, sons of soil, etc."

Commission says, "Mandal is a divisive philosophy. You must not rely on Mandal as a political leadership of this country." Mandal recommendations are something which have almost been unanimously accepted by this country and implemented. The judge has a bias on his past reservations and postings. How was this connected?

The issue is, the gentleman investigating the facts and circumstances leading to the events on 6th December, 1992, now has a whole theory on Mandal. It is not an isolated observation. Read recommendations on page 970. Read the two paragraphs together, that is, para 173.8 and para 173.9. In para 173.8, he says that the recruitment policy of the Government of India must change. Recruitment must be on merit alone. He does not want to lose over Mandal here. He has said it in the body of the Report. He says, "merit alone", and in next paragraph, he says, "The civil servants, who are posted at the helm of affairs, ought to be picked for the skills that they are required to exercise, rather than for completely unrelated academic skills or for casteist or regional basis."

The ATR says, "This recommendation will be referred to the UPSC." - para 6.6. I do not know whether these are the ideas of Justice Liberhan or the *gyan* of one *gyani* because it is still not clear as to who wrote this report.

I am only substantiating what are really the contents of this Report and I will now come to the key contents in the context of conspiracy. Just read page 540. At page 540, he now refers to the political leadership of India. The discussion starts at 539. How is it concerned with the events of 6th December and events leading to that? I will just refer to the relevant sentences and this is not on the BJP or RSS; this is on the entire political leadership of the country. I quote, "The loss of political neutrality and the convenience with which justification can be found for every action has rendered all objectives of peaceful civilised society as enunciated by intellectuals, leaders, philosophers, thinkers since ancient times, obliterated. 79.4. The law — common or constitutional, morals, ethics, epics and everything else is being examined in the scales of politically desirable results. It is immaterial whether those results are legitimate or healthy for democratic governance. Everyone is out to become a Politician rather than a Statesman." And, in the next sentence he says, "The politician has become the epitome of the proverbial rags-to-riches story. 79.5. The common Indian has formed the firm belief already that the ills that face us can be traced to the political leadership and can be cured by a voluntary reform in the political parties in India...". I repeat: Was he a truth investigator or a political pundit?

It is clear that he was dwelling on a political path not concerned about other things because when it comes to the question of who demolished it, he says that he cannot identify a single person.

After seventeen years of wasting public time and money, Commissions are not trivial errors. Dr Singhvi says, "Oh, he has made some trivial errors." You made trivial errors. But the whole Report is a compilation of howlers, the whole Report is a tragedy of errors, rather than a comedy of errors, and, there are hundreds of these kinds. What does he say about Gulzari Lal Nanda? The last I heard of Gulzari Lal Nanda was that after being the Prime Minister of this country for a short duration, he lived in a *barsati* in Defence Colony, and, he was dispossessed, and his luggage was on the road before he passed away.

About Gulzari Lal Nanda, Commission says on page 336, Rajendra Singh, the RSS leader, Dau Dayal Khanna, and, Gulzari Lal Nanda, die-hard Hindus — was there any evidence against Gulzari Lal Nanda in connivance with people with similar thoughts, started conceiving and exploiting a local dispute at the national level, maybe for their selfish political needs, — what was Gulzari Lal Nanda's political need in 1992 — or, for achieving the old theory of Hindu rashtra. He was the Prime Minister belonging to the Congress Party. When did he become a supporter of Hindu *rashtra*? If you are given to head a Commission of Inquiry, how can you pass any comment about anyone without having gone through a procedure? Some were very agitated that something has been said about Deoraha Baba, and, Dr. Singhvi said, "Oh, it is a mistake in that list of 68 people, where he uses the word 'culpable'." I am afraid that is only half-truth. Let me quote the full sentence which he has written about Deoraha Baba at page 427. "Open threats by exhorting the dacoits to take on arms for the Ram temple were made by Ashok Singhal, Deoraha Baba, and, Harishbhai". Deoraha Baba asked the dacoits to pick up the arms and come in support of Ram temple. Can the Home Minister please show us the evidence which led to this conclusion?

When the Report says that there is no evidence of a conspiracy and no facts to this effect have been established, then how come the Commission indict Shri L K Advaniji and others? Therefore, everything is not believable. It betrays the mindset of the Report. On page 23 he says that it is generally believed that Ayodhya is the birth place of Lord Ram. On page 63 he says that since 1934 no *namaz* was performed here. There is also a reference to a verdict of the British judge saying:

"It is most unfortunate that a *masjid* should have been built on a land sacredly held by the Hindus, and as it occurred 356 years ago, it is too late to remedy the grievance" Even after taking note of all these facts, Commission goes on say:

"The History books produced before the Commission as well as the White Paper of the Government of India and the BJP and the various contentions of various counsels are unanimous". There is unanimity that "In 1528, there was a Ram Janmabhoomi temple and Emperor Babar ordered Mir Baqi, his commander, to erect a mosque at Ayodhya".

(The writer is the Leader of Opposition in Rajya Sabha and an eminent jurist)

This piece is based on the speech he delivered in the Rajya Sabha

□

Reforming Governance in India

—**Jagmohan**

Meaning and Ambit

Few people understand the true meaning of the term 'governance'. Still fewer understand how deep and extensive its roots are and how inextricably it is enmeshed with the mind and soul of a nation, and its capacities in various spheres of life. Most of its definitions are rather restrictive and structural in their ambit. Governance in all its aspects, with national ethos and national capacities dug deep in its outward frame, is seldom considered.

The span of governance, it needs to be fully understood, extends to the entire canvas of the life of a nation. It involves not only administrative or managerial capacities but also social, political, intellectual, cultural and moral capacities of the system in its entirety. And the best governance machinery is the one which harnesses all these capacities and directs their focussed beam on the resolution of the problems that confront the nation. If, for example, the intellectuals provide no fresh or creative ideas or if the culture of a nation is not generative of values of honesty, dedication, compassion and the like, the quality of governance would suffer, no matter how perfect its institutional arrangements are.

Present-day India, by and large, has failed to recognise the vital role which the intellectual, cultural and moral capacities of its system play in determining the quality of its governance. It does not understand that unless the system is productive of constructive urges and is propelled by values of fairness, justice and compassion, its governance would not improve. So far, whatever little attention has been paid by the national leadership to the issues of governance has been devoted only to the framework of administration and management. That is why the Indian governance today is devoid of originality and is neither being propped up by intellectual vigour nor fertilised by the culture of service, dedication and cleanliness in public life.

India's structural frame-work, too, has many infirmities and its administrative and managerial capacities need to be improved substantially. But the cardinal flaws of its governance machinery are to be found in the total neglect of the leadership to build intellectual, cultural and moral capacities of its system and to create a reservoir of ideas and lofty ideals which could continuously lubricate it. The main challenge that India faces today in the area of governance is, therefore, three-fold:

(a) How to make structural improvements and strengthen its administrative and management frame-work.
(b) How to build, upgrade and elevate the intellectual, cultural and moral capacities of its system as a whole.
(c) How to ensure emergence of leadership at different levels of national life that could undertake and successfully complete the tasks indicated above.

Prevailing Conditions

To understand fully what I am going to say with regard to the structure of reforms and the motivational force that is required to effectuate them, it seems necessary to invite attention, albeit briefly, to the prevailing conditions in the key areas of governance.

Ideals of the Constitution and Reality

The Preamble of the Constitution, which reflects its ideals, declares: "We, the People of India, having solemnly resolved to constitute India into a Sovereign, Socialist, Secular, Democratic Republic and to secure to all its citizens...". But what is the operational reality today, after over 60 years of independence? How are the ideals of the Constitution being translated in practice?

"We, the people" are sovereign, says the Constitution. But how do we give expression to this sovereignty? By electing our representatives to legislatures who have criminal records, or who obtain money for tabling questions in Parliament, or who receive bribes for voting in the House in a particular manner, or who indulge in human trafficking, or who take oaths and other pledges only to break them with impunity, or who are too deficient in intellect to understand the complex problems of India and of the world around her!

And even when we elect a 'great' leader, we soon make him, or he himself is willing to become, a prisoner of the social and moral evils that reside within us.

So far as socialism is concerned, we cannot even make a pretence of it. A World Bank Report of 2007 has observed: "India, a country with low initial inequality, is headed for one of the fastest increases in income inequality anywhere". In a country where millions remain hungry and diseased, the combined wealth of 36 richest Indians had touched 191 billion in the year 2006.

What about the solemn pledge of making India a secular state? Has it not been turned upside-down? Are not the political parties and their leaders taking every vital decision on the basis of caste, creed and community?

Equally spurious is our democracy. T.S. Eliot, in his philosophical poem, *Choruses from the Rock*, has reflected:

"Where is Life we have lost in living?
Where is Wisdom we have lost in Knowledge?
Where is Knowledge we have lost in Information?
The cycles of Heaven in the twenty centuries
Bring us farther from God and nearer to the Dust."

I do not think it would be wrong to entertain a similar train of thought and say that we have virtually lost our democracy in the very process of establishing it. Our electoral system and the forces that propel it are the major culprits. The more the cycles of elections move, the further we recede from the true purpose of democracy.

Broken Window Syndrome

The internal security situation continues to be serious. Apart from the festering sores of Kashmir and Assam, the Naxalites are posing a grave threat. The position with regard to public order and general law and order is also far from reassuring. Lord Wavell had once observed that India could be governed firmly or not at all. The experience of the last sixty years shows that we have yet to learn the art of governing our country firmly and fairly. The soft and permissive attitude of the state is reflected in what has come to be known as the 'broken window syndrome' in governance-literature: "If a window is broken and left unrepaired, people walking by will conclude that no one cares and that no one is incharge. One unrepaired window is an invitation to break more windows, and lawlessness spreads outward from buildings to streets and then to entire communities."

Termites in the Table

Quite a few commentators of the economic scene, of late, have been observing that the optimists in India see the glass as half-full, while the pessimists see it as half-empty. However, observations of this nature, though attractive, tend to ignore a more significant aspect of Indian reality. If the table on which the glass is kept gets weaker by the day on account of its wood being eaten away by termites, it would soon collapse. The glass itself, whether half-empty or half-full, would fall to the ground and break. The massive and all-round damage that is being caused to the over-all system is bound to obliterate whatever few lines of hope that are still being seen by the optimists on the palm of India's destiny.

Political Executive and Bureaucratic Executive

Once reputed to be one of the best in the world, the civil services in India are rather in a poor state of health. After the early period of freedom, when the quality of leadership was comparatively high and influenced, though to a limited extent, by Gandhian ethics, reverse gear came into play and both politicians and administrators began their long descent to inefficiency and injustice. They began to compound each other's flaws. Performance shown in the records does not tally with the ground reality. Malpractices abound.

Superficial Concern for Reforms

The civil services and their political masters have shown a marked disposition to maintain status quo, though both of them have been talking incessantly of the reforms and the need for change. So far, about 600 Commissions and Committees, dealing with some or the other aspects of administrative reform or of the administrative machinery as a whole, have been set up from time to time by the Central and State governments. But the net outcome of these Commissions and Committees has been negligible.

Reforms in the UK and other Western Countries

How a strong leadership and favourable social and intellectual environment can cause basic changes may be seen from the developments that have recently occurred in the United Kingdom and a few other western countries. In these countries, a determined leadership came on the scene. The intellectual ferment was provided by what is known as a philosophy of the New Public Management.

And far-reaching changes took place. One of the noted scholars of the subject, Donald F. Kettl, has described these changes as "stunning in breadth and pace".

On account of constraint of space, I would deal with only one such change – a programme called Next Steps. Under this programme, a number of freestanding, semi-autonomous, executive agencies were created. The head of an executive agency was not necessarily a civil servant promoted on the basis of his seniority or performance in government service, but was chosen on the basis of competition from the best available talent in the public or private sector. The executive agency enjoyed internal flexibility and could function on the basis of business principles, adopting management practices that it considered best to secure the desired results. At the same time, it was held fully accountable for its performance and achieving key targets that were defined and laid down beforehand.

Overall, the impact of this reform was wholesome. By the end of 1997, there were 138 executive agencies, having staff strength of 325,575. The chief executives of these agencies were recruited through open competition. In 1997, about 34 per cent of them were from outside the normal civil service. They were employed on renewable, fixed-term contracts, with salaries linked to performance. They virtually constituted a new breed of civil servants, with a different culture, motivation and management skills.

The Labour government, led by Tony Blair, which came into power on May 2, 1997, did not alter the basic framework of the civil services reforms introduced by the previous regime. But it toned down the earlier dogmatic approach and presented the package in a more acceptable form – "Ms Thatcher, without a handbag".

The civil services reforms have come to stay in the United Kingdom. The new Labour government has lapped it up as much as the Conservatives of the Thatcher era and most of its attributes have been institutionalised. There is now a more open, diverse and professional civil service which is dynamic, economical and performance-oriented. Both the structure and culture of the civil services has been upgraded. The protagonists of the reforms claim, with substantial justification, that in the last 25 years or so, the UK has witnessed a quiet revolution, the biggest shake-up of the civil services.

Canada, Australia and New Zealand have also been influenced by the new public management. A set of solid reforms have been carried out. In Canada, for example, Prime Minister Mulroney declared: "If Canada is to survive and prosper, it will be in part because it enjoys the benefits of a committed, modern, flexible and professional public service. This will be one of our most important legacies to future generations".

No New Pattern in India

In India, the commitment to reforms remains skin deep. Neither the political executive nor the civil service has risen above its narrow interests. A leadership with constructive vision and iron will, like those provided by Mrs Margaret Thatcher in UK, Helmut Kohl in Germany and Lee Kuan Yew in Singapore, has not appeared on the scene.

Despite the huge pay-rise and increase in other expenditure, neither the work-culture of the employees nor the over-all productivity of the system has improved. And the game of extending mutual benefits to each other continues to be played by the political executives and the civil services. In fact, it has gained momentum. The bureaucrats are extending subtle help to the political executives to enable them to attain their political and personal ends, while the former are being rewarded for their help, albeit imperceptibly, by giving them lucrative posts, even after retirement.

It is this game of extending mutual benefits that is at the root of various afflictions which have weakened and uglified the present system of governance in India. It is this game that has caused a large number of cases of corruption to be covered up. It is this game that has enabled the powerful business houses to manipulate government decisions both at the bureaucratic and the political levels. It is this game, again, that has created a network of vested interests which has ignored even the most well-meaning reforms suggested by different high-level Commissions and Committees.

Many other unwholesome features have crept into the system. A tendency, for instance, has developed amongst the IAS officers to enlarge the field of their posting. While the progressive countries have evolved new ways and means to inject new blood in the fixed cadre system, the senior officers of the IAS have been managing to corner posts which should go to the experts in other fields. This, besides promoting unmerited elitism, has caused demoralisation to the specialists and lowered their overall capacity to do creative work. In the process, the overall potential of the nation to move forward speedily is not being tapped.

Take, for example, the post of Director-General of Archaeology. During the British regime, it was held by talented professionals like John Marshall and Mortimer Wheeler. The former remained at his post for 25 years and made a historic contribution to the task of unravelling antiquity of the Indian civilisation. About his work, it has been appropriately observed that "he left India about 3,000 years older than he found it". Currently, the post is given in routine to an IAS officer of the rank of an Additional Secretary who remains on it for a short time. He or she is either on the verge of retirement or on the look-out for a promotion to the next rank: Secretary, a 'post of crucial significance is treated like a parking lot. In the process, not only is frustration caused to the professional experts but also the opportunity to present the ancient Indian culture and civilisation in better light is lost. The damage caused is far more pervasive than can be seen on the surface.

Curing the Maladies

How do we cure a set-up which is beset with multiple disabilities? While the fundamental remedy lies in treating the inner pollution that has fouled the mind and soul of India, a few structural changes, could help in improving the system.

At the field level, special units of management and development for carrying out well-defined jobs should be established. These units could be placed for a specific period, say five years, under the overall charge of an officer who has the requisite calibre and commitment. Such an officer could be selected from private or public sector or academic institutions, by an independent statutory Board or

Commission. He could be vested with full powers to run the unit and achieve, within the framework of overall government policy and its budget provision, plans and programmes formulated for that period. He could be allowed total flexibility and freedom in executive action. If after the expiry of the fixed period, the officer is found to have under-performed, his services could be ended. In the event of his performance being good or outstanding, he could be suitably rewarded and given another five-year term. For path-breaking work, national honour could be conferred.

As an illustration of my suggestion, I refer again to the Department of Archaeology on which I have made brief comments earlier. If the Directorate of Archaeology is converted into a special unit on the lines indicated and if the Director-General is appointed for a period of five years, after selection, through an independent Board or Commission, from a wide range of candidates who may belong to any Central or State government cadre or private company or management institute or university or non-official body, he could remain on the assignment for a period of five years. He could be vested with full powers to run the department on principles of management. The only obligations that he would have to discharge would be to function within the budget provisions and in accordance with a policy that would be outlined for his guidance by the government, beforehand. At the end of the five-year term, his performance could be thoroughly evaluated. Bad performance would result in termination, good in extension and outstanding in reward.

The proposed system would yield a number of salutary results. First, it would enable the government to secure the services of the best available talent in the country for the job. The incumbent would have an opportunity to develop a deep association with a particular unit, feel proud of it, acquire expertise and even act virtually like Plato's Philosopher King, bringing into play all his special knowledge and skill. He could become a model of executional excellence all over the country.

Secondly, the new system would check the tendency towards smugness, which is generally generated by the fixed cadre of an elite service, like IAS, with reserved posts and virtually assured upward movement after a given number of years. All officers would have to stay competitive and make special efforts to upgrade their knowledge and skill. At the same time, the officers belonging to other services, academic institutions and other organisations would become conscious of the fact that they, too, could secure higher assignments by outshining members of the elite service.

Thirdly, with full power being available to the head of the unit, he would not be able to advance, at a later stage, a plea that he was handicapped by political or ministerial interference or hemmed in by rigidities of the usual bureaucratic patterns. The area of responsibility would thus be clearly defined.

Fourthly, the national set-up as a whole would become more energetic, more enterprising, more creative and more constructive, and thus help in development of a responsible and focussed leadership at crucial levels of governance.

All key field agencies of the central and state governments, all their public sector undertakings, all urban development authorities and local bodies etc need to be converted into the type of management and development units, the broad outlines and the merits of which I have indicated. If this is done, our public sector undertakings and authorities would become competitive, our field agencies would get rid of the menace of frequent transfers and acquire result-orientation.

The basic principles of New Public Management, the practical application of which in the United Kingdom and other countries I have already analysed, should be accepted. Keeping in view these principles, the pattern of special units of management and development that I have proposed, and the recommendations of the various high levels commissions and committees made from time to time, the Planning Commission should formulate its own package of concrete reforms and make it a part of the Five-Year Plan. The package should be divided into two parts — 'Obligatory' and 'Discretionary'. The latter part could be implemented by the States with whatever modifications they consider appropriate to suit the local conditions. But the implementation of obligatory part would be necessary if the States have to remain entitled to the plan assistance from the Commission in a few specified areas.

Regeneration of the Indian Mindscape

The mother of all reforms is the reform and regeneration of the Indian mindscape. After the publication of my book, *Soul and Structure of Governance in India* in 2005, I had the privilege of addressing at the India International Centre, New Delhi, a group of eminent political analysts, retired civil servants, jurists, university professors and the like. At the end of my exposition of the main theme of the book, I was asked, as is usual in such cases, a number of questions, particularly about the 'soul' aspect of governance. I replied that by soul I meant an inner controller who held the compass of life and shaped man's conscience and underpinned his thought and action and that it could be reckoned as a melody that was composed by the invisible sanctum of the mind. I also raised a counter question: "How is it that despite your repeated denunciation of corruption and malpractices in public life by way of newspapers articles and courts' judgements, and despite creation of several new institutions like Central Bureau of Investigation and Enforcement Directorate, the menace of these evils has been growing both in scale and intensity?" Since there was hardly any response, I provided what I thought was the right answer:

"All this is happening because no one in India has prepared the soil on which the seeds of constructive and noble ideals could be planted for the fruitful harvest to grow. The waste-land that India has become due to a long period of social and cultural degeneration cannot respond to even the healthiest of seeds. The primary task is to reclaim the waste-land and fertilise it with a strong dose of reform and regeneration. Then alone, exhortations of well-meaning persons would get registered on the mindscape of the common people; then alone, the institutional frame-work would attain animation and yield positive results."

Clearly, it is not possible to establish an honest administration without an honest mind or a beautiful edifice without beautiful instinct. Swami Vivekananda has rightly observed:

"You may make thousands of societies, twenty thousand political assemblages, fifty thousand institutions. There will be no use, unless there is that sympathy, that love, that heart, that thinks for all. But where is that heart to build upon? Where are the foundations?"

Fall-outs of the Debased Mindscape

The message that comes out of the past sixty years of the country's life is loud and clear. It is largely because of the debased mindscape of India that hosts of formidable problems have arisen in almost all walks of life. It is this debasement that is preventing growth of governance capacities, causing corruption to extend its tentacles in all organs of administration, giving rise to myopic and irresponsible leadership at both the Central and States' levels, letting loose forces that are fomenting subversion and terrorism and crippling the efforts of the few saner elements that still remain on the scene. Like the bull in a china shop, a loose mindscape damages every item with which it comes in contact.

History's Transmissions

Let alone the above message, what do the transmissions from history say? They tell us in no uncertain terms that every turning point in the march of civilisation has been preceded by a fundamental change in the mindscape of the people. From the mid-fifteenth century, Europe commenced its long journey from the medieval to modern age, when the Renaissance started unleashing forces that stimulated the public mind and made it intellectually vigorous, culturally sensitive and socially humane. From the awakened mind sprang the scientific temper, the spirit of inquiry, the ideas of progress and disposition to shake off the unjust impositions of the Church and the State.

Personal Experience

During my long years in public life, one common perception stood out: there were too many irons in the Indian soul and its mind had been badly clogged by the stagnant material that it had collected during the long period of degeneration that its civilisation had undergone. I noticed that it was on account of these 'irons' and 'stagnant materials' that almost all sections of the Indian society and all organs of the Indian state had become morally sick and were malfunctioning. I got convinced that unless the Indian mind was regenerated and the Indian soul freed of its impurities, the country would continue to have an irresponsible citizenry, selfish leadership and corrupt politics.

Revolution or Renaissance

Sometimes, I am driven to think that our problems are so formidable, so deep-rooted, that nothing short of a revolution would do. But India's past history and heritage show that its ethos are more in tune with renaissance than revolution.

There is a fundamental difference between revolution and renaissance. The former comes like a storm, a tornado, that sweeps everything before it – old values, old attitudes, old institutions and old edifices. It dynamites the past. But it destroys more than it constructs, and extracts a very heavy price. What is worse, more often than not, it enthrones a 'God' that may turn out to be false. It has often happened that "the scrupulous, the just, the virtuous, the noble do not remain the leader of the revolution; they become its victims."

A renaissance, on the other hand, is like a fresh breeze that flows gently into a dark and suffocating night, and begins to remove its dust and haze, giving birth to a clear dawn – a dawn that is new but not unconnected with the dawns that are now resting in the lap of history.

During the late nineteenth and early twentieth centuries, India experienced a renaissance which was at the root of its successful struggle for freedom. But it lost its verve and vitality in the post-1947 period. The social and cultural order which was undergoing a new impulse of reform and regeneration was neglected. The leaders were obsessed with politics and its power. The Gandhian attempt to inject noble strands of Indian culture in the task of all-round national reconstruction of the country was virtually thrown in the dustbin of history.

None of the leaders of any stature of the post-1947 period pondered over the fact that the social order which was dominated by the forces of obscurantism, casteism and general ignorance could produce only a weak and venal political order. In the absence of healthy social and cultural roots and with poisoned blood stream flowing in its veins, the body-politics of India was bound to develop deformities and give rise to a number of chronic ailments. And this is exactly what has happened. Every component of the state machinery is getting out of joints and exposing the system to a grave risk of total collapse. The outward facade may not look in an alarmingly bad shape, but the signals emanating from the inner recesses are ominous.

Second Renaissance

I have no doubt that if the fundamental aberrations of the State and the society have to be corrected and if the arteries of the system, clogged as they are at present with a lot of degenerate stuff, have to be cleaned up and restored to health, India would have to experience another renaissance, a renaissance which is far more potent and pervasive than the first one.

It must penetrate every nook and corner of Indian life and help in creating a new set of national ethos which would elevate its mindscape and underpin, albeit imperceptibly, all societal and state actions.

Pivotal Measure

The pivotal measure that needs to be taken to bring about another renaissance is to reform the religious order on the shoulders of which largely rests our social order which, in turn, determines our political ethos. If the religious order serves as an incubator of superstitions, dogmas and irrational practices, neither the social nor the political order would be healthy. By leaving the religious order alone, what is being left untouched by the Indian state in post-1947 period, under the cover of practicing secularism, are all the evils which entered the system during the period of decay and degeneration of the Indian civilisation. Reform of the religious order is a must if the mindscape of India has to be regenerated and if the social and political orders have to be purged of their pollutants. For doing so, reform of Hinduism, which is the religion of about 80 per cent of the Indians, must be accorded top priority. That would go a long way in fashioning out a new building-block for a new national edifice.

Reform of Hinduism

I would grade the current Hindu thought and practices at three levels. Level I would cover the core of Hinduism, that is, the ethical principles contained in the philosophy of Vedanta. These principles indicate:

i) That every individual is potentially divine and that he or she can tap this potential to enlarge his or her divinity;
ii) That every item of life and nature, of mind and matter, is inextricably enmeshed with the other and interwoven in an organic cosmic web;
iii) That there is One in All and All in One;
iv) That since every individual is part of the other, any injury to the other would also be an injury to the Self;

v) That Jiva is Shiva – service to the man is service to the God'
vi) That discovery of the Ultimate Truth is the ultimate goal of life and one should move towards that goal by continually striving to widen the aperture of one's mind and obtain a higher level and larger dimension of Truth; and
vii) That every acquisition of higher level and larger dimension of Truth would further improve one's knowledge and insight and thus result in better and better quality of life in this universe.

These seven principles as would be elaborated subsequently are, in spirit, not only wholly scientific, secular and humanistic but also generative of equality, liberty, fraternity and human dignity.

In level II would fall all the beliefs and practices which are not contrary to the basic philosophy of the aforesaid ethical principles but which came into existence in response to the religious needs of the common folk who could not grasp the intellectual content of its core and who had to depend on temples, images of gods and goddesses and their symbols.

In level III would come all the spurious rituals, rites, cults, castes, gender-discrimination, superstitions, prejudices, magic, sorcery and other degenerate stuff.

Reform of Hinduism would involve total elimination of level III, refurbishment of level II, and simplification of level I. The Vaishno Devi Temple reform is a good example of putting level II in the right orbit.

So far as level I of Hinduism is concerned, I have spelt out above its seven basic principles. These principles are in perfect harmony with the constitutional goals of liberty, fraternity, equality and justice. In fact, they provide the spiritual basis of these goals.

As regards the goal of equality, for example, if the same divinity permeates the personality of one person as well as that of another, they cannot but be equal. Likewise, it would be unthinkable for the divinity in one person to starve the same divinity in another person or do injustice to it in any manner.

If the propagation of the above principles has the State backing, they would certainly help in orienting the mind of the individual towards service, compassion, non-acquisitiveness and the realisation that he is a part of the greater Self and that he should not do anything that has the effect of injuring a part of his own Self. In other words, they would help in creating a purer and nobler heart, which, working in unison with other purer and nobler hearts, would give rise to a force that would push society and the state towards purer and nobler goals.

It has been rightly observed: 'If there is no purity, fairness and justice in your heart, these qualities will not be in your home; and if they are not in your home, they will not be in your society; and if they are not in your society, they will not be in your State.'

Corrupting both 'Ceaser' and the 'God'

The post-1947 leadership, be it in political, social, cultural or intellectual arena, has largely treated the above seven principles, which constitute the core values of Vedantic philosophy as Hindu religious values and ignored them under the mistaken notion of espousing secularism, forgetting all the time that these values are themselves necessary for making India a truly secular, humane and enlightened state, and for creating a society with character, conscience, compassion and commitment. In the inspirational vacuum, in our attempt to give unto 'Caesar' things that are 'Caesar's' and to 'God' things that are God's, we are actually doing nothing but corrupting both 'Caesar' and 'God' and entrusting our maladies for cure, not to the surgeons but to the butchers.

Reform of other Religious orders

What I have reflected and enunciated above pertains to Hinduism. But this does not mean that I am excluding Islam and other faiths from the purview of my proposition of regenerating the mindscape of India by injecting right kind of values in its society. Islam needs to be correctly interpreted, keeping in view the principles of harmonious and dynamic construction of its various tenets.

The seven principles, the parameters of which I have explained above and which embody both spiritual secularism and spiritual pluralism, are as much in harmony with correctly and constructively interpreted higher tenets of Hinduism as with the correctly and constructively interpreted tenets of Islamism or Sikhism.

Instrument of Change

Having indicated the lines on which the current religious and social orders could be reformed and their elevated values made the motivating force for running the State institutions honestly and with a sense of mission, the next question to be considered is who would bring about the necessary change. Would it be political leadership or intellectual class or social and cultural organisations or upcoming younger generation with a fresh mind and an innovative outlook? Obviously, it would have to be a combination of all these elements. Each one of them has to acquire a new motivation, a new sense of direction and act with a new zest and zeal not only in its own but also in allied fields.

For effectuating a second Renaissance, a positive interaction between healthy urges within the society and the leader who mobilises them is absolutely necessary. A truly great leader is one who commences his mission by tapping the healthy forces that are already hovering around the mind of a section of the people, organises them into a cohesive force and propels them to a higher horizon to build up a grand vision for reform and regeneration.

Renaissance Heroes

What India needs today is a great leader who would put himself or herself at the vanguard of a new renaissance which, by virtue of its own dynamics, would give rise to a band of 'renaissance heroes' in education, culture, politics and other walks of life, and fertilise and regenerate the mindscape of India.

Educational System

For emergence of 'renaissance heroes' the role of our educational system would be particularly significant. If this system is so designed that, besides promoting normal studies and cultivating scientific temper, it engenders respect for ancient nobilities of India and revulsion for products of its degenerate past, then a strong foundational plank for the second renaissance would be created.

Regeneration

Let me, in the end, reiterate that in the noble heritage of India lie embedded a powerful and profound mind and a pure and punctilious soul. The impulses generated by the combined impact of the measures and movements that I have outlined earlier would rekindle that power and reawaken that soul. With this rekindling and reawakening would commence the process of injecting fresh blood in the dying institutions of the State and society, and making them vital and vigorous.

New capacities — intellectual, moral and social — would be created in the system, and India would move from strength to strength, from imbalance to balance, from callousness to compassion, from casualness to commitment and from degeneration to regeneration.

Many of us may think that what I have suggested about regeneration is impossible. But this would be a defeatist belief, a virtual admission that we are gripped by forces we cannot control. Our problems are man made, therefore, they can be solved by man. And man can be as big as he wants. "No problem of human destiny", as John F Kennedy once observed, "is beyond human being".

(The writer is a former Governor of J&K and a former Union Minister)

□

Worth throwing in to the Bay of Bengal

—M. Venkaiah Naidu

With the death Shrimati Indira Gandhi, her plan suffered a setback with regard to Ayodhya. Her son took over as Prime Minister and another colleague of his took command of the Ayodhya matter. From then on, a series of disastrous steps followed. Until the court order, the temple agitation remained almost a unilateral affair; but the opening of the locks triggered off a great deal of controversy. Many described it as a State managed affair which proceeded with undue haste to pre-empt the VHP plan. Compare it with the lightning speed with which the case filed by an unknown advocate was heard and disposed of. Within hours of passing of the order, the temple was unlocked and even the Doordarshan cameramen were present to cover the occasion which was widely telecast across the country.

How did this case move at this speed? How did the Government acquiesce in this case? How did the Faizabad locks open, in a matter of two days, when the Hindus have been pleading for nearly 37 years? How did the Doordarshan cameras click the opening of the locks within an hour of the court orders? These are not Venkaiah Naidu's words. These are the words of the then Prime Minister of India and the Congress President, who said that with the demise of Indira Gandhi, her son took over as Prime Minister and a colleague of his took command of the Ayodhya matter, and from then on a series of disastrous steps followed. The Commission had no time even to look into this matter. The Commission had no time even to inquire into the sitting Prime Minister at that time. This is from the book of Shri PV Narasimha Rao, '*Ayodhya 6th December, 1992*'. All my friends are saying no, it was a misjudgement, wrong judgement. If it was a wrong judgement, none of the Congress leaders had the guts to stand up and say that it was a wrong judgement. Even the present Home Minister, even the present Prime Minister, even many of the present Ministers, they were all there in that Government and they happily enjoyed the power. Suddenly, now it occurs to them that it is a national shame. At that time, they were calm. Now they say, Shame. What is this? Who are they trying to deceive in the country? Who did all these things, is a matter of history. Simply, this report is not even worth reading by any human being.

This Report has no support. Everybody has condemned this Report. This is a commissioned Commission. It suffers from absence of facts and it is full of politicking. The Report has no legal support. I do not know why a learned man like Shri Kapil Sibal was, time and again, referring to a document which has no legal validity, which is full of politics, sermons, preaching and teachings without even knowing the fundamentals of politics and public life of the country. The Congressmen are dumbfounded after Shri Arun Jaitley debunked the Report. They have no answer whatsoever. They cannot rebut any of the points raised by him. So they start now talking about others, sadhus and saints and then make comments about them. From the day one I had the doubt that this Report was outsourced to somebody. I am wondering who is the man who prepared this Report. *Giani* or *agiani*? There are so many factual mistakes in the Report. He does not know when the RSS was started. He does not know who was the founder of the RSS. He himself has named the founder of the RSS. Fortunately, he did not say that he himself was the founder. He can say that also.

This Report deserved to be thrown into the Bay of Bengal. We have seen so many Commissions in this country. Truth has become an omission; facts were given remission and assumptions and presumptions are the emissions in the Report. His conclusions conflict with evidence. These 17 years mean 6,036 days. Every day has 24 hours and every hour has 60 minutes and every minute has 60 seconds. What was this man doing for all these years? I do not know whether he was writing 000.6 pages per day and spending this valuable time. In contrast, see the Shah Commission. It was appointed on 28.5.1997. The number of sittings they held was 100, the number of complaints recorded was 46,261 and the proceedings were completed by

31.12.1998. Within one year and six months the entire report was prepared and then given to the Government. What did this great champion of Commissions do at that time? They have disbanded the Commission after coming to power. We also could have done it. But we did not do it.

We are *Ram Bhaktas*. If that is our fault, then, let it be so. It is like digging a mountain and catching a mouse. The Liberhan Report is a Report for the vote bank politics. It is a Commission which was wrong on every front. To be frank, there is nothing left in the Commission to speak about. It is because the Report is full of mistakes and these were pointed out by Parliamentarians and senior legal luminaries alike in the country.

Commission has imagined things. Shri Sunder Singh Bhandari, Shri Sikander Bakht and other senior leaders were in Delhi. He imagined things and took them to Ayodhya. The Chief Secretary was taken there. The Chief Minister was taken there. He changes the founder of the RSS. He changes the philosophy of Deen Dayal Upadhyaya and, suddenly, brings in Jinnah, and inserts it. What sort of a Commission is it? I can understand some small, small mistakes, grammatical mistakes, or, some historical mistakes here and there. But, on each and every front, there is total ignorance. What did the important people say about this Commission? Shri MN Buch, a former civil servant, said, "If there is any justice in the world, then, Liberhan and others must be made to cough up Rs.8 crores spent on the Commission." This is the recommendation made by a senior civil servant.

"It is an idiotic report." This is the opinion of our senior colleague, who is also a veteran journalist, Shri Arun Shourie. "The Report must be consigned to the archives at the earliest to avoid political damage." This is the opinion of Shri Arun Nehru, who was a part of the ruling class. "The Liberhan Report is a thousand-page gossip." This was said by Shri Cho M Ramaswamy. It has now become a *tamasha* in the country to appoint Commissions. Whatever credibility the Commissions of Inquiry had earlier, when we compare the Thakkar-Natarajan Commission and this particular Commission, I dont think, anybody in this country will henceforth accept appointment of any Commission of Inquiry to go into any matter. This is the greatest service Mr Liberhan has done for this country. He has brought so much discredit, not only to the Commissions of Inquiry but also to the Report that nobody is going to ask for it any more. In a way, this is the best service he has rendered to the country.

How has this leakage taken place? Is there a package behind the leakage? Why was it done? He had one copy and the other was with Shri Liberhan, who prepared this report. There must have been one copy with his assistant. Now from where did the copy go into the hands of the journalist friends and to the electronic media? The Government really brought shame to Indian Parliament on such a sensitive matter.

There was selective leakage. The idea at that time was to divert the attention from the spectrum, divert the attention from Madhu Koda, divert the attention from price rise and the strike of sugarcane farmers of Uttar Pradesh and, subsequently, of other parts of the country. Government tried to divide the Opposition parties because everybody, in the Opposition, has got his or her point of view. So, that was the purpose.

For six months the Government was never bothered about the Report. Instead of that, Government passed it on to some selective friends in the media and made the Parliament a mockery. The country became a laughing stock.

This Report has chosen to defame the highest court of the land, the Supreme Court, and yet people in the government claim, 'great Report, great man'. It is a non-sense. This government defamed every institution; it defamed all the sadhus and saints in the country.

"No Conspiracy"

The Congress White Paper on Ayodhya says, "No conspiracy". It is not BJP White Paper. It is Congress Government's White Paper. The, then Home Minister, father of the present Chief Minister of Maharashtra, Mr SB Chavan says, "There was no conspiracy". Shri Satyanarayana Reddy, the former Governor, serving at that time in Uttar Pradesh says, "No conspiracy". The IB told the Supreme Court, "No conspiracy". The CBI ruled out any conspiracy and the charge-sheet filed in the court did not have any charge of conspiracy. The Bahri Tribunal set up by the Government to review the ban on RSS came to the conclusion, "There is no evidence to suggest any conspiracy and quashed the ban on the RSS." It was a slap on the face of the

Congress Government at that time. The Trial Court of Rai Bareilly in its judgement in 2001 has dismissed the conspiracy charges against the leaders of the movement in the year 2001. But now, surprisingly, the Government says that there is a conspiracy. Government has no faith in the court, but trusts only its own person, the person who is defaming the Supreme Court.

The UP Government filed an affidavit in the Supreme Court stating that the charge that demolition of the structure at Ayodhya was done under criminal conspiracy by any specific community or political party is wrong and denied. The Allahabad High Court upheld the trial court order. The order was then challenged in the Supreme Court. The Supreme Court did not give any adverse judgement. The Supreme Court refused to intervene in this matter in 2009. So, legally, there is no conspiracy.

Everybody — the Governor, the Supreme Court, the High Court, the lower court, the CBI, the IB, the White Paper, the then Home Minister, the then Central Government at that time -- says there is no conspiracy. Now, after the demise of the former Prime Minister, a former Congress President, the ruling family does not like that man who is no more.

Foreign invaders always construct churches to demonstrate their political victory over the country. I humbly submit that I am not a regular religious person; I was president of the BJP, I am a senior member of the party. I can confide to you, that I am not a person who performs regular *pooja*. At the same time, we need no certificate of 'secularism' from the ruling party and other so-called 'secularists'. In my own village Kasimoglu, there is a Mastanwali Dargah. As a family, we all go there. My father's name was Mastanaiah Naidu. His brother's name is Pedda-Mastanaiah Naidu, elder Mastanaiah Naidu. We live together. We go to the Dargah. They come to the temples. We live together. This is the tradition of India. Then, how has this tradition been broken? Efforts are being made to create ill-will in the minds of the people to show that something has happened. There are 20 more mosques in Ayodhya. Not even one was touched! Why? There was no frenzy to destroy mosques. That is why no other mosque was touched in Ayodhya by any of these people, over all these years. Why this particular structure?

Mr Arnold Toynbee a great historian of the century, while

addressing the Azad Memorial lecture, said, "While I have been speaking. Some vivid visual memories have been flashing in my mind and one of these is a mental picture of the Principal Square in the Polish city of Warsaw, some time in the late 1920s. In the course of the first Russian occupation of this city, the Russians built an Eastern Orthodoxcathedral on this central spot in the city, that had been once the capital of independent Roman Catholic Christian country Poland. The Russians had done this to give the Poles a continuous ocular demonstration that the Russians were now their masters. After the establishment of Poland's independence in 1918, the Poles had pulled this cathedral down. The demolition had been completed just before the date of my visit. I do not blame the Polish Government for having pulled down the Russian church. The purpose for which the Russians had built it had not been religious but political and the purpose should also have been intentionally offensive."

Theocracy Alien to India

Warsaw is a historical fact. It is a famous historian who was speaking in Azad Memorial Lecture. BJP believes that theocracies are alien to our history. India being secular is not because of Indira Gandhi or Atal Behari Vajpayee or this Government or that Government. It is because of the blood of the people of this country. People who want to think on religious lines have gone to Pakistan. They have chosen Pakistan as their motherland. But the remaining people thought that this *Bharat Mata,* this India to be their country and that they should live here. There is no discrimination on the basis of religion in this country; some people are trying to create false propaganda and arouse the feelings of the people. What happened in 1527 is that the invader who came from outside destroyed the Rama temple. Lord Ram is adored by millions and millions of people across the country. The entire world adores Him. There is *Ramayana* festival even in Indonesia and everywhere. There is Garuda Airlines in Indonesia. There is the Kubera Bank in Indonesia. There is picture of Ganesha on the currency. Some time back, after seeing this, I asked them, 'What is this? What is your religion?' They said, 'Our religion is Islam.' I asked, 'Then, what is all this?' They replied, "they are our ancestors, our forefathers". That is the respect Rama commands everywhere in the world. That is why Mahatma Gandhi wanted to usher in Ram-

Rajya in the country. That is why, Rajiv Gandhiji, after performing *Shilanyasa*, started a campaign for *Ram-Rajya* at that time.

Is speaking about Rama something communal? This Government has the support of the people who ridiculed Rama, who ridiculed Rama Setu, who also raised doubts on the very existence of Rama. The Government filed an affidavit in the Supreme Court and later it had to take it back. That is the situation. It is true our approach is different and government approach is different. Let us agree to disagree. It is a democracy and there is nothing to feel ashamed of. What is there to feel shamed? I would like to know, if somebody from outside comes and then constructs something, and he asks, 'who are the people'. It is the people of India. Who demolished it? It is the people of India belonging to all hues, the *kar sevaks* and the other people who gathered there. They all did it because the matter is getting delayed for years together and political parties are using it for political ends. The Congress Party got the locks opened. The Congress Party allowed *pooja*. The Congress Party took the Doordarshan staff there to show it to the entire country saying that, 'see, we have allowed *pooja*.'

In 1984, when thousands of Sikhs were massacred in Delhi, what was the reaction? The Congress leaders need to search their soul. It was then said that when a big tree falls, the earth below shakes. If a big banyan tree falls, then the earth shakes. Was it not all planned? We talk about not one person but about the belief of millions of the people across the country and the world. But it is we who are branded communal! Who? This Government has been friendly with the Muslim League. It has an alliance with Mazlis-e-Ittahadul-Muslimeen. Alliance with those who oppose *Vande Mataram*, with those who object to *Saraswati Vandana*. Congress does all these things and then attributes in reverse to the Bharatiya Janata Party. Shri Chidambaram said the other day, "the National Executive in 1991 recorded its appreciation of the attempts made by some Shia leader to persuade the community that it was contrary to the tenets of Islam to have a mosque built upon a place of worship of another religion and that therefore, the site of dispute should be handed over to the Hindus and the mosque should be built at some other suitable place". Let the people decide who is communal and who is secular.

The President of India went to do *shilanyas* at the Somnath Temple there. Was he communal? Was that not destroyed by foreign invaders? What Congress preaches is not secularism but peculiarism. Now the Liberhan Commission says that religion should not be used for the sake of politics. If there is one party which is using religion for the sake of politics, number one is the present ruling party. My charge is that Congress has an alliance with Muslim League. Can Congress say that Muslim League is a secular party? Great! BJP is communal, Muslim League is secular. Mazlis-e-Ittahadul-Muslimeen is a secular party to Congress.

Shri Chidambaram claims people voted for Congress in 2004 and 2009 and rejected BJP. Babri incident had happened in 1992. There were elections in 1996, there were elections in 1998 and there were elections in 1999. Congress and many of their allies were rejected by the people. BJP and its allies got the majority and ruled the country for six years. What did we do when we got an opportunity to rule at the Centre? We gave the people air connectivity, rail connectivity, highway connectivity, rural connectivity, telecom connectivity, television connectivity, port connectivity and we got political connectivity with all parties together in the North, South, East and West. That is what we have done. We have taken every party along with us.

There has been an abnormal delay. Even now the best way to settle the issue is, we have to live together. We have to work together. We have to take the country forward. We cannot look back forever continuously to the pages of earlier history; though we should not forget history. Why, during the VP Singh Government, during Chandrashekharji, during Narasimha Raoji, Sadhus, Saints, VHP and Babri Action Committee were called for discussion? It was to find out an amicable solution and also, time and again, you are giving some space for poojas in 2 odd-acres which was declared as undisputed area. There was no problem in that.

The Government records, the Gazette, the White Paper, the official statement all mention the disputed site as Ram Janambhoomi. In the site map of Ram Janambhoomi-Babri Masjid Complex, Ayodhya, Faizabad, UP there is Sita Rasoi Temple. It is in the Report. There is Seshavtar Temple. Is such a temple in a mosque? Then, there is Ramacharitamanas Trust. Then, there is the Hanuman Mandir. Then, there is the Ram Chabutra. Then, you have a number of institutions which are functioning within this area. In Ayodhya, there are so many other temples. We believe that it is the birthplace of Lord Rama. In this country, Rama is a household name. Rama is Maryada Purushotama.

Shri Lal Krishna Advani did the greatest service to this nation for the cause of country's unity by bringing in the concept of cultural nationalism. He is the man in Indian politics who tore the pseudo-secularists and vote-bank politicians into pieces. We are proud of Shri Advani. We are proud of our leader Shri Atal Bihari Vajpayee. We are proud of our colleagues. There is no doubt about it. We are proud of our association with Ram Janmabhoomi Movement. We want to see that there is a magnificent temple in the birthplace of Lord Rama. But, at the same time, we have no disrespect for Muslims or Christians. We want to have their mosque at a suitable place. We are not asking for handing over all the temples which were destroyed earlier. There is a psyche of Hindus also who are majority in this country. Unfortunately, they have to come to streets and they have to take up agitation. Is it the respect that you have for Hindus? Secularism does not mean irreligiousness. Secularism does not mean anti-Hindu. But, some parties, some people in this country, unfortunately, say, anti-Hindu means, secularism. If you talk of Hindutva, it is wrong. What is wrong in Hindutva? Hindutva is a way of life. That is what the Supreme Court said. The highest court of the land said this. Sir, the Supreme Court said that Hindutva is synonymous with *Bharatiyata*.

What is wrong with this? Muslims, Christians, Hindus, are all there in the country. We are all one irrespective of caste, creed, sex and religion. India is one, one nation, one people. Even if I go one step forward and I want to exceed, a Common Civil Code like in the State of Goa should come to the country, at the earliest, after an agreement by all the people.

I have list of places where communal tensions have taken place from 1947 to 1990. Thousands of people lost their lives. Do you want this to continue further? Or, do you want a permanent friendship, understanding, harmony between the two sections of society? Do you want to perpetuate this sort of psychology and continue your vote bank politics or do you want to address the core issue? Settle this issue once and for all. Forget it. Stop this ritual. Every 6th December, some demonstration takes place, somebody comes on to the streets and then some protests take place and some incident happens. Stop this ritual. Be realistic.

Let the Congress Party be frank. Let it say, yes, we will reconstruct the disputed structure. If not, why do you deceive the people?

Let us come to an understanding. Put an end to this, which you know pretty well that nobody is going to do anything. For 50, 60 years, courts also did not do anything. One of the courts said that it is not a matter which is justiciable. It cannot go into the beliefs of the people of this country. It is a dispute about a site of 2.3 acres. Give and take approach should be there, because we want to live together, we want to live happily, we want to prosper, we want to compete with the so-called great countries of the West or the other countries and we want to become a strong nation.

So, please allow a proper atmosphere for construction of a Great Rama Temple there. Let us be proud of it and wherever other places of worship are there, we all go there. I go to Kerala; I go to famous churches; it is part of our history and I go to some other places, in my own village. I am going to a Dargah, Ajmer Dargah Sharif. Thousands of Hindus go there.

If you want harmony, if you want social harmony, there is only one way. But if you want to derive political points like this even after 17 years and if you want to bring that back and then want to settle the scores, then be sincere, If government wants to try us, to punish us, come on, do it; but dont base it on a waste paper like Liberhan. Have something concrete and then come forward. We know how to fight it out; we have seen many such things; the RSS has also seen many such onslaughts. It is a democratic country.

The country has a history of Emergency; 1,60,000 people were put behind bars. What has happened to the perpetrators of Emergency? That part of history I need not explain. I am also one of the products of Emergency; I was in jail for seventeen-and-a-half months. We came back; fought against authoritarianism, and, finally, the people accepted democracy. So, that is the principle. So, please be sincere, don't try to offend the feelings of the majority community in the country and don't try to mislead the minority community of the country as if something is happening to them.

Whether it is minority or majority, they are equal part of this country. We had six Presidents; Dr Zakir Hussain Sahib; Fakhruddin

Ali Ahmed Sahib; then you have Bharat Ratna Abdul Kalamji, President of this great country; and then you have Mohammad Hidayatullahji, the former Chief Justice of Supreme Court; you have Air Marshal Latif; you have Mohammad Azharuddin, the former Indian Cricket Captain. They are all the products of India, not of Pakistan. It is because they have the talent not because of Muslim or Hindu; but because they are the icons for many people in this country. That is the spirit of India. Don't spoil the spirit of India. Dont try to create divisions further. Don't bring in communal reservations. Communal reservations is against the wish of Jawaharlal Nehru; Late Rajiv Gandhi, even Mahatma Gandhi; Sardar Patel and Dr Ambedkar. They all opposed communal reservation. You want to bring communal reservation now. You want to have communal budgeting now. What is this! 'Justice to all, appeasement of none' — that is our motto.

(The writer is the President of Dr Mookerjee Smruti Nyas, a Rajya Sabha Member and a former BJP President)
This piece is based on his speech in Rajya Sabha

□

Judicial Reform for Ensuring Speedy and Satisfactory Disposal of Cases

—Justice Dr. M. Rama Jois (Retd.)

During the period when the country was ruled by Britishers, they inaugurated Anglo-Saxon judicial system in our country and it came to be established throughout the country. Undoubtedly the system has got its own merits but at the same time after we secured independence we should have modified/reformed the said judicial system so as to be in conformity with our ancient judicial system with necessary modifications suited for the present day. In fact, Mahatma Gandhi had pleaded that after securing independence, in every field of national activity there should be '*swadeshi* stamp'. But unfortunately, the same judicial system established by the Britishers with English language as the court language has continued and no changes have been made in the justice delivery system. In fact, after we secured independence, for two decades, in the law degree courses the law students were being taught mainly about the judicial system brought into existence by the Britishers and Roman Law was one of the compulsory subjects giving an impression that we had no legal, judicial and constitutional system of our own. Fortunately, some time in 1966 the Bar Council of India replaced Roman Law by the subject Legal and Constitutional History of India. It is at that stage I became an Hon. Reader on the establishment of a private law college where I was entrusted with the teaching of Ancient Indian Legal, Judicial and Constitutional System. After this subject was allotted to me for teaching in the law college, at the inspiration and guidance of Sri. ES Venkataramaiah, who was the Principal of that college and who later on became a Judge of the High Court, Judge of the Supreme Court and Chief Justice of India, I undertook the study and wrote a book on ancient legal, judicial and constitutional system. It took practically 12 years for me to write the book incorporating legal and constitutional system prevalent in ancient India which happened to be the oldest legal and judicial system in the world. Our ancient Indian legal and judicial system was embedded in a comprehensive word called "*Dharma*". Accordingly, the civil and criminal law including procedural law came under the title "*Vyavahara Dharma*" and the constitutional law governing the administration of any State was called "*Raja Dharma*". The book has been recommended as a text book on the subject by the Bar Council of India. The book was published in the year 1982 with the aid of National Book Trust and as many as four reprints of the book have been published.

Unfortunately, after securing independence no attempts have been made to reform our judicial system so that it is not only in conformity with our thoughts, philosophy and principles evolved from times immemorial, but also suited to our own present requirements. In this article, I am not attempting to deal with various aspects of administration of justice required to be reformed as this has been done in various articles, seminars, but only refer to a few important problems and also suggest some reforms so as to ensure speedy and satisfactory disposal of cases.

In the first instance, I shall refer to the administration of justice in the High Courts. Prior to independence there were a number of British provinces and Princely States. There were separate High Court Acts with different constitution and organisations. Having regard to the fact that an appeal had been provided against the decision of the High Court in the British Provinces to the Privy Council which was far away in England, an internal arrangement was made in the High Court to the effect that an appeal shall be provided against rendered by a single judge of the High Court to the two judges of the High Court which was called Letters Patent Appeals for the reason that the High Courts concerned were established under the Letters Patent issue by the British Crown.

But there was enormous changes regarding the status of the High Courts under the scheme of our Constitution. Article 214 provided that there shall be a High Court for each State. Article 216 provided that every High Court shall consist of a Chief Justice and such number of judges as decided by the President. In particular, under the wide writ jurisdiction conferred on the High Court under Article 226 of the Constitution under which power was conferred on the High Courts to issue various kinds of writs including the power of judicial review of both executive and legislative action. In exercise of such power, the High Courts are empowered to strike down a law enacted by the State legislatures or Parliament if the High Court comes to conclusion that the law enacted was ultra vires the power of the legislature concerned or violative of the provisions of the Constitution.

The resultant position has been that the Chief Justice and all the other Judges of the High Court are of the same rank with same conditions of service and none of them is superior to the other. But strangely, the provisions for appeal from the decision of one judge of the High Court to two judges in the guise of letters patent appeal which were in existence prior to the commencement of the Constitution, which ought to have been abolished with the commencement of the Constitution has been continuing. As held by the Supreme Court in AIR 1970 SC 1, the very concept of appeal is entering a superior court against the decision of a lower court. How the two judges of the same rank and who are judges of the same High Court can sit in appeal against the decision of the High Court just because the decision was delivered by a single judge is untenable and wholly unreasonable and also per-se unconstitutional. For illustration, writ jurisdiction is conferred on the High Court. Whether a writ petition is decided by a single judge or more than one judge, it is the decision of the High Court. Constitution does not provide an appeal. A Division Bench is neither a senior High Court nor a Junior Supreme Court.

A plain look at the provisions of the Constitution indicates that the two judges of the High Court have no jurisdiction under the Constitution to interfere with the order of the single judge whose decision is as much a decision of the High Court. It is unfortunate that neither the Supreme Court has frowned upon such appeals nor the legislature has considered this aspect and has taken any necessary steps in conformity with the provisions of the Constitution.

Even after six decades after the commencement of the Constitution, different High Courts are functioning under different enactments or letters patent issued by the British Crown calling themselves as chartered High Courts notwithstanding the fact that Entry 78 of the List-I of the 7'th Schedule Constitution provides that power to make law on the topic of Constitution and Organisation of the High Court has been conferred on the Parliament so that it may enact a common High Court Act in conformity with the provisions of the Constitution as applicable for the whole country. As a result, some High Courts have original jurisdiction and a few others do not have it. Not enacting a uniform High Court Act and abolishing the so called intra court appeals which is patently unconstitutional is contributing to the enormous delay in the disposal of cases at the High Court level. This is one of the matters in which the Parliament should take interest immediately and enact a Uniform High Court Act in which all such provisions which are necessary for the speedy disposal could be incorporated.

As the High Court happens to be the highest court in the State, it would be appropriate that the cases coming before the High Courts should be decided by a bench of two judges finally in respect of all ordinary civil and criminal matters and an appeal to the Supreme Court should be provided only in respect of cases involving interpretation of the provisions of the Constitution or the Central law or in respect of issues which are of national importance. As the highest court of the land is burdened with all ordinary civil and criminal cases, the said unbearable workload prevents the Supreme Court from deciding cases involving important questions of Constitutional law at the earliest. As a result, such cases are pending for more than decades and it is needless to mention that if the Supreme Court were to decide one important case involving provisions of the Constitution, hundreds of cases pending before the High Courts would automatically get decided.

Secondly, after providing that, the minimum number of judges to decide at the High Courts should be two. It is appropriate that minimum number of judges to decide the appeals before the Supreme Court should be three instead of two as at present. As far as the questions involving interpretation of the provisions of the Constitution are concerned, clause (3) of Article 145 provides that the minimum number of judges to decide such cases is five.

Unless and until the vast jurisdiction of the Supreme Court

regarding ordinary civil and criminal matters is restricted and confined to matters of constitutional and national importance, it is impracticable for the Supreme Court to decide important matters within a reasonable time. A look at the type of cases which are pending before the Supreme Court would show that number of matters of constitutional/national importance involving interpretation of the provisions of the Constitution are pending for more than 12 to 14 years. Even if such cases are decided after such a long time and an unconstitutional law were to be struck down by the Supreme Court, the injury caused to the nation during such long period of pendency is incalculable. Therefore, it is imperative that a uniform High Court Act is enacted and also to make necessary changes in the jurisdiction of the Supreme Court to ensure speedy disposal of cases.

Unanimous or Majority Decision instead of Several Judgements

The present practice of delivering separate and concurring judgments by benches of more than two judges, entails avoidable debate which take considerable time and delay in ascertaining the opinion of majority. Article 145 of the Constitution should be amended as also the statutes regulating exercise of power of High Courts to ensure that there shall be unanimous or one majority judgement in each case. This would save considerable time of the Courts as in the event of there being several concurring judgements, the arguments by parties on the basis of such judgement would occupy several hours and days and if instead there is only one unanimous or majority judgement in each case, there would be no doubt about the position in law which constitutes an easy precedent to be followed in subsequent cases both by the Supreme Court as well as the High Courts/Lower Courts.

Recruitment of Judges

In the ultimate analysis, the efficiency of administration of justice in the Courts depends upon the quality of persons appointed. Further, transparency in the conduct of judges is of utmost importance. This can be secured by the existence of transparency in the appointment of judges. Therefore, recruitment procedure should be such so as to secure the services of honest and efficient persons as judges at all levels.

District Judges

The appointment of District Judges should be made on the basis of recommendations of the High Court concerned which would be solely on the basis of performance in viva-voce conducted by the full court or by a committee of judges constituted by full court of the concerned High Court in respect of direct recruitment from the bar. In the case of promotion, it should be made from amongst the persons in the cadre of civil judge on the recommendations of the High Court.

Lower Court

The appointment for lower judiciary should be made by direct recruitment based on competitive examination comprising of written test and viva-voce from those with minimum qualification of a law degree and minimum three years experience as an advocate or teacher in recognised law college. The selection should be made by High Court through a committee of judges constituted by full court.

Simplification of Execution of Decrees

The bane of the Civil Procedure has been that the procedure prescribed for execution of decree under Order 21 of the Civil Procedure Code. The procedure prescribed in Order 21 of the Civil Procedure Code is so cumbersome in that even though a person is able to secure a decree from the Court after considerable time, he would not be able to get the fruits of the decree easily. There are cases in which even after 50 years after the passing of the decree, they remain unexecuted.

In this behalf, the procedure practised in ancient Indian Judicial system is worthy to be followed by deleting Order 21 of the Civil Procedure Code and providing that the Court which passed the decree was under an obligation to execute the decree and secure the fruits of the decree to the successful party.

The provision under ancient Indian legal system was that immediately after the Court passes the decree it was required to post the case for execution of decree unless in the meanwhile there is a stay order from the appellate Court. The Court which passes the decree was required to proceed with the execution of the decree. In cases where the appellate Court had granted stay order, the Trial

Court had to proceed with the execution of the decree after the stay order comes to an end if the decree passed by it had been confirmed by the appellate Court. If there was any alteration of the decree by the appellate court, the Trial Court was under a duty to execute the decree as modified by the appellate Court. This one area of procedural law requires to be amended in such a way so as to secure justice to the litigants which alone inspires faith in the administration of justice.

There are many other reasons for the delay in disposal of cases and the consequent accumulation of arrears leaving a feeling in the minds of the litigants that their cases are not going to be decided in their life time and they are not going to secure any reliefs from the Court.

The problems which the judiciary is facing are:

1. Increase in number of cases having due regard to the increase in population but not creating required number of judicial posts.
2. Inordinate delay in making judicial appointments even regarding existing posts as a result of which much of the time during which the cases could have been disposed off and the judges claimed experience is lost.
3. Dilatory attempts of the Advocates in that whenever a advocate has got a weak case, his tendency is to secure some interim orders and seek innumerable adjournments to delay the final disposal of the case.
4. Failure to make full use of the legal provisions to expedite the disposal.

Therefore, attention ought to have been given by the Government, Judges and Lawyers to these aspects jointly to remedy these problems. Failure to do so is responsible for mounting arrears and consequent inordinate delay in disposal of cases, which is resulting in the people losing the faith in the efficiency of judiciary. It is well said that it is never too late to mend. Let us do so atleast hereafter.

These are some of the aspects which are required to be attended to apart from various other steps which have been recommenced by the Bar on various occasions.

(The writer is BJP Rajya Sabha MP and former Governor of Jharkhand and Bihar)

□

Strengthening the Spirit of Nationalism in Politics

—Balbir Punj

The national level parties, with starry-eyed ambitions, would espouse nationalism as the last virtue. Secularism, minorityism, regionalism and casteism are more likely to dominate their discourse. Prime Minister Manmohan Singh ironically chose the birth anniversary of Netaji Subhas Chandra Bose, India's supreme nationalist, on January 23, 2007 to moot his 'Muslims First' policy. Muslims, he said, have the first claim on the country's resources making thus a mockery of right to equality enshrined in the Constitution. Ram Vilas Paswan made a facetious but dangerous suggestion of extending citizenship to Bangladeshi infiltrators. He and Lalu Prasad Yadav, both of whom had used an Osama bin Laden look alike to campaign during last Bihar elections, tried to project SIMI as innocuous as a bunch of Buddhist monks. The revelations by Gujarat Police that Indian Mujahideen (IM) is a clique within SIMI framework might have put them on the defensive. They went on to, not for the first time, to equate the image of SIMI to reality of RSS and Bajrang Dal. To them, apparently, calls for *Nizam-e—Mustafa* and *Bharat Mata ki Jai* appear the same! It betrays a ton load of perversity that has mutated the national political discourse.

COST TO THE NATION

Since the spirit of nationalism in politics in the country has been weak, our chequred history is replete with blunders which cost the nation enormously. Gandhiji's unstinted support for restoration of

Caliphate in far away Turkey in the 1920s ultimately led to the partition of the country in 1947. Not only did India lose one of its vital parts (where vedic hymns were composed and Buddhism flourished), a lethal foe was born. The Communists supported the demand for Pakistan because their understanding of the society was "international" and NOT national.

Within two months of its birth, Pakistan invaded Kashmir. When the Indian army was on the verge of throwing out the invaders to the last man, Pandit Nehru ordered ceasefire and took the matter to the UN, with disastrous consequences, both for Kashmiris and rest of India. While Sardar Patel, fired by his nationalistic zeal was able to integrate over 500 princely states into the country successfully, Pandit Nehru, in absence of nationalist fervour, has left Kashmir as a festering sore in India's polity.

India's humiliating defeat at the hands of China in 1962 was also on account of the fact that both, the then PM (Pandit Nehru) and the Defence Minister, V K Krishna Menon had more concern for "global peace" than the security of the country. And the Left in India supported Red China against their own country. Their commitment to their ideological doctrine Communism was obviously more than their sense of belonging to their country of birth.

It was the strong sense of nationalism which motivated Indira Gandhi to go in for Pokharan I in May 1974, wage an all out war against Pakistan and Balochistan In the process Bangladesh was born and all this was done in spite of the US pressure. The Pokharan II, ordered by Atalji in May 1998 was also accomplished against the wishes of America on one hand that of the Left and Congress led by Sonia Gandhi, on the other. It's ironical that the Left had hailed China when it had gone nuclear! For them it was a "people's bomb" in case of China and Pokharan II was born out of a "War-monger" mindset of the BJP.

NDA's all out war against terrorism was fired by a strong sense of nationalism. Those devoid of nationalism opposed POTA, and dropped it from the law book after coming to power. Its again the absence of nationalism which prods a section of our people to treat the security agencies as suspects when they are involved in anti-terror operations and terrorists as innocent youth.

PARTICIPATORY POLITICS

Participatory politics in India is a post-1857 development. Nationalism, on the other hand, is an ageless virtue inherent in Indians, as the *Prithvi Sukti* (Hymns to Mother Earth) of the *Rig Veda,* the sage proclaims that he is the son of Mother Earth. Love of his country comes as naturally to a human being as the love of his home. It was an upsurge of nationalism in the land of five rivers in late 4th century BC that saw Alexander's hegemony in Punjab collapse as soon as he had departed. It was the nationalist spirit that made ancient Hindus to defeat the Sakas, Kushanas and Huns even after they had consolidated their rule in parts of India. Nationalism, although inverted, survived during Muslim rule as sons of soil protected their religion, culture, and way of life.

Famous historian Dr Radha Kumud Mookerjee, who also graced India's first Rajya Sabha, in his book *Local Government in Ancient India,* refused to accept a 'Muslim period' in Indian history for an interesting reason. The invaders i.e. Turk, Pathans and Mughals, entrenched themselves in the cities and directed the political destiny of the country. The villages, however, remained in the hands of the Hindus who preserved their native lifestyle, thought process and customs. The Hindus maintained their world of their ideas where a Turk or Muslim had no place. Even today, if the national ethos is being preserved in India, it is not due to the 'secular' governance of Westminster model, but despite it. Nationalism is kept alive due to the people, whose moorings go deep into this land, and not due to the political leadership. There is a need for nationalism to be inculcated in the political leadership more than in the people.

Participatory politics began in India with the establishment of the Indian National Congress in 1885. The establishment of British Indian Association (curiously its membership was not open to British) in 1851 and Indian Society in 1867 both in Calcutta who later merged themselves into the Congress were a preparatory drill. The objective of Congress was to appeal to the British government through petitions, resolutions and speeches to address the problems and aspirations of Indians. It worked for 'reformation' of the Viceroy's Executive Council, provincial legislative councils and corporations etc which meant induction of more Indian faces. It wanted ICS (Indian Civil Services) exams to be held in India at par with England for convenience of the

Indian aspirants. The whole exercise was thus meant to co-opt the Indians into British-run system. But curiously not even the biggest nationalist wanted to return to pre-British political system of monarchy or one-man rule. The exercise was seen as a rehearsal for evolution of responsible government in short term and democracy in long run.

ALIGARH LOBBY

The Congress, which was catalysed by a British civil servant AO Hume, was a body to 'apprise' the British authority about Indian public opinion. It was not allowed to 'build' a public opinion. The Congress fell out of favour and ran into difficulties within three years when its President proclaimed that it would mobilise public opinion by reaching out to masses. The British also promoted the Aligarh lobby led by Sir Sayyid Ahmed Khan who remained a trenchant critic of the Congress, and near successfully dissuaded the Muslims of India to join it. The Congress, although it claimed to speak for the entire nation, failed to convince the Muslims to join it. The division between national interests and Muslim interests emerged distinctly clear in the field of politics from the beginning. The gulf was about to increase with the formation of Muslim League in 1906, and until the partition became a reality in 1947.

BENGAL PARTITION

Nationalism first hit the streets in 1905 during the Bengal anti-partition movement. Viceroy Lord Curzon's move to divide the large province of Bengal (it included Bihar and Orissa as well) into Western and Eastern parts triggered a mass upsurge of protests from the Bengalis. But the unique feature of this movement was that it exceeded its agenda of reuniting Bengal. The songs and philosophic writings that grew around this movement were thoroughly national rather than provincial. They spoke of a 'Divine Mother India' with a mission in the world and wanted the complete independence of India. The idea was advanced for its age, from the point of view of Congress who represented the political mainstreams.

The rumblings of the Bengal anti-partition movement were heard far outside Bengal like Maharashtra (where the young VD Savarkar organised a bonfire of foreign clothes) and in Punjab. The Congress had to pass resolutions against the partition of Bengal. But it was the public who set the agenda for the leadership to follow. It was perhaps the only movement of India that succeeded in its objective. Bengal was reunited in 1911. The movements led by Gandhiji from Non Co-operation to Quit India ended in failure or compromise. Even today we find some movements in India where the public is setting agenda for the leadership to take note of. A recent example is Jammu's Sri Amarnathji Sangarsh Samiti's movement; Salwa Judums and outburst in Orissa and Karnataka against evangelism. This is perhaps the best way to restore nationalism in politics.

The complete and inalienable independence for Indians 'as an Englishman is free in England and French in France' (which Sri Aurobindo spoke about in 1905) did not become Congress creed until the 1929 Lahore session. The Bengal anti-partition movement spawned the first generation of Indian revolutionaries. It made revolution as integral part of freedom movement. But these revolutionaries, with dim view of Congress obsequious methods, remained outside the mainstream of politics. The romantic nationalism that they espoused would not fit into the politics of Congress. And although a section of 'extremists' grew in Congress like the famous Bal-Lal-Pal (Tilak, Lala Lajpat Rai and Bipin Chandra Pal) they were ousted from the Congress by the moderates. Thus nationalism remained in exile from politics.

ADVENT OF GANDHI

The worm turned in the 1920s with advent of Gandhi. Gandhi was the first person with an agenda of the moderates and methods of the extremists. He started mass contact programmes to furrow through the un-reached hundreds of millions. But the humble Indian masses who idolised Gandhi were not often interested in his political views. That Gandhi's kept the meaning of his '*Swaraj*' obscure did not matter to them. (it actually meant Dominion Status within British rule, *Purna Swaraj* adopted in 1929 Lahore Congress meant freedom). They saw him as a saint promising some kind of deliverance from British rule.

But Gandhi placed a high premium on Hindu-Muslim unity that sometimes appeared more important than attainment of Swaraj. But the sad reality is that Muslims and Hindus joined the Khilafat Movement and Non Co-operation Movement for two different reasons.

While Muslims were interested in restoration of Caliphate in far-off Turkey, Hindus were agitating for freedom from British rule. The Congress committed a grave political sin by asking for restoration of the deposed Caliph (an autocrat and a sponsor of Pan-Islamism) while espousing the cause of democracy in India. This blurring of line between Pan-Islamism and nationalism has marred India's future political development. It was the genesis of Muslim appeasement even if it meant distorting the Indian body politic. In 1974, India made an unsuccessful attempt to join the OIC (Organisation of Islamic Countries), the consortium of Muslim countries. Manmohan Singh's 'Muslim first' policy is a continuation of the same original sin.

CONGRESS AS PLATFORM

The pre-independent Congress was more a platform and less a party. From Hindu Mahasabha to Forward Bloc, every shade of clique could be floated from there. But Gandhi bent backwards trying to accommodate the Muslim aspiration in the Congress. Despite this not more than four percent Muslims ever joined Gandhian Congress.

Rather he was vilified by Muslims when his Non Co-operation movement failed to restore the Caliphate. From Sir Sayyid Ahmed Khan to Jinnah, Congress had been dubbed as a 'Hindu Party' despite Congress' claim that it was national.

The 1946 interim elections showed the Muslims were with Muslim League asking for Pakistan. When Pakistan was attained the Congressmen had to relocate lock, stock and barrel from Pakistan. They were not spared for their secular pretensions. The Communists, who had provided intellectual arsenal like 'right to self-determination' that Jinnah needed to justify his Pakistan demand, too had to flee Pakistan for their dear lives. Communist Party ceased to be in West Pakistan almost immediately after partition, whereas in the East it was suppressed within a few years as a 'Hindu movement meant to break up Pakistan'. The Congress and Communists should be constantly reminded why they had to flee Pakistan if religion is no factor.

TARGETS OF ISLAMIC FUNDAMENTALISM

The growing Islamic fundamentalism today makes no distinction between BJP, Congress, and Communists. If Advani and Narendra

Modi are on hit list, there was a plot to abduct Rahul Gandhi from Congress headquarters of Lucknow and Maharastra Congress Chief Minister Vilas Rao Deshmukh has received a mortal threat. The same is true for his NCP deputy minister RR Patil. The secular vilification of BJP won't make a Congressman or Communist less kafir in the eyes of terrorists. The Indian Mujahideen e-mails which profusely quote from the Quran makes it amply clear that their war is against Hindu India. It's the right time to constantly remind the secular Hindu politicians of this aspect. This may either be done by BJP or apolitical nationalists.

The mission to strengthen nationalism in politics goes much beyond a Muslim-centric debate. But understanding the debate may be the key to solve many other problems. Independence in 1947 effected a major change in Indian politics. From being agitators, we became the rulers. The political authority if it brought power, brought many responsibilities. One of them was to harmonise the number of contradictions and conflicting interests. The issue of state reorganisation on linguistic lines, uplift of the scheduled castes and tribes, emancipation of women, balancing between interests of rich and poor, between development and conservation opened up Pandora's Box.

CONTRADICTIONS OF DEMOCRACY

The contradictions of democracy are going to stay, they can at best be managed. But at times, ill-conceived political decision or lack of political will have struck at the roots of nationalism.

The Khalistani Insurgency in Punjab in 1980s; the insurgency in Kashmir; the foreign inspired Dalit campaign against Hinduism; the ULFA insurgency in Assam have all tried to hit at the concept of India. Indian authorities suffered from lack of core conviction about nationhood. The Congress version of unity in diversity saying India is a multi-religious, multi-ethnic, multi-lingual country had somehow stretched out the concept of nationalism.

Pandering to minorities has actually obscured the majority in India, which meant falsifying Indian nationhood. It never pronounced the idea that what lies at the core of Indian nationalism. At the core of Indian nationhood are the Hindus. Hindus are not spoken of here in the religious sense of the term, but historic, philosophic and civilisation sense. India cannot be a called a nation at the cost of Hindus.

The ideologically motivated Jihad and Maoism we are witnessing today are because of our political hypocrisy. Our trying to glorify Akbar, and absolve Aurangzeb, hasn't prevented the rise of Indian Mujahideen.

Moreover, the multi-party system often degraded into a competition for Muslim votes. Congress nationalism, Communist party's anti-religiosity, Lalu and Mulayam Singh Yadav's OBC amelioration programme, Paswan's Dalit upliftment, all seem to end in Muslim appeasement.

REASSERTION OF NATIONALISM

It would take an intellectual movement to disabuse the Indian politics of it perversions of minorityism. To strengthen nationalism in Indian politics the dignity of the word Hindu should be restored. It is due to the Hindus that India remains India, it has not become Islamic republic of Pakistan or Bangladesh. It is after all the Hindus who went to gallows and suffered incarceration for freedom of India. The story of evolution of India is essentially a story of the Hindus. Even in 19th century the word Hindu was used as a synonym for national. We had Hindu colleges, Hindu schools, and newspapers called *Hindu Patriot, Hindu Chronicle,* and still extant *The Hindu.* But from Gandhi onwards, Hindus have become just a community, even a word of reproach.

Indian history has shown wonderful reassertion of nationalism at the hour of adversity. The tumultuous time that we are living in, I believe, won't prove an exception.

This time, I believe, public will set the agenda for political leadership to execute. This is possibly the best way to restore nationalism in politics. And nationalists in politics will have to do their bit to remind fellow politicians that neither minorityism, nor provincialism, nor even internationalism has not been able to supplant nationalism. India is an ancient country that is now renewing itself. The rules of politics may be rewritten.

(The author is a National Secretary of BJP and Rajya Sabha MP)

□

Role of the Media in Our Democracy

—**Chandan Mitra**

The role of the media in a democracy is continuously evolving. It was essentially a medium of information till the middle of the last century. And information meant everything – from advertisements to official notifications. As a British newspaper baron once commented "News is the stuff to fill up the space between ads"! In fact, even in India, the front page of newspapers till the 1940s consisted of ads, with news reports placed on the inside pages. Ironically, that trend seems to be returning with many newspapers now coming wrapped in advertisement supplements.

Although in India many newspapers championed the cause of freedom and moulded public opinion against British rule, such journals could not match the circulation of mainline publications, which were mostly pro-British. Regional newspapers like *Aaj*, *Amrita Bazar Patrika* and, of course Bal Gangadhar Tilak's *Kesari* struggled valiantly to keep the nationalist flag flying under perilous conditions that included frequent censorship, stoppage of Government advertisements and other official impediments aimed at curbing their economic viability and public impact. In established democracies like the UK, US and France, the media was in awe of their respective Governments and reflected conservative and pro-status-quo opinion.

It is only since the mid-1950s that newspapers and journals began to realise their power to influence opinion and make the Establishment accountable. It is in this period that an adversarial relationship between the Government and the Press began to emerge in Western democracies, culminating in media opposition to Britain's ill-conceived intervention in the Suez Canal dispute (1956), France's conflict with freedom fighters in Algeria (1961) and, most importantly, America's war against Vietnam in the late-1960s. Apart from political issues, the media began to function as a true watchdog of society on various issues such as access to information, health and education policy, regulation of the market economy and so on.

In India, the media underwent a gigantic transformation as a result of the Emergency (1975-77). Till then the jute press, so called because its ownership was vested largely in the hands of industrialists who owned jute mills, was generally subservient to the Government. Investigative reportage was unheard of and newspapers consisted primarily of Government press handouts or inputs from Government-funded news agencies.

Although Indira Gandhi was displeased with the criticism she faced from many industry-owned publications because of her socialist rhetoric in the aftermath of the first Congress split of 1969, the attacks on her were fairly muted till the early 1970s. But disturbed by the media's refusal to toe her and son Sanjay's line in the mid-70s, she imposed stringent censorship laws during the Emergency and even took over the managements of some newspapers like *Indian Express* and closed down pro-Opposition papers like *Motherland*.

The Emergency came as a shock to the entire media fraternity. Particularly distressing was the manner in which the demi-gods of the press kowtowed at the feet of the Establishment, shamelessly defending the curtailment of civil liberties, stifling of judicial independence and wanton arrest of suspected political opponents. Upon assuming charge as Information and Broadcasting Minister in the Janata Party Government, Shri LK Advani made a telling remark when he said, "The Indian media crawled when asked to bend". Consequently, there was a virtual revolution as soon as the Emergency was lifted. The Indian media suddenly flowered, etched a new identity for itself and, for the first time started to become the voice of the underdog.

This background is necessary to understand how the role of the media has been redefined from time to time. It is only in the post-Emergency era that the media has become qualified to be called the Fourth Estate or the fourth pillar of democracy after the legislature, executive and the judiciary. In fact, today the media plays a role in society that is no less important than the other three. In the process, however, certain distortions have emerged.

Although the print media is not entirely blameless, much of the new disturbing trends have been caused by the advent of satellite TV and an incredible number of 24/7 news channels in English, Hindi and regional languages. The media boom has resulted in rank commercialisation, cut-throat competition for circulation or TV eyeballs and, finally sensationalism.

The new genre of sting operations that began with the motivated hidden camera expose of a fictitious scandal by *Tehelka* has snowballed. People have been blackmailed, reputations damaged and organisations politically targeted. *Tehelkas* 'Operation Westend' was followed by various copycat stings, some aimed at personal vilification – such as a recent fake report of a woman teacher running a sex racket and some earlier instances of Bollywood actors being lured with temptations in order to catch them in acts that they would not have done had they not been allured. These actions have resulted in sections of the media straying from the path of responsibility that is essential for it to perform as a credible Fourth Estate in a vibrant democracy.

In the wake of a recent sting operation, again by *Tehelka*, on the eve of the 2007 Gujarat Assembly elections, I wrote an article in *The Pioneer*, which deserves extensive quotation in this context: "Yet another politically motivated sting operation has set the Delhi media's tongues wagging. I have no intention of coming to the defence of the perverted criminals who have bragged on hidden camera about their "exploits" during the post-Godhra riots of 2002. The communal frenzy that gripped Gujarat, caused by the burning alive of 52 kar sevaks inside two bogies of the Sabarmati Express at Godhra was despicable and heinous. The mass targeting of members of a particular community in its aftermath cannot be condoned even if the provocation at Godhra was extreme.

The judicial system can do without unsolicited assistance from secular fundamentalists who evidently have no faith in the system's ability to deliver justice. Therefore, the masterminds of the sting operation resorted to deceit and subterfuge to procure "confessions" from select perpetrators of the violence. That the alleged rioters blabbed relentlessly indicting themselves in the process is another matter.

"The first and most questionable aspect of the sting is the timing of its public release. Polling dates for the Gujarat Assembly have been announced and voting is due in just about a month. Why did the makers of the sting operation wait till now since they have been working on it for quite a while? A DCP, one Mr Gadhvi's rejoinder to the queries posed to him is a dead giveaway. Accused of having wilfully fired upon some Muslims in a ghetto, the DCP said that since the event was "three years old" he would have to rack his brains to recollect the precise sequence of events although he categorically denied having ever met a VHP functionary who claimed he had prodded the policeman into action. The Godhra incident happened on February 27, 2002, which means it is well over five years old. This suggests that the sting operation has been continuing for more than two years.

The "stingers" themselves say "evidence" was collected over several months. Why was it timed for release just a month before polling?

"Apparently, the operation was mounted in the guise of a research project on the rise of Hindutva in Gujarat. The reporter posed as an ardent Hindu research scholar gathering material for a book. Having been a student of history, I too had extensively interviewed surviving participants of the Quit India movement of 1942 in Ballia, Ghazipur and Varanasi in UP and some districts of Bihar during my fieldwork in 1982. People were very forthcoming in their responses. None had any objection to being tape recorded. But while cross-checking later, I found that individuals tended to grossly exaggerate their role in the incidents, often lying brazenly about their importance. Much of these tall stories had to be modified and even totally deleted from the final version of my doctoral thesis. The rigorous examination field data was subjected to by our supervisors made it essential to be extra-careful while putting down oral assertions into the text of the thesis.

"I have narrated this personal experience to point out the unreliability of oral "evidence" proferred by alleged activists who are prone to build myths around themselves and love to brag. This is a tendency common in India, particularly in small towns and villages. This is not to suggest that the entire body of "confessions" gathered by the sting operation is false or exaggerated. It is possible that some of the people captured on hidden camera actually perpetrated those gruesome acts. My limited point, however, stands: Unverified information can be highly misleading and will certainly not stand scrutiny in a court of law. So, the exultant reaction on the part of the multi-million Gujarat Riot industry may be premature and misplaced.

"It is obvious that Lalu Yadav will demand Narendra Modi's arrest and prosecution. But the attempt by the sting operators and their media cohorts to force the judiciary to take suo motu cognizance of their handiwork is aimed only at self-publicity. Anybody can claim that he or she has indulged in grossly criminal acts; that their "connections" with higher-ups have ensured early release from detention or dilution of cases against them; or that top people in Government, including the police, encouraged them to act in a particular manner and even congratulated them. Unless proved with the help of corroborating evidence, such claims are not worth the paper they are written on or the film on which they are recorded.

"Those who mounted the expose are not babes in the wood. In fact, they are veterans of India's burgeoning sting industry who dispatched call girls and crates of Scotch whisky to lubricate the tongues of army officers. Subsequent stings by them, their offshoots and other copycats have been equally mired in controversy. They know very well that such hidden camera "confessions" will never result in conviction of the accused. So, why did they conduct the operation and then time it for pre-poll release? It hardly requires investigative genius to crack their motives. The BJP and its associates have been systematically targeted in almost every significant sting operation from the inception of this genre of journalism. Even in the cash-for-queries scandal, we were never told how the MPs were selected by the "stingers". That only one Congress MP was trapped, while the rest belonged to non-Congress parties, particularly BJP, carries its own tale.

"The pre-poll release of the "findings" may undoubtedly horrify many people; indeed, most decent human beings will be shocked by the grotesque claims of the alleged rioters. But, contrary to the intentions of the stingers, it could also have a reverse effect. Narendra Modi has tried hard to live down Godhra and its aftermath. He has been asserting with considerable public resonance that those who keep reopening the wounds of 2002 are hell-bent on preventing Gujarat's spectacular economic progress; that they are conspiring to destroy Gujarat's asmita (self-esteem). Recalling the riots, no matter in howsoever gruesome a manner, may well bring communal polarisation back on the agenda. It is for the sting masterminds and their political mentors to ponder the eventual electoral cost."

I have quoted this at length to underline what the media's role in a democracy SHOULD NOT be. Unfortunately, we are drifting steadily into a situation in which unsubstantiated, often fabricated and politically motivated material is passed off as news with damaging consequences. We need to guard against this even if it means imposition of some guidelines and restraints on the media. At least a regulatory body is needed to cover the entire gamut of print, TV and new media (Internet), so that a grievance redressal mechanism is put in place. As I&B Minister, Smt Sushma Swaraj had proposed the creation of the Media Council of India to act as an independent regulatory authority. Unfortunately, no effort has been made in that direction since the NDA demitted office in 2004.

I believe the role of the media in a democracy has to be based on the following guidelines:

1. Upholding the national interest: This is especially relevant in view of the terrorist challenge facing the country. Demoralising the security forces by describing every encounter as fake – for example the recent incident in the aftermath of the Delhi blasts of September 13, 2008 in which a valiant police officer, ML Sharma laid down his life – is unacceptable to society. Promotion of terrorist and secessionist causes, such as giving Azadi to Kashmir Valley, are equally reprehensible and must be questioned.
2. Treating facts as sacrosanct: Unfortunately, commercialisation and sensationalism has introduced too many distortions in media coverage of events. The health of a mature democracy is dependent on a healthy media. If the media loses its credibility and seriousness, it spells doom for democracy.
3. Acting as a bridge between the ruling Establishment and the ruled – that is, ordinary people. The media must faithfully represent the cause of the underdog and draw attention to injustice, high-handedness and other forms of exploitation in a balanced, constructive manner. While the media is expected to demand accountability from the Establishment, it cannot take upon itself the role of prosecutor, judge and hangman – all at the same time. The balance between the media's responsibility and the

demands of the system's stability must be maintained scrupulously.

A mature, vibrant democracy can march ahead only when an independent and self-assured media recognises that its role goes beyond profit-making and circulation wars. If it is to be taken seriously, it must function as a critic but not as an enemy of the system. If it goes overboard, the system, namely democracy itself, will be endangered.

(The author is Editor, The Pioneer and MP (Rajya Sabha))

□

Six Decades of Indian Republic

Time to have a reality check of our Republic

—Prabhat Jha

Republic Day comes every year in the life of the nation. Every Indian wishes that our Republic should be immortal, *amar*.

At the same time, it is also an occasion to review the successes and failures of our republic every now and then. We should not evade it nor should it be perfunctory lacking the element of honesty in its evaluation. If the exercise is done on the plain of reality, we can measure the extent of our progress in the real sense.

Where do we stand today, where have we to go to reach our goal and how have we to strain our nerves to attain it? We should all know it too well. Every Indian has the inalienable right to know his country. The country does not belong only to those who are members of Parliament or of State assemblies. It is also not the sole property of those in politics. The country belongs to all those who consider themselves Indians by all counts.

We only have a superficial and not an in-depth view of the republic. The fault lies in the fact that we considered that the country belongs to those who run it. We speak very loudly about our rights but we are always evasive of our duties.

If we have to usher in change for the better, we have to ponder over the present conditions in the country. We have to be face to face with the stark realities.

To which Direction is Agriculture moving?

After we won our independence, we have throughout been saying that Indian economy is predominantly agricultural. The foundation of our economic edifice stands on agriculture. Yet, where do we stand as far as agriculture is concerned? In 1951 our per capita cultivable land holding was 0.46 hectare which went down to 0.19 in 1992-93. Today it stands at just 0.16 hectare.

70 per cent of our population in 1952-53 was dependent upon 102.09 million hectare of agricultural land. At that time 18.1 per cent of the land was irrigated. Agricultural production was 59.2 million tonnes and average production was 580 kilogram per hectare. At present with 45 per cent of 122.4 million hectare of agricultural land as irrigated, the total agricultural productions stands at 230.3 million tonnes with per hectare production at 1854 kilogram. The percentage of population subsisting on agro-based industries stands at 56.

Fighting Hunger and Malnutrition

Addressing a joint session of the two houses of Parliament in June 2009 Her Excellency the President of India, Smt Pratibha Patil declared that Government will come out with a new law called National Food Security Bill. But this law has as yet to see light of the day. 53 per cent of our population, out of which 20 per cent belongs to backward classes, is suffering from hunger and malnutrition. According to a latest survey, 1.5 crore children in rural India are on the verge of malnutrition. 27 per cent of the world's population afflicted with malnutrition belongs to India. 20 lakh infants (2.8 per cent) die every year because they cannot get potable water vital to sustain life.

How alarming is the situation and how complacent are the people can be seen from the fact that in India food grains worth Rs. 58,000 crores get rotten, unfit for human consumption just because we lack the modern technique for storage. Could we not have taken adequate and effective steps all these years to prevent this loss while crores of people are suffering from hunger? What a paradox that among 119 countries in the world India stands at No. 94 in the matter of hunger and malnutrition. What was our aim and where have we gone?

Rising Poverty Graph

We may claim that poverty in the country is on the decline. But facts speak otherwise. Increase in poverty is keeping pace with the increase in economic development in the country. According to a report released by the Prime Minister's Economic Advisory Committee's Chairman, Shri Suresh Tendulkar, 37.2 per cent of India's population is very poor. This figure, according to the Report, is 10 per cent more than the assessment made in 2004-05 which stood at 25.5 per cent. In other words, in the last 11 years 11 crore more people have joined the population living below the poverty line.

41.8 per cent of the population, that is 45 crore people, according to Tendulkar Committee report, are subsisting on a monthly per capita expenditure of Rs. 447. In other words, these people are unable to meet their daily basic essential requirements of life. This situation only makes us to think as to how many republic days need we to wait to usher in a life of plenty and prosperity for each and every citizen in the country.

Widening Disparity between Rural and Urban population

Villages are not progressing the way and on the lines they should. This is what the official figures indicate. In urban areas 77.70 per cent people live in *pucca* houses and in rural areas, only 29.20 per cent. 81.38 per cent of urban population enjoys the facility of drinking water, while in villages only 55.34 per cent population is lucky to have this privilege. 75 per cent of urban population has the benefit of power supply while only 30 per cent of rural population has their houses illuminated. In 6 lakh villages in the country the literacy percentage is 59 while in 5,161 cities it is 80 per cent. We have to work very hard to narrow this gap between the urban and rural population. We know that even today 72.2 per cent population of the country lives in villages. Therefore, villages hold the key to India's progress. Without the villages moving forward, the country cannot march towards progress. India as a whole cannot be strong without rural areas being made strong and prosperous.

Increasing Foreign Debt

Our boasting cannot hide the reality. The country continues to be under debt. Till December 2008 India's debt liability had gone up to $230.80 billion which was not far from our foreign reserves of $254.6 billion during the period under review. According to official estimates, the external commercial borrowing (ESB) has jumped to

$66.16 billion from $4.6 billion and till September 2008 the share of ESB in the total national debt has gone up to 28.7 per cent from 27.4. Why are we not worried about these mounting debts? Why are we not serious to bring back the illegal money stacked by Indians in Swiss banks? Why have no concrete steps been taken to get the country out of the debt trap? These questions are crying for answer from the government.

Population to touch 150 crore

According to a UN estimate, by 2025 India's population will grow to 150 crores, half of which will be living in cities. Speaking in a seminar on disaster management, experts have opined that the urban population will be the worst hit if our cities were exposed to any disaster. But we seem to be least concerned about this threat. Government seems little interested in saving the country from the threat of population explosion. How long shall we wait? How long can we wait?

Asia's Fourth most Corrupt country

In the list of the most corrupt countries of the world we stand at 85 and in Asia at 4. Last year commenced with the explosion of a scam worth Rs. 7,000 crores in the country's largest IT Company, Satyam Computers. Then followed a series of scandals, like the spectrum scam in the Communications Ministry, scandals involving the former Jharkhand governor Shri Sibte Rizvi and the former chief minister of Jharkhand Shri Madhu Koda, former union minister's son Sweety; and recently Parliament echoed with the scam involving Justice Dinakaran and senior Army officers involved in land scam. All these have only lowered the esteem of the country in the comity of nations.

Education System that Inspires no hope

Government claims that the percentage of admissions in primary schools is touching 90.95. Presence of children in schools is increasing. At the same time the number of children and youth is also witnessing a marked spurt. Based on this assumption, India is in the forefront of the youthful nations in the world. But that is not the reality. On the contrary, the fact is that one-third of the youth in the country continue to be illiterate or they have not been able to complete their primary education. Irony is that the picture of a young India that is being projected is only limited to the youth living in cities having received education in information technology, computer, software, management etc. 70-80 per cent of the youth living in villages and slums in urban areas still stand deprived of such elite education. Of which *Bharat nirman* are we speaking without the emancipation of the really young India?

For various social and economic reasons, about 40 percent of our children are forced to leave the schools without completing their primary education. Most of these get engaged in child labour. In other words, only 60 per cent of the children are able to reach the middle standard of education. Even among these, 50 per cent of children leave their middle school education midway. This leaves only 30 per cent of the children who are able to reach the secondary school education. Further, among these students 30 per cent students who complete their secondary school education, only 15 per cent are able to get admission in colleges. To sum up, out of 100 students who get admission in primary classes only 10-12 are able to reach for college education.

Pitiable State of Higher Education

According to an Assocham report, more than 4.50 lakh students go to foreign countries, like the USA, UK, Australia, Canada, Germany, Singapore etc and spend about Rs. 48,000 crores. The reason for this outflow of students is the lack of facilities for high quality professional education within the country. Government will have to chart out a roadmap to meet this shortcoming. Otherwise, Indian students will continue to be the target of racial discrimination, as in Australia, and Indian money will continue to strengthen the economies of other countries.

Poor Health Facilities

As per the 2008-09 economic review, according to the 2001 census standards, India is short of 20,856 health sub-centres, 4,833 primary health centres and 2,525 community health centres. 34 per cent of the existing health institutions are also functioning from rented accommodation. Even the health institutions functioning at present, are severely handicapped by an enormous shortage of doctors, nurses and other para-medical staff. Hundreds of hospitals are functioning without doctors, specialists and nurses.

It is unfortunate that in a country where about one thousand people die every day, the government is spending only one per cent of the country's GDP on health facilities as compared to our neighbour China which spends 6 per cent of its GDP.

Acute Shortage of Housing

According to a figure released by the national housing organisation, about 2.5 crore urbanites (about 37 per cent of urban population) have no house of their own. According to data released by the National Sample Survey Organisation (NSSO) 32 per cent of India's urban population has lesser space to live in than the space available to people in jails in USA.

In villages 39 per cent houses provide 65 square feet of space per person. But during the last fifty years the space available in a house per person has got further squeezed both in villages and towns. Today 55 percent of people in urban areas and 56 per cent in rural areas have to make do within a space of just 10x10 feet per person. According to UN Habitat report, 17 crore people live in slums in India. The life in the slums, we all know, is worse than that in US jails.

Republic Day is a national festival. We gave to ourselves this Constitution on that day. We had vowed that administration will ensure a better life for the people and will be answerable for it. We have tried to bring to the notice of Government the problem of *roti, kapda, makan,* education and health being faced by the *aam aadmi*. Despite all that is available in the country, still people are facing with the problem of hunger and want. We have to ponder over why this situation still persists. If we are able to overcome all the hurdles and difficulties that lie in the way, we will certainly be able to chant loudly: *Mera Bharat Mahan*!

(The writer is a BJP National Secretary & Rajya Sabha MP)

□

Commitment to Ideology

—Prof Om Prakash Kohli

Among the qualities that are expected of activists, one is the commitment towards ideology. Political party is such an organisation that has some goal in public life. This goal cannot be only winning elections and coming to power. To win elections and to come in power can only be a medium, the end is to realise the goal on which the party is based.

In the constitution of Bharatiya Janata Party the goal of the party is inscribed in the following terms: 'Party is committed to build a *Bharat* which will be strong, prosperous and self reliant nation, which will have modern, progressive and intellectual vision and which will proudly seek inspiration from ancient *Bharatiya* culture and values and which is capable of emerging as great power of the world which plays effective role among the comity of the nations to establish an international system based on justice and world peace.' It is further stated that party shall work with the aim of establishing a democratic state and maintain the sovereignty, unity and integrity of *Bharat*.

Other parties also have their own goals. But in sum it may be said that the goals of the political parties are or should be in the interest of the society and nation. There may be different paths to fulfil the interests of the society and the nation which we term as principle or ideology of the party. By analysing the ideology and principle, the voter in a democracy decides as to which party can better serve the interest of the nation. Here we are not discussing about those political parties whose only aim is to gain power. However, these kinds of parties also claim of having larger national goals.

For increasing the commitment of the people towards party, for its expansion and victory, it is the foremost requirement that activists have firm faith in the party ideology.

There is always some inspiration that works behind a person. This inspiration may be either higher or ordinary. Ordinary inspirations are those in which a person seeks to pay attention to one's self interest. Higher inspirations are those in which a person works in the interests of others, society, people and for nation. We can also call it '*Dharma*'. Politics is also a *Dharma* which aims a public good. The politics of Ram was for public good, inspired by *Dharma* and oriented towards *Dharma*. Tulsidas in *Ramcharitmanas* defined *Dharma* as pertaining to the interests of others and public good:

"Parhit saris dharma nahi bhai"

(There is no greater *Dharma* than serving the others)

Today in the field of politics we experience opportunism. The aim of the political parties is now confined to somehow gaining power and enjoying it. Such political party and its leadership fail to set high standards for its activists. Opportunism has superseded ideological commitments. While distributing tickets, the emphasis is more on winnability rather than on ideological commitment. Those who fail to get ticket from their own party, manage to get it from other party, therefore it is not the ideological commitment that counts but the issue is to win elections and to increase power. Those who manage to get ticket from anywhere fail to command the respect from the people as an ideologically committed activist gets in the society. The situation turns from bad to worse when a party tries to shamelessly offer inducements to those belonging to other parties and ideologies. Recently large sums were given to the MPs and amoral agreements made with them to win the vote of trust in Parliament. Politics without dignity is shaking the faith of the people in the system. It is a serious challenge for Bharatiya Janata Party to maintain the commitment of the activists towards ideology in the era of distorted politics.

Generally we find two kinds of individuals. One, who keep swinging like pendulum, they have no commitment to any ideology or principle. People of such unstable mind have no compunction in giving up the ideology in the name of practical politics. These peole are inspired by the allurements of posts and strong desire for power. On the other hand we have such examples when an activist moved ahead with great commitment to the ideology and could not be swayed away any kind of allurements. For having such faith for the ideology it is required that the ideology for which one is committed should be for the welfare of all and fit in all aspects. Commitment arises from excellence in ideology. One who is committed to ideology never keeps himself in the centre of his activities but his work is ideology-centric. He derives satisfaction by gaining wider acceptability for the ideology irrespective of his personal gains. He never gets tired of working for the ideology without expecting anything in return. He considers himself to be a medium and a tool. The selflessness of Pandit Deendayal Upadhyaya and sacrifice and resignation from the central cabinet by Dr Syama Prasad Mookerjee are examples of politics inspired by high values.

Change of party is a distorted form of political opportunism. Changing party has led to unstable politics in India. Only few governments are able to complete its terms. Political instability is affecting the national life. People are losing faith in the political leaders and political establishments.

Indian politics is passing through a phase of coalition. The mandate of the Indian voter is getting divided among the national and regional parties. As a result no single party is getting majority. Situation leads to coalition politics. To widen the base of coalition, parties of different ideology are sought to be accomodated. The parties are forced to give up their ideological positions and programmes in the interest of coalition governmetns. In the BJP led NDA coalition, BJP gave up its programme of abrogating article 370, construction of Ram janmabhoomi temple and implementation of common civil code. To form the government in 2004, the congress had to give up the programme of economic liberalisation started by Narsimha Rao government. In such a political situation political convenience supersedes commitments towards ideology and principles.

It is necessary to practice the ideology repeatedly for enhancing the commitment towards it. Practice gives firmness. Practice means to test the ideology on the scale of public good and national interest. The process of testing should be strong and ruthless. There is difference between faith and blind faith. The view that develops from following a ruthless process of testing is different from the one from artificially adopted ideology.

For a healthy democracy, a voter has to take into account candidate, party and ideology. Candidates represent the party. If a candidate is not committed to the party ideology and somehow manages to get the ticket then he would not be able to promote the aims and ideology of the party. Political parties are not only a group of people but they are the organisations with definite goals. The faith of the activists in the goals of the party instills a sense of commitment and discipline in him. Today we find self interest in place of commitment and unruly behaviour in place of discipline in the political parties.

All these happen due to lack of commitment towards ideology and principle. If commitment and discipline remains in tact in the activists, then factionalism would never find place in the party. Self interest and party interest would become one. Factionalism and differences in opinions emerge due to conflict between self interest and party interest.

A good activist never compromises the principles of party for immediate gains. For ideological commitment he is prepared to forgo immediate gains. It has been commonly seen that when the self interest is not served or when the ticket is denied, an activist starts criticising the party. Sometimes he doesn't even desist from leaving the party. On being denied the ticket, he confines himself to his home and doesn't make efforts for the victory of the party candidate. He publicly criticises the party creating problems for the candidate. If one's interest is served, he finds everything well with the party and if something goes against the interest everything appears wrong in the party.

To have commitment for the ideology it is necessary that there is no doubt left for the excellence and competence of the ideology. If doubts remain then we would not be able to respond appropriately to the attacks of the adversaries of the ideology. Commitment is such a thing that transforms into permanent world view. Mechanical acts are different. Real commitment inspires and person and gives him the confidence.

In our scriptures, faith has been eulogised as the best virtue. One can have faith on an individual as well as on essence. In political parties and organisations like this, sometimes faith is towards the leader and not to the essence. Faith in essence is better and durable compared to that of leader or individual. If behaviour of a leader fails to measure up to one's standard then one loses faith in him and becomes discouraged about the party. If our faith is centred on essence then we remain committed even in the face of the leader having lost his credibility. In the *Geeta*, it has been said " *Sanshayatma Vinashyati*". In *Geeta* intelligence and stability had been enumerated as qualities of knowledge. Stability is the basis of will power. Stability is the quality of a determined person. Ideologically committed activists working selflessly are found in every political party. They do not expect any post or ticket, they continue to serve selflessly to make party ideology stronger. The respect which one gets from good behaviour is better than the respect one gets due to post. Such activists become ideals for others. Shri Deendayal Upadhyay ji is an example of an ideal activist.

The identity of Bharatiya Janata Party and Jana Sangh was shaped by commitment towards ideology and excellence in behaviour. In our ideology the view of "*Lok Sangraha*" is implicit. "*Lok Sangraha*" means stopping people from getting into undesirable activities.

For this, commitment to the goal is required. What is our goal? We are engaged in securing for India its rightful place in the comity of nations. We believe that we can achieve our aims on the basis of Indian values and best elements of our traditional culture. The direction of our efforts is determined by safeguarding the Indian values and eternal elements of our traditional culture.

The philosophy of integral humanism propounded by Pandit Deendayal Upadhyaya describes the traditional Indian values in newer context. This is our ideological and principled position. It is what we call cultural nationalism. By following it we can preserve the identity of our party and give expected contribution in nation building.

(The writer is BJP Delhi State President & former MP)

□

The Smile of the Poor holds Mirror to Nation's Prosperity

—**Ruddar Datt**

This requires a two-pronged strategy – (i) The expansion of sectors which promise higher labour absorption and (ii) Empowering the poor with education, skill formation and health so that they can enter sectors which require higher competence and provide better remuneration which enable the poor to cross the poverty line. The following strategy can solve the problem of poverty.

Adopt a strategy of pro-poor growth instead of emphasizing liberalization and GDP growth

Former Prime Minister Atal Bihari Vajpayee in his Independence Day Message (15th August 2001) candidly stated: "The fruits of liberalisation have not adequately reached the poor and the people living in rural areas. Inequalities have increased." It would be, therefore, futile to pursue the failed strategy of liberalisation which has a focus on only 8 per cent of labour force in the organised sector. The need of the hour is to take care of the 92 per cent of labour force engaged in the unorganised sector. Liberalisation has driven more and more people from the organised sector to the unorganised sector. There is a need to reverse this process and more and more units in the unorganised sector are enabled to graduate and join the ranks of the organised sector. The government should re-appraise them and give priority to the removal of unemployment and recognising the 'Right to work' as a basic human right. For this, a new model of development reconciling GDP growth and employment should be developed.

In this model, emphasis should be laid on development of irrigation and watershed development with people's participation. Similarly, degraded and wastelands should be developed through participatory efforts of panchayats. Agricultural co-operatives should be strengthened to undertake food processing industries and KVIC should be assigned the task of marketing. SSI sector should be helped on the lines suggested by SP Gupta Study Group. Greater emphasis should be given on housing for the poor and economically weaker sections. Rural infrastructure in the form of roads, provision of power in rural areas should be strengthened and a programme of social infrastructure should be undertaken.

Besides, there is a need for promoting informal sector which is major source of self employment and absorption of casual labour.

Stimulating Agricultural Growth

Indian Government has been fixing the target of agricultural growth during the Ninth and the Tenth Plan at 4 per cent per annum, but in practice realised 2.7% in the Ninth Plan and only 1.7% in the Tenth Plan. To identify the causes of sluggish growth of agriculture, it appointed a high power Commission under the chairmanship of Dr M S Swaminathan, world renowned agricultural scientist. The National Commission on Farmers suggested the following 5-point action Plan:

1. Undertake Soil health enhancement through integrated measures in improving organic matter and macro-and-micro nutrient.
2. Promote water-harvesting, conservation and equitable use by empowering panchayats to become '*pani panchayats*.' A sustainable water harvesting system should be established in rain-fed areas lacking assured irrigation.
3. Keeping in view the decline in profitability and farmers distress, the Government should reduce the rate of interest on crop loans to 4 per cent.
4. Bridge the growing gap between scientific know-how and field-level do-how both in production and post-harvest phase of farming. This could be accomplished by training farmers through the agency of Krishi Vigyan Kendras (Agricultural Science Centres) in both production and post-harvest technologies.

5. The gap between what the rural producer gets and the urban consumer pays should be narrowed down, as has been done in the case of milk by Dr V Kurien.

Besides, the National Commission on Farmers placing the unfinished agenda in land reform first in its list of five factors central to the present agrarian crisis states "The first and foremost task of the National Policy on Farmers should be in the area of land reform with particular reference to tenancy laws, distribution of ceiling surplus land, attention to common property and wasteland resources and consolidation of holdings.... Giving access to land and homesteads not only reduces poverty but is the best way to bring dignity in the lives of today's excluded." (Quoted by the *Approach Paper of the 11th Five Year Plan*, p.29).

But the greatest irony of the Indian polity is to include land reform as a part of agricultural strategy in every plan, but to conveniently forget it at the time of implementation, since neither the Central Government nor the State Governments are keen to take up land reform as a priority concern. Even consolidation of holdings programme has been abandoned. Neither is there any progress in the distribution of ceiling surplus land. But for the Left front Government of West Bengal which implemented 'Operation Barga' in 1977, no other state government has taken up the issue of land reform with the much-needed urgency. West Bengal did benefit in the form of a big boost to agricultural productivity thereafter. With the new wave of economic reforms introduced after 1991, emphasising liberalisation, privatisation and globalisation, the State Governments have practically abandoned land reform in their agenda of agricultural policy. However, there is a need to pay attention to this issue. But alas! This requires strong political will which is conspicuous by its absence.

Increasing the Productivity and Job Quality of the Unorganized Sector

The NDA government appointed 'Special Group on Targeting Ten Million Employment Opportunities', under the chairmanship of Dr SP Gupta, the then member of the Planning Commission which submitted, its report in 2002. The Special Group emphasised a shift in the strategy of development by emphasising the growth of unorganised sector as the surest method to reduce unemployment and poverty.

To quote:

"The only answer to this situation is to increase productivity and job quality of the unorganized sector. It means that all attempts should be made to implement those policies which will release the basic growth constraints and by ensuring a level playing field for this sector.... In the attempt to increase the labour productivity, more emphasis should be on the growth of this sector rather than for substituting labour by capital. Further, to improve the job quality and its security, major changes in legislation will be needed regarding basic social security measures, working conditions, minimum wages and protection of labour interests."

The Special Group Report was unique in many ways:

- It rejected the reform process as a panacea for all ills of the economy, especially referring to unemployment.
- It rejected the thesis of the reformists that the organised sector, more especially the corporate sector, could usher an era of zero unemployment and removal of poverty.
- It focussed attention on the unorganised sector which provides employment to 92 per cent of labour force and has remained neglected so far.
- It repudiated the theory that amendment of the Industrial Disputes Act to give powers to the employers to hire and fire shall lead to enlargement of employment. Rather it would result in more firing than hiring.
- On the basis of international experience and the imperative need of our country, the Report brought out the fact that small and medium enterprises are not only to co-exist but should also become the principal contributors of industrial growth, removal of poverty and unemployment.
- It underlined the need for providing special incentives for the unorganised sector and stopping the decline in the share of bank credit from 57% to 37% in a short-span of 6 years. (1993-94 to 1999-00)

- It highlighted the fact that the employment elasticity of the unorganised sector visa-a-vis the organised sector was 3.23 times and thus the state must strengthen it because it is a sure method to reduce poverty and unemployment.
- Besides, the normal expansion of employment as a result of high growth of GDP, it focussed on Special Programmes for the poor to provide them employment.

There is a need to immediately implement the recommendations of the special group so that reduction in the rate of poverty reduction with higher GDP growth is halted and a reverse trend is generated.

Improving the Share of Wages in the Process of Growth to Achieve Poverty Reduction

The saddest finding in the Approach Paper of the Eleventh Plan is: According to Annual Survey of industries, real wages declined even for workers in the organised sector although managerial and technical staff did secure large increase. *The wage share in our organised industrial sector has halved after the 1980s and is now among the lowest in the world.* (Emphasis added)

In this connection, the Report of the Secretary General, United Nations for the 2006 Economic and Social Council of the United Nations highlighted the centrality of employment to sustainable growth and poverty reduction. Accelerating employment growth is crucial for reducing poverty, as the Report pointed out, labour income constitutes the main source of income for the poor.

Professor Sheila Bhalla in her article *Note on Employment, Poverty and the Structure of Aggregate Demand in South Asia* presented in the International Conference on 'Universalising Socio-economic Security in South Asia', New Delhi 17-20 February 2008 presented the share of profits and wages in net value added in organised manufacturing in India.

Figures given in the Table reveal that wage share declined from 50.8% 1989-90 to 38.9% in 1994-95 and further declined to 32.4% in 2004-05. As against it, the share of profits which was merely 19.1% in 1989-90 rose to 40.65 in 1994-95 and further shot up to 55.6% in 2004-05. This dramatic rise in the share of profits as against fall in the share of wages is the cause of slow-down in poverty reduction.

Table: Share of Profits and Wages in Organised Manufacture in India

Value in Rs. crores at current prices

	Net value added	Profits Share (%)	Wages Share (%)
1989-90	42,663	19.1	50.8
1994-95	1,05,852	40.6	38.9
1999-00	1,54,974	30.5	38.2
2000-01	1,43,621	24.9	43.1
2001-02	1,44,302	24.2	44.0
2002-03	1,72,340	35.9	39.7
2003-04	2,02,954	45.5	35.7
2004-05	2,59,907	55.6	32.4

Source: CSO, *Annual Survey of industries,* various issues

Professor Sheila Bhalla also mentions: "The savings rate of the private corporate sector rose sharply every year while the trend for household savings component was flat. A large part of the private sector's investment has been financed out of its retained earnings or savings. Increases in retained earnings, in turn, have been achieved on the strength of rapidly rising share of corporate profits largely in national income accompanied by rapidly falling share of wages."

To put it more bluntly, the growth of the corporate sector is fundamentally based on exploitation of labour in the form of real wage reduction, by employing over 20 percent of the workers as temporary or casual workers without any social security.

The question arises: Should the State remain a silent spectator to falling share of wages in the face of rapidly rising share of profits and still claim that it intends to follow the philosophy of 'inclusive growth'?

Obviously, this entails a larger role of the state for encouraging productivity-wage bargaining with the fundamental premise that the workers have a right to equitable share of the fruits of economic progress. Along with this, if the state deliberately and in an effective manner can promote growth of the unorganised sector, this is likely to achieve the objective of full employment. The arm of the state has to be on the side of the weaker section i.e. labour so that it can negotiate a compact with the corporate sector to evolve a mechanism for the equitable distribution of net value added. Unfortunately, the role of the state after liberalisation has been to provide support to business magnates, this role needs a reversal if 'inclusive growth' has to be made just and equitable. Only then a fall in the share of wages can be halted and reversed into a rising and equitable share in net national product.

In fact, the entire policy of liberalisation was based on 'survival of the fittest', the law of the jungle, whereas a civilised society should follow the law of 'survival of the unfittest' as the hallmark of its policy of inclusive growth. The policy permitted unlimited growth of profits, while denying labour 'decent work' as the ILO intended to achieve by assuring an equitable share of wages. In this, the government as a matter of policy should try to enter into a compact with industrial lobbies regarding sharing of high growth and productivity gains with labour.

Empowerment of the Poor through Education and Skill Formation

As a consequence of sustained growth in expenditure on education, there has been a remarkable growth in educational institutions at all levels – primary, secondary and tertiary. The country was able to achieve a Gross Enrolment Ratio of 96% at the primary level, though the drop-out rate for class I to VIII was 51 percent which is quite high.

At the secondary and higher secondary level, total enrolment for the age-group 14-18 years was about 40 percent, though the drop-out rate for class I to X was as high as about 62 percent.

Gross Enrolment Ratio in higher education reached a level of about 11 per cent in 2004-05, though world average is 23.2 per cent. The country has huge infrastructure in education with 378 universities and 18,064 colleges.

The country was able to establish institutions of excellence in the field of engineering, medicine, management and also create national level research institutions in agriculture and science. As a consequence, the country produces second largest educated and skilled manpower in the world, only next to China.

The development of a huge educational structure of 378 universities and 18,064 colleges, 1.52 lakh secondary and higher schools, and 10.43 lakh primary and upper primary schools is a matter of legitimate pride.

Glaring Failures in Education

However, there are glaring failures which deserve urgent attention.

- Despite nearly 58 years of development planning, the country has failed to achieve universalisation of Elementary Education – a goal set by the Constitution to be achieved by 1960. Even after nearly six decades since independence, the number of children outside schools in elementary education is quite large.
- Drop-out rate among STs and SCs was even higher at 65.95% and 57.3% respectively which is much higher than the overall drop-out rate.
- Although secondary education up to class X is not the real terminal stage, even then drop-out rate (I-X) was as high as 62%; 64% for girls and 60% for boys.
- Enrolment in secondary and higher secondary level taken together was only 39.9% in 2004-05 – 44.3% for boys and 35.1% for girls which is very low.
- Mid-day meal scheme which covers about 18 crore children in primary and upper primary schools, has improved attendance and retention rate, but serious weaknesses about the implementation of the scheme to provide standard meals have been highlighted by NGOs which need remedial action.
- Glaring inter-state variations in enrolment, drop-out rates and access to secondary and higher secondary level need remedial action so that these variations can be narrowed down.
- A sharp shift in the management pattern of the schools has been noticed. The share of unaided public sector schools has doubled from 15% in 1993-94 to 30% in 2004-05. As against it, the share of government and aid schools has come down from 85% in 1993-94 to 70% in 2004-05. This implies that parents are prepared to pay more for the education of the children, if they perceive of good quality education in a particular category of schools. Thus, there is a need to make more investment in government and aided schools for improving the quality of education.
- To reach the objective of universalisation of secondary education as our goal in future, it is necessary to strengthen the school infrastructure, both physical and human in a substantial manner.

- Even in government and aided schools, there is a need to charge some reasonably affordable fees so that the management is provided more resources, besides state grants to improve quality of education.
- There is gross failure in the provision of vocational education since only 5% of the population in India of age-group 19-24 in 2004-05 acquired some skill, whereas the target set by the Education Commission (1964-66) was 25% by 1986. There is a need to develop effective strategies so that demand-driven vocational education programmes in partnership with employers can be drawn. These glaring shortages of skilled human power are being experienced in the rapidly computerising knowledge economy.
- Higher education continues to be elitist since Gross Enrolment Ratio is only 11% of the population in the relevant age group against the world average of 23.2% and for the countries in transition at 36.5% to which India belongs.
- The share of private unaided higher education institutions increased from 42.6% in 2001 to 63.2% in 2006. Their share in enrolment also rose from 32.9% to 51.5% during the same period. Since these schools operate purely for profit and charge very exorbitant fees, they price out the weaker sections of the society and become elitist. This militates against our goal of inclusive development and is thus a conspicuous failure of the educational system.
- The dispersal of technical education in the country is highly skewed. Andhra Pradesh, Tamil Nadu, Karnataka and Maharashtra account for nearly 55% of engineering colleges and 58% of the enrolment in country.
- Distance education was adopted to provide opportunities for the deprived sections of the society, but universities are using these institutions as milk cows to provide huge surpluses for their development. Even IGNOU is charging very high fees for BCA, MCA, MBA and other vocational courses to either make them self-financing or surplus generating.
- Despite the target set for 6% of the GDP to be devoted to public expenditure in education by 1986, we have reached a level of 3.49% of GDP in 2004-05. This is another gross failure

of our priorities toward education which is a potent instrument to promote inclusive growth.

It is heartening to know that in the Eleventh Plan, the Central Government envisages an outlay of Rs. 2.37 lakh crores at 2006-07 prices for education. This is a four-fold increase over the Tenth Plan expenditure of 0.54 lakh crores at 2006-07 prices. The relative share in the total Plan outlay will correspondingly increase from 7.7% to 19.4%. Around 50% of the outlay is for elementary education and literacy, 20% for secondary education (IX to XII) and 30% for higher education (including technical education). The big boost to education proposed in the Eleventh Plan priorities will take care of the resource constraint and the country should devote its energies to improve effective implementation of the professed goals.

Empowerment through Provision of Better Health

The strong link between poverty and health needs to be recognised. Long-term illness and expensive illness can drive even the non-poor, into poverty. To improve health care, a comprehensive approach is needed which comprises individual health, public health, sanitation, clean drinking water, and knowledge of hygiene and bringing up of children.

Although India has achieved significant improvement in various health indicators like life expectancy, infant and maternal mortality rate, yet countries in similar stage of development as China, Indonesia and Sri Lanka performed much better. During 2002-04, 20% of India's population was malnourished and 47.9% of its children under age 5 years suffered from malnutrition.

42.6 million persons lived in slums in urban areas, accounting for 15% of urban population. Lack of sanitation and poor quality of drinking water lead to high incidence of diseases among slum dwellers.

Although India has developed a huge infrastructure of 1.45 lakh sub-centres, 22,670 primary health centers and 3,910 community health centres, yet due to shortage of staff and inadequate diagnostic equipment, rural population has to approach towns and city hospitals for treatment.

In recent years, as against public hospitals, private hospitals are growing at a faster rate and in 2004-05, about 58% cases for treatment approached private hospitals in rural areas, and the figure for urban areas was higher at 62%. Despite high cost in private hospitals, about three times as compared with public hospitals, people prefer private hospitals.

National Rural Health Mission (NRHM) and National Urban Health Mission (NUHM) are the two major initiatives to help the poor in the availability of health facilities.

In secondary and tertiary health care, both public and private sector are involved, but the system is overloaded due to shortage of primary health care facilities in rural areas especially.

Household expenditure on health is 6.1% of total household expenditure in urban areas and 4.9% in rural areas. Out of this the share of expenditure on drugs is 77% in rural areas and 69% in urban areas. The poor are the worst affected because they are frequently affected by diseases and are least able to purchase and utilise the health services and the drugs. There is a need to set up mechanisms so that at least essential drugs are made available at affordable prices.

Eleventh Plan enthusiastically recommends public-private partnerships, but experience shows that the private sector which operates with an eye on profits, cannot redress the concerns of the poor, except such experiments where private sector is motivated by a charitable and social purpose.

There is a need to extend health insurance for workers in the unorganised sector so that the weakest sections of the labour force are provided assured benefits in the form of insurance cover and thus can be saved from falling into poverty trap, because periods of prolonged illness result in fall of incomes but rapid rise of expenditure.

Combined expenditure of Centre and State governments declined from 1.01% of GDP in 1992-93 to 0.99% in 2003-04. However, it has improved to 1.13% in 2006-07. There is a need to raise it further to 2.3 percent as per the target set by the Eleventh Plan so that it can serve the ends of social justice in a more effective manner.

There is a need to provide clean drinking water and sanitation, especially in slums, backward and remote rural regions so that they do not carry water-borne diseases. India's record on sanitation is very poor since only 33% of India's population has access to improved sanitation.

A R Nanda and Almas Ali conclude their survey on health issues and challenges: "Detailed analysis of the NSS data shows that untreated illness among the poor has clearly increased due to financial constraints. Inequality as measured by figures of household consumption expenditure group appears to have worsened, and the divide between the rich and poor in terms of untreated illness and expenditure on health services, as well as their use of both public and private health care institutions, has grown. The rich are now the major users not only of private but also of public hospitals. Increased drug costs and rising fees for different health services in both public and private sector seem to have played a major role in this." (Government Health Spending in India, *Economic and Political Weekly*, June 28, 2008). This is the major challenge for reproductive health agenda which should help the poor.

Our achievements on health indicators are encouraging, but we have miles to go before we sleep.

Empowering the Poor through Provision of Housing

There is a need to remove the shortage of permanent houses in the rural as well as urban areas. Not only that, an effort has to be made to provide the basic amenities of life such as drinking water, toilets and electricity. The country must launch a massive programme to provide housing and basic civic amenities.

The situation is much worse in rural areas than in urban areas. Government should subsidise housing for the poor and weaker sections of the society and recover the cost as part of rent and instalments over a period of 20 years. At present, the amount of Rs. 30,000 being given for the construction of a house under Indira Aawas Yojana is too meagre in view of the rising cost of construction to provide a two-roomed house, with a kitchen and toilet. This should be the minimum that is required by a family. This requires the limit of Rs. 30,000 to be revised.

Since rural areas are not offering enough employment opportunities, there is a push factor working and as a consequence, the urban population is increasing. In the urban areas, housing property has become so costly that it is beyond the reach of the majority of population. Most important is the price of land whose price has been sky-rocketing. The way out is that the government acquires land and does not add it as a charge from the poor and lower middle classes and starts a massive programme of housing. Construction cost should be charged from the people and price paid by the government to acquire land be treated as a subsidy for housing. It is only such an affordable price which can help the country to achieve the target of "housing for all" in a period of 20 years. This will also generate massive employment and thus raise the income of the poor who will be drawn to build houses.

In case, this is not done, the poor will usurp some land and put up *jhuggies* and this will lead to further growth of slum population.

Empowerment through Skill Formation for our Expanding IT Sector

In view of the increasing use of computers and Information Technology in all walks of life, the demand for skilled labour is on the increase. Since this requires access to higher education and vocational training, only those who can afford costly education and vocational training are able to benefit from the expanding opportunities of employment. Consequently, the poor are being priced out because they cannot afford expensive higher education and vocational training. Thus, the State should:

- provide subsidised higher education and vocational training for the poor;
- institute a large number of merit-cum-means scholarships for the poor; and
- help such institutions, both financially and otherwise, which provide education to the poor.

Such measures, if taken on an emergency basis as a national priority, can help the poor to rise in life.

Providing employment through National Rural Employment Guarantee Scheme (NREGA)

NREGA was started by the UPA Government as a national programme to provide 100 days of employment to begin with, through asset-creating public works every year at minimum wages to one-able bodied person in every rural poor class household. For this purpose, the Government passed the Employment Guarantee Act, 2005. Jean Dreze who was a member of National Advisory Council is of the view that NREGA is very different from Employment Assurance Scheme (EAS) and Jawahar Rozgar Yojana (JRY) etc because under the existing schemes, people have no rights, and, therefore, no bargaining power. By the same token, the administration is not accountable. But NREGA gives people work entitlement as a matter of right, indeed a legal right enforceable in court. Another important thing is that NREGA is the first attempt on a national level to work out an Employment Guarantee Scheme with 80 percent funding by the Central Government.

The National Rural Employment Guarantee Act came into force in 2006 in India's 200 most backward districts. In 2007, it was extended to another 130 districts and with effect from April 1, 2008, the Act is to cover all districts.

NREGA has been reviewed by the Comptroller and Auditor General (2007) and certain NGOs, especially the National Consortium of Civil Society Organisation (CSO), have also undertaken several reviews.

The following are the major short-comings of NREGA:

- Lack of adequate professional staff
- Lack of project planning
- Bureaucratic resistance of NREGA on account of the widely held belief that it is much more difficult to make money under NREGA as compared with other employment programmes
- Lack of transparency and absence of social audit
- Inappropriate rates of payment.

It is, therefore, vitally necessary that measures be initiated to remove these shortcomings so that the programme can deliver the benefits intended from its implementation.

However, Prof Kaushik Basu questioning the very concept of NREGA mentions: "No country in the world has ever succeeded in providing full employment. The chances of India – with its poor quality of governance and high corruption – being the first is zero. Hence, granting people the right to employment is to devalue the meaning of 'right'." (Kaushik Basu, *Hindustan Times,* April 13, 2008, – Not much of a Guarantee'). However, social activists do not agree with Prof. Basu.

Concluding Observations

Jeffrey Sacks in his famous work; '*The End of Poverty– How can we make it happen in our life time*' (2005) mentions:

The extreme poor lack six major kinds of capital:

- **Human Capital**: health, nutrition and skills needed for each person to be economically productive
- **Business capital:** the machinery, facilities, motorised transport used in agriculture, industry and services
- **Infrastructure:** roads, power, water, sanitation, air transport and sea ports and telecommunication systems that are critical inputs into business productivity
- **National capital:** arable land, healthy soils, biodiversity, and well-functioning ecosystems that provide the environmental services needed by the society
- **Public institutional capital:** the commercial law, judicial systems, government services and policing that underpin peaceful and prosperous division of capital
- **Knowledge capital:** the scientific and technical know-how that raises productivity in business output and the promotion of physical and natural capital.

The public sector should be mainly focussed on five kinds of investments – human capital (health, education, nutrition), infrastructure (roads, power, water and sanitation and environmental conservation), natural capital (conservation of biodiversity and ecosystems), public institutional capital (a well-run public administration, judicial system, police force), and parts of knowledge capital (scientific research for health, energy, agriculture, climate, ecology).

The general lesson of successful economies is that governments are wise to stick mainly to general kinds of investments – schools, clinics, roads and, basic research – and to leave highly specialised business investments to the private sector.

If the government is able to successfully discharge its general functions, it sets a process in motion which shall lead to elimination of poverty.

Basically, what is needed is a commitment to end poverty within our life time. Human forces, if set in motion, by leaders who show gigantic will, are destined to transform human society. All that is required is make poverty the central objective and all measures should be designed to end it.

Poverty reduction requires a pro-poor strategy of growth which implies creation of more and more productive employment opportunities in those sectors which help the poor-to raise their level of income. This entails:

- Strengthening agriculture which provides nearly 60 per cent of employment by raising its growth rate to 4% per annum
- Strengthening a system of land tenure which provides greater security to share croppers and peasant proprietors
- Increasing the productivity and job quality of the unorganised sector
- Improving the share of wages in the process of growth as against unrestricted growth of the share of profits
- Empowerment of the poor through education and skill formation
- Empowerment of the poor through provision of better health
- Empowerment of the poor through provision of housing
- Empowerment through skill formation for our expanding IT sector
- Extending continuous employment to the poor through employment guarantee programme, not as seasonal programme but as a regular and more sustainable durable assets programme which increases productivity.
- To alter the role of state from supporting liberalisation models to those in which the state assumes a more pro-active role to create five forms of capital i.e. human capital, infrastructure, natural capital, public institutional capital and knowledge capital that can lead to end poverty.

If all these measures are taken, one can reasonably hope that a large number of poor people will be able to smile in their life time. But we have miles to go before we achieve the result.

(The writer was a well known colummist particularly writing on economic issues. He sent this piece a few months before his sad demise. Kamal Sandesh pays homage to the departed soul)

□

Freedom from Populism and Electoral Compulsions

—**Vinay Sahasrabuddhe**

All over the world, democracy appears to be well-entrenched and despite the fact that autocratic regimes continue to exist for decades, none of them is accorded any legitimacy. It appears that democracy has become something sacrosanct, notwithstanding the fact that people under some democratic regimes may be thoroughly disgruntled about the quality of governance. Many a time, people are given to understand that they have to tolerate all the lacunae in democratic governance since that is the cost of liberty that they enjoy under it.

Increasingly, people under many democratic regimes including India are becoming pessimistic as they think that no political party can really solve their problems and make their life easier. In response to this observation, political parties say that they cannot help the situation because they are the victims of the present-day system. Their political behaviour is conditioned by the system in which they operate. An impression is building that political parties are essentially incapable of coming out of populist and electoral compulsions. Although certain sections of the political class may have developed some vested interests in the system in which they operate, it is prudent to consider that the majority of politicians would like to transcend the present mould of politics. With this presumption, it is further required that a systemic solution to the crises emerging out of populist and election-oriented politics is thought of. Unless this is attempted and a road-map to convert democracy in India into a delivering democracy by way of salvaging political parties from the trap of populism and electoral compulsions is visualised, people may start losing their faith in democracy.

Making Democracy Deliver

Are all those whose stakes are involved in democratic governance aware of all this? Do they realise that they have to act fast if they are serious about making democracy deliver? Chances are that persons at the helm of affairs are aware of the perversions that have crept in India's political system but they have apparently either –

1. Chosen to ignore these threats and compromise with the situation albeit unwillingly.
2. Surrendered to the circumstances helplessly and have almost abandoned efforts to transform the situation.
3. Decided to make the most of this situation since changing the same is considered as just not possible.

Indepth probing into certain aspects of functional democracy in India is required before one finds solutions to the current crisis in our polity where we have a democracy that functions but hardly delivers. These aspects could be listed as follows—

1. Has political leadership in India grasped the enormity of the manifold crises emanating from a decadent political system? Are Indian political leaders aware of the gravity of the impact of institutional degeneration of political parties in India?
2. Have influential leaders who are in commanding positions in their respective parties for a long time and who are seriously into politics, completely lost motivation to transform the situation particularly in their own party and in Indian polity in general? Has this lack of motivation also resulted in an absolute lack of political will for reforms?
3. Is the overall absence of any structured efforts for salvaging political parties and party politics in India from its present mould, a result of inertia and a feeling of helplessness? Or, has the establishment in general and particularly India's politicians developed a vested interest in maintaining a status quo?
4. Are there any possible systemic solutions to the problem of political parties in India succumbing to populist pressures

and electoral compulsions? Would the political class be accepting such solutions?

On this background it is necessary to establish a clear link between efficacy of democracy and effective organisational functioning of political parties. The central argument here being that in India if democracy is to be consolidated, it has to deliver and if it has to deliver, the state of political parties need to be markedly improved upon. Populism and electoral compulsions are the two main obstacles in the way of good governance and effective party organisations alone can withstand these forces. True, building effective party organisations is easier said than done, mainly because of the system in which political parties operate. Hence it is all the more important to find out as to what kind of systemic changes can help strengthen political parties so as to withstand populist pressures and electoral compulsions. In that context, here an attempt has been made to suggest different sets of reforms for bringing about systemic changes that would help arrest the process of degeneration of parties.

Discernible Trends

To start with, there are certain clearly discernible trends in the present day politics in India. They could be surmised as —.

1. **Politics sans purpose**? Diminishing role of idealism and ideology in the functioning of political parties lead to a situation where people no more believe that politicians pursue politics for some great cause.
2. **Apparent similarities in party functioning.** With power-seeking becoming a great leveller, there is a growing similarity in the overall conduct of political parties in India, whether in power or otherwise.
3. **Weak party organisations**. With dynastic politics ruling the roost, organisational characters of political parties in India are fast weakening. With parties becoming a family affair, cadre and cadre-building have become irrelevant, face apathy and neglect.
4. **Decline of leadership** Erosion of authority of the leadership that gives way to personality cult; charismatic leaders attaining more importance as those working behind the curtain, for party organisation.

5. **Perennial electoral mode**. With ideology being pushed to the periphery, unprincipled coalitions on the rise add to instability. This has contributed to the atmosphere of permanent election mode adding to the tendency of politicising all and sundry, with a view to taking political advantage at any opportune time.
6. **Diminishing popular participation in democratic process**. Similarities in political parties make voters realise that the emerging situation eventually denies them the element of choice. All this adversely affecting popular level of participation in elections and thereby in the overall democratic process.

Political parties are at the core of most of the arguments made above. In addition to these macro-level issues concerning the quality of party competition and representative democracy, there are other key factors supposedly responsible for degeneration of political parties. Generally speaking, these key factors could be described as organisational impact of excessively election-oriented party politics in India. These factors are as follows—

- Growing tendency to always "play to the gallery". Excessive insistence on factors such as image building, publicity mileage and remaining in the limelight.
- Inability and dis-inclination of political parties to educate the masses. Lack of courage to take unconventional, bold/unpopular sounding decisions.
- Growing dominance of money and muscle power making electoral victories as a technique.
- With power-seeking as the prime agenda party competition taking different shapes. At certain times, it involves fierce hate mongering whereas at other occasions, it just remains make-believe with an element of match-fixing. Popular belief that all politicians are hand-in-glove in reality, has added to the increasing tendency of intense dislike or hate towards the entire political class.
- Lack of ideological motivation having a cascading effect on policy formulation processes. It has lead to a dearth of political will for governing with a particular set of principles. With compromises for continuing in power becoming an order of the day, marked erosion in the quality of governance.

- An individual's ability to get elected (Electability) taking precedence over all other factors. Consequently, unabated erosion in the quality of political leadership.
- With most parties realising that money enables them to hire 'activists', abysmal neglect of cadre building or training of the activists becoming an established trend.

Democracy is, without doubt; a way of life in the sense that it adheres to a set of values of the human life. But then it can never be denied that democracy after all is, first and foremost a system of governance. Democracy after all has to deliver the goods. The question then is whether democracy has established itself as a far more superior system of governance in the context of its ability to bring about a real change in the living standards of the people at large?

Widening Gap

As pointed out by David Broder, there are five distinct factors behind the "widening gap between acceptance and effectiveness of democracy."[1] These factors are death of ideology, decline of state, decline of religion, low esteem of politics as a profession, and the irresponsible role of media in general. Notably, of these five factors, three (death of ideology, decline of state and low esteem of politics) are directly related to political parties.

On the performance count, or what is being lately described as the "delivering" aspect of democracies, new and emerging democratic governments have more often than not, met with failures. Even after a decade of democratization, here, power is wielded with the same old style that smacks of authoritarianism, elections are still less fair and rule of law continues to be fragile.

Even in established democracies there appears to be an underlying yearning for reforming the system. Not for no reason, as recently as in November 2007 Manmohan Singh, Prime Minister of India had to appeal researchers to explore whether one-party rule as against multi-party rule is more conducive for countries like India.[2] People who are generally satisfied with democratic governance too are looking for some improvement in the way democracy is implemented or practiced. This also reinforces the issue of quality of leadership in democracies. Dissatisfaction about the political leadership in general, their ability to handle critical issues, their moral bankruptcy and poor quality of performance, etc are some of the key issues that democratic process needs to address. With ability to get elected dominating all other factors, consideration of leadership qualities while selecting a candidate has been taking a back seat. This compels one to look into the organisational character of the political parties.

Early attention

In India too, the situation warrants early attention. Having tasted almost all the available political parties as parties in government, people are now wondering about the next alternative they can look at. It was certainly not for no reason that when Shiv Sena supremeo Bal Thackrey[3] used to advocate the necessity to switch over to *Thok Shahi* (dictatorship) in place of *Lok Shahi,* (democracy) people used to respond positively. This, without any doubt, does not augur well for democracy in India.

There is a necessary interrelationship between political culture and the fundamental organic linkages between parties, populism and electoral compulsions. It is this interrelationship which shapes political culture of a country. It is on this setting that one has to view the organic relationship between democracy, parties, populism and elections in the context of India. If elections, parties, electoral campaigns and peaceful transfer of power are the instruments of democracy, India certainly can boast about them. However, whether these instruments have effectively contributed in developing a culture of democratic functionality is the moot question. If the overall quality of functioning of political parties, voluntary organisations and institutions, legislatures, and media organisations in India today is any indication; institutionalisation of the intrinsic democratic spirit is yet to come about.

On the whole, following aspects could be identified as principal features of political culture in India. These are as follows—

1. Leader-centric organisations and Leader-Follower-Voter relationship.
2. Good people with good intentions no more sustainable in power politics.
3. Promoting sycophancy, converting party cadres into cheer leaders.
4. Emotional-issue-centric electoral politics and the resultant domination of identity issues.

5. Greater role of media in shaping political culture.
6. Politics becoming a business with increased role of money power.
7. Growing domination of market-friendliness in socio-cultural life and public life in general.
8. A general apathy towards duties as voters and citizens of a democracy. Lack of civic initiatives in general.
9. Lack of an institution-building approach in conducting party affairs.

Lack of institution-building approach is the end product of excessive electoral orientation that political parties in India have acquired. Partly, it is the electoral system and the Westminster model of democracy under which the present FPTP system operates, responsible for this. Hero worship, sycophancy, greater stress on emotional issues and greater impact of media are direct results of populism. As one can see, populism and electoral compulsions are both, reasons behind the unabated degeneration of parties as well as the effect of this degeneration. The sum total of the overall consequences of this situation is reflected in increased levels of apathy and cynicism on the part of the common citizenry.

Recruitment

Here comes the discussion question of recruitment in political parties. Recruitment of individuals to politics is one of the most important functions that parties perform. Joining a political party still remains the most effective option for any one deciding to play an active role in democratic governance especially at the implementation level. Generally speaking, an attraction for a particular ideology, or a leader with a charismatic personality or a liking developed for a set of persons associated locally with a political party, etc, could be the reasons for an individual's entry in a political party. However, in none of these cases, the new entrant is either formally told about the aims and objectives of the respective party or is informally asked about his intentions behind joining the party. As a result, several political parties end up just as any other organisation with few office bearers, several storm-troopers and no particular direction to follow. No wonder, such parties fail in generating any confidence in the minds of the people.

With party affiliated candidates, cultivation of principal-agent relationship is likely to be served more effectively. While it is true that competitive indulgence in partisan politics and its horrendous consequences have prompted some Indian leaders like Jai Prakash Narayan (JP) call for promoting a party-less democracy, the concept has largely been looked at as just another Utopian idea. Moreover, if parties are considered as an important part of the problem of degeneration of our polity, they also have to be considered as equally important part of the solutions to the crises. The success of representative democracy mainly hinges upon political parties since they constitute its most significant vehicle. For the simple reason that in any democracy, where the number of electorate runs into several millions, what is always required is a "linkage" institution that "organises, distils and translates" public opinion.[4] When political parties allegedly fail in doing this job properly, two significant aspects of representative democracy viz. popular control and responsiveness are bound to suffer.

Prey to Populism

Reasons for political parties falling prey to populism and the damage that this trend may cause to the classical notions of representative democracy also warrant attention. Populism and electoral compulsions are intertwined. At times, basic populist stand points make parties surrender before electoral compulsions while at other electoral compulsions compel parties to take a populist path. Just as populism, electoral compulsions also greatly impact the functioning of political parties. Again, electoral compulsions have an organic relationship with the system in which political parties operate. In India, for example, populism has played the role of a great leveller making our major political parties look alike and function alike. This has discredited them in the eyes of the masses towards whom, ironically; populism is directed. As a consequence, a large section of the voters understandably consider that almost all the parties as unworthy of unstinted support at the national level. With fractured verdicts, parties are forced to go for coalition politics. In the cases of both the major parties in India, the Congress and the BJP, their electoral alliance with regional parties has undoubtedly stunted their growth in those particular regions. Further, their electoral presence has remained limited to constituencies in which they contest as also coalitions have denied them the chance to compete with their alliance partner.

In the Indian scenario, the organic relationship between present electoral system and political parties indulging in populist politics for electoral gains, is much more evident. With abundance of regional, linguistic and religious diversity, parties find it convenient to identify more closely with one (or many of the same type) of the diverse groups or communities and ensure support of the voters belonging to them. This tendency has come to be known as indulging in Vote-Bank Politics. A populist appeal to regional and linguistic identity is the key to Dravidian politics in Tamil Nadu, Telugu Desam in Andhra Pradesh, Mizo National Front in Mizoram as also capitalizing the agony, the underdevelopment of Assam by the Assam Gana Parishad in Assam, and the slogan of "*Marathi manoos*" (Marathi people) given by Shiv Sena. Playing on religious identity has always remained central to the politics of Akali Dal in Punjab and of course the Muslim League in Kerala and elsewhere. Shah Bano case of 1987 was a classic example of populist religious politics indulged in by the Congress. The success of political *Hindutva*[5] of the Bharatiya Janata Party (BJP) was a response to this. BJP and its earlier incarnation, Jana Sangh was always known for Hindu-oriented politics but it was only after Shah Bano that political *Hindutva* started yielding. No wonder then 'minorityism', 'pseudo-secularism', 'minority appeasement' etc. became a part of the BJP lexicon, and BJP leaders like LK Advani and others could popularise *Hindutva* only after 1987.

Electoral Compulsions

Electoral compulsions are closely related to the electoral system. Also, as underscored by the famous Duverger Law, the number of parties in a country and consequently the nature of the electoral competition depend on the electoral system a country adopts. With parliamentary democracy under the Westminster system with a First-past-the-post voting system being practiced in India, many have observed that political parties here are perpetually in an election mode. At any given point of time, in one part of India or the other, parties are always preparing for elections and this greatly impacts upon their style of functioning. Also, stability of a government depends on the electoral system and if voters realise that in spite of their participation in voting, elections have been throwing only fractured verdicts, it reflects on their enthusiasm for voting. Generally speaking, behaviour of political parties is governed by the electoral system and both these factors together impact upon the quality of democracy. Arend Lijphart's research clearly brings out that "Consensus democracy may be considered more democratic than majoritarian in most respects."

New Trends

Fifty-seven years after India became a republic, some new trends are becoming discernible. Following the break-down of the Congress system, there is now a clearly perceptible shift. Indian party system has now moved from hegemonic to a competitive multi-party at the national level. Broadly, three coalitional alternatives are emerging although durability of these alliances is always uncertain. At the states, an independent party system is emerging and at times and in certain states it is totally different from the national system. Three clear typologies are emerging. In a large number of states, it is Congress+ versus Regional Party+. In some others, it is Congress+ versus BJP+ and in the remaining; it is between two largely regional alternatives.[6] In other words, while Congress is declining in some key states like Bihar, UP and Tamil Nadu, BJP is still to find an effective foot-hold in Kerala, and many states in the North-East. Absence of BJP consequently leads to a vacuum which regional parties come forward and fill. This has added to the fertility of political ground resulting in greater political fragmentation. Obviously, this does not augur well for the evolution of a sound two-party system. Another notable trend is that of anti-incumbency. While this particular element has reinforced the process of polarisation of polity, it has also created an altogether different kind of challenge in front of representative democracy. With anti-incumbency becoming an established trend, the element of deterrence of the voters'- power, which is inherent to the electoral politics, is getting diluted for obvious reasons. Those in power, now indulge in corruption for a huge collection of illegitimate funds since any way 'they have to forgo power', while those in opposition afford to remain docile since 'anyway the next turn is theirs'. In the emerging scenario, all serious political parties are facing challenges. If Congress has to maintain its pan-Indian supremacy, it has to institutionalise itself in a sound way. BJP has to emerge as a pan-national alternative while constructing a national consensus about its own acceptability. All other parties, mainly the Communists have to concentrate upon expanding their base and appear as a credible third alternative.

In the absence of any serious efforts to meet these challenges, for a large section of the people democracy may be reduced to just a partisan competition to win formal popular support. This disillusionment about democracy will, as compared to any other developed nation, cost India more heavily and hence a quest for solutions is all the more important in the context of India. Before going deep into the relationship between democracy, political parties, populism and electoral compulsions; the discussion will also look into the salient features of political culture in India.

On this background the necessary link between efficacy of democracy and effective organisational functioning of political parties needs to be institutionalised. Since the present system has effectively blurred this link, enhancing the quality of party-functioning rarely finds a place on the agenda of national discourse. Across the political spectrum, senior and old politicians appear to have lost the zeal for taking initiative for reforms. Those who are young and have at least 20-30 years of active politics ahead are vary of reforms since they apprehend that reforms (and within the party, even asking for a debate on reforms) may affect their political career. Besides, if political parties, organisations or individuals clamour for reforms, there is always an apprehension that motives will be attached to their demand. The circumstances in which NDA government abandoned any follow-up of the National Commission for the review of the functioning of Constitution are a case in point.

For those who take pride in regular holding of elections and anti-incumbency as an established trend, it is noteworthy that thanks to this trend, some clearly undemocratic traits are emerging. As observed by Justice CS Dharmadhikari[7]: "Those in power, ignore public interest and work on an obviously selfish agenda because they consider it a certainty that they are going to be dethroned no matter how best they govern. Similarly, those in the opposition also ignore genuine public interest and indulge in all sorts of wheeling and dealing as they believe that in any case the next term in the government is any way theirs. This has taken the perversion of politics to a new low."

About inertia for systemic change, there appears to be an overriding feeling that the present Westminster model has no better alternative. Although this feeling is baseless, in an atmosphere where political reforms have hardly occupied any central position in India's national public discourse, doing away with a sense of resignation is extremely hard.

On this background, it makes sense to reommend initiating a national debate on the need for political reforms and later, on the nature of reforms. Having established that unless parties are compelled to function in a systematic way, representative democracy can not free itself from its shortcomings, this essay makes some concrete recommendations along with some general suggestions.

Recommendations—

A. Constitutional reforms:

1. Defections at every level and whether that of an individual or a group, should be banned making vacation of seat by the defector, mandatory. Even for an independent candidate, switching loyalties once declared, should automatically attract disqualification.
2. A system of 'Constructive vote of no-confidence' should be introduced.
3. A system of recognising a pre-poll alliance should be in place. Issuing a joint public-declaration explaining the objectives of the alliance and the nature of understanding should be made mandatory.
4. All post-poll alliances should be primarily disallowed. The election commission should have the discretion of allowing such alliances, only in exceptional cases with a view to breaking the constitutional deadlock and after filing due affidavits about the common minimum programme and common policy perspectives with a clause for conditions under which alliance could be dissolved.

B. Constitutional reforms for better functioning of parties:

It is urgently required that possibilities for introducing a comprehensive law regulating and disciplining the functioning of parties are thoroughly explored. Such legislation should include aspects like recruitment, internal democracy, leadership, human resource development, policy shifts, coalitional arrangements, financial transparency and accountability as well as a strict code of conduct for elected representatives and party office bearers.

On the lines of party-supported foundations in Germany (stiftungs), efforts should be made to explore establishing training and research foundations for and by parties with a partial financial assistance from the government. By the time all these reforms are given a serious thought, what can be done urgently is establishing an independent organisation called "Political Party Watch" to monitor parties on certain important counts.

This essay recommends following concrete reforms—

1. Reforms for making the process of establishing a new political party more serious and elaborate with a focus on transparency, accountability and internal democracy.
2. Mandatory publication of annual accounts of parties, at the national and state levels.
3. Mandatory publication of Annual report of Party activities.
4. Mandatory maintenance of Party Membership Register at the state and district levels.
5. Mandatory holding of elections for party office bearers under the supervision of Election Commission at least once in every five years.
6. Mandatory establishment of an internal Training, Research and Development Department for every national party, with clear guidelines about some basic Training in Democracy for all party functionaries.
7. Mandatory comprehensive training for all first-time elected people's representatives and party office bearers. Making a provision that no elected official could seek re-nomination without undergoing training.

C. Electoral Reforms

Measures like Code of Conduct of the Election Commission are in vogue for quite some time. While the focus of this Code of Conduct is mainly on preventing the use of public money/facilities for partisan purposes, that itself is not enough. With a more positive and truly democratic approach, following measures with a clear focus on educating the masses and bringing transparency, could be introduced—

1. Giving incentive for publishing Report to the Electorate by every elected representative at every level, every year.
2. Mandatory publication of the details of candidates' assets in local newspapers and on local channels.
3. Mandatory publication of a manifesto by contesting parties at respective levels followed by a mandatory Action Taken Report (ATR) on the manifestoes (even parties that have lost the elections can inform about their efforts to follow up on their promises) by every political party.
4. Considering MCPR as an alternative. In our quest to find solutions to the problems inherent in the FPTP system, probing as to whether introduction of Mixed Compensatory Proportional Representation (MCPR) will do away with most, if not all; the ills of FPTP merits deeper analysis. Apart from a constant danger of instability and taking recourse to all kinds of unethical tactics to thwart instability, FPTP system also has several lacunae. It over-represents the majority while denying any adequate space for scattered minorities. In a bid to avoid political marginalisation, minorities tend to vote en-bloc, leading to some kind of a perpetuation of vote-bank politics. Merits and demerits of PR vis-à-vis the present system of FPTP also merit elaborate discussion.

A Case for Proportional Representation

There are many individuals, political scientists and constitutional experts, and also organisations, which have been advocating switching over to Proportional Representation (PR). According to them, as compared to the present Westminster Model, PR is more likely to help improve the quality of democratic governance and in effect arrest the growing indifference towards the democratic process, leading to cynicism and eventual lack of faith in democratic ideals. TM Joseph, a researcher; after reviewing the relationship between democratic representation and electoral system in India, strongly recommends that "the German model is well placed to feature strongly as it ensures stability, allows constituency representation and provides outcome far more proportional"[8] than our present system.

Organisations like *Janadesh,* a platform for National Campaign for Political Reforms have been very strongly advocating that India should switch over to PR. Claiming hat under PR, parties are under almost no pressure to be the biggest and loudest voice and hence less expenditure is required to win, advocates of PR argue that PR is best suited to reduce corruption.

Even under the Westminster system, competent and honest persons who prefer to remain away from direct electoral politics for obvious reasons can easily enter the legislatures via the upper houses. But, as past experience shows, the parties have largely abused this particular provision of the constitution. Upper houses in state legislatures in India are often used as back-door entry points for veteran politicians who have either failed in the direct elections or who are not confidant of facing the electorate. Constitution-makers have provided for nominations of certain number of individuals from different walks of public life in the upper houses (In the Rajyasabha and in the Legislative Councils in states). However, past experiences show that this provision has been abused by nominating hardcore politicians under the same.

PR has also been recommended in the 170th Report of the Law Commission of India (1999). The report says, "we feel that a combination of FPP (FPTP) and the list systems... may best meet our needs."[9] In order to find solution to this crisis through changing the electoral system, the Law Commission reviewed all the 212 parliamentary electoral systems listed in *The Global Distribution of Electoral Systems* in order to assess what might be the most suitable for us. After an elaborate analysis the commission has recommended a combination of both the present FPTP system and the List system. Besides, as claimed by *Janadesh,* several political parties including CPI(M), DMK, MDMK, The Indian Union Muslim League and Shiromani Akali Dal have also supported PR.[10]

Proportional Representation could perhaps be described as the most likely answer in this quest for systemic solutions to India's democratic deficit. As compared to FPTP, PR will provide greater political stability and more certainty about the schedule of elections. PR provides for a simultaneous voting for an individual as well as for a party and this element is more likely to reduce the technique element that has gripped our electoral system. With the provision of List System, chances for consideration for the ability of a candidate are in a way reinstated. This will automatically encourage entry of good, well meaning and quality people in politics.

Implementing at least some of these reforms and attempting a healthy debate on the advisability of Proportional Representation is a tall order. Ironically, the hurdles in the way of these reforms are again those very factors against whom systemic solutions need to be found out. Again and again, it is populism and populism alone that has prevented a public discourse on the issues that concern majority of Indians.

(The writer is a Member, National Executive, & Convenor, All India Training Cell, BJP.)

References

1. David Broder. Senior journalist and commentator from the US in his Lecture at the Salzburg Seminar session 384, on Democracy. June 13, 2001.
2. Report about Manmohan Singh's speech in International Conference on Federalism in New Delhi as appeared in *The Times of India*, Mumbai dated November 6, 2007.
3. Bal Thackrey, is the octogenarian founder-supreme leader of Shiv Sena. Shiv Sena is the main opposition party in Maharashtra. Started as a party that staunchly advocated the sons-of-soil theory initially; Shiv Sena is also known for the radical sounding views and out-of-box thinking of its leadership. Shiv Sena had not opposed the Emergency of 1975 and Thackrey has repeatedly and publicly expressed his disenchantment with democracy and preference for some kind of a benevolent dictatorship.
4. Everett Carl Ladd "Where Have All the Voters Gone?". xxi (New York. London, WW Norton and Co.1982)
5. This is a term used by many, including political commentator Swapan Dasgupta with a view to describing the politicization of aggrieved feelings of the majority Hindus in India. Although *Hindutva* literally means Hindu-ness, the political connotations of the term vary from person to person.
6. Jammu and Kashmir, Haryana, Andhra Pradesh, Kerala, West Bengal, Meghalaya, Orissa, Sikkim and Mizoram come in the first category where the polarization is between Congress and regional alternatives. In Himachal Pradesh, Punjab, Uttarakhand, Rajasthan, Madhya Pradesh, Delhi, Gujarat, Chhattisgarh, Maharashtra, Bihar, Jharkhand,

Karnataka and Orissa it is Congress + versus BJP+. In states like Tamil Nadu, and now Uttar Pradesh, it is a fight primarily between two regional party conglomerations.

7. As told to the author in an interview in Mumbai on June 27,2007.
8. TM Joseph, "Democracy and Representation in India: Does Electoral System matter?" in *Gandhi Marg,* Oct-Nov. 2006, p.321.
9. 170th Report of the Law Commission (India), http://www.lawcommissionofindia.nic.in/lc170.htm as on Jan. 2, 2006
10. A pamphlet by *Janadesh,* Lok Satta (movement), Maharashtra.

□

Women in India Today : Need for Refreshing Our Mindset

—**Nirmala Sitharaman**

There is a need for refreshing our mindset, our national mindset, on women. We pride ourselves that women are worshipped here; even the Supreme is conceptualised as '*ardhanari*'. Not just worshipped, but accepted and honoured as great Gurus, Sages and Seers. Gargi, Paulomi, Vishpala are a few names from over thirty who gave us our eternal *Vedas*.

Consider the five women of yore, whom we are taught to recall every morning as exemplary: Sita, Mandodari, Tara, Draupadi, Ahalya. Add Kunti and Savitri; they are well known for their womanhood and dedication to their beloved husbands. But the greatness of our civilisation lies in the fact that *we did not exempt* them from this hoary list of great women for their striking individuality, self-confidence, scholarship, audacity to question authority, perseverance or even for their occasional adventurism.

Take a step forward. Padmini, Rani Chennamma, Rani of Jhansi were more brave than were many of the men rulers of their times. For Honnamma, Molla and Vengamamba, caste was no barrier to scholarship. Tarabai Mohite and Chandbibi were sparkling administrative genius and strong characters.

Our contemporary history too is crowded with women of grit and distinction who have risen to become the President, Prime Minister or Chief Ministers, judges, legislatures, litterateurs, reporters, journalists, sportspersons, mountaineers, astronauts and entertainers. They head international businesses. By default or by choice, women continue to anchor families, do the chores of the households, and effectively or otherwise function as the storehouse of the culture and tradition of their families.

Fear is that these are achieved at a great cost. Several million unknown and unseen women are bearing this cost. The cost is that of being bypassed, left unreached and uncared for. We have failed miserably to reach out to them; are we not even sensitive to their basic needs?

Notwithstanding our noble attitude towards our women, almost every 30 minutes one rape is committed in India. Every hour 18 women are victims of crime directed specifically at them. The most shameful fact is that in nearly 75.1% of the rape cases the offenders were known to the victims.

The National Crime Records data reveal that 7,618 women were killed for dowry in 2006. This marked a 12.2% increase over the previous year. Death is only a culmination for the victims who most certainly endured verbal, psychological and mental abuse and stress before this ignoble end. Didn't Manu, the lawmaker, leave us in the care of fathers before marriage and husbands after?

We are talking of refreshing our mindset on women. There are innumerable references in the *Mahabharata* which can help us make a start. One such says, "*Bharya hi paramo hyarthah...*" (*Shanti parva.144.14*), meaning, the greatest wealth of a man is his wife.

Shakuntala of Dushyanta fame eloquently says, "*Ardhe bharyaa manushasya, bharyaa sreshtatamh sakaa; Bhaarya moolam trivargasya, bhaarya mulam tarishyatah.*" (*Aadhi Parva, 74.41*). The wife is a man's other half; the wife is his best friend. The wife is the root of all order, of material prosperity, of the fulfilment of desires.

These are not occasional references; our Epics, Puranas, and Upanishads are replete with such noble thoughts. What have we done to ourselves? Why this decadence? Can a strong Dowry Prohibition Act deal with our mindsets? Laws are expected to deter the exceptional misconduct or punish the black sheep in the flock.

Our fathers and brothers who demand and take dowry are unable to give the same when it comes to their daughters and sisters! Do they appreciate the difference between *streedhan* and dowry? Is it *streedhan* for daughters and dowry for daughters-in-law?

Can we explain the "missing girl child" from our census data over the last few decades? Why don't we want the *Ghar ki Mahalakshmi?* Women from Kerala and Bihar are being married off to men in Haryana because they have very few women of marriageable age now. Except for a few heart-warming stories of inter-regional harmony, trade in women with lure or duplicity is growing. This has led to social tension of an unimaginable scale.

If this is how families and friends treat their women, look at what institutions, due to their inefficiency, are doing to them. Lack of access to proper medical care, absence of assistants and indifference charecterise our public health. This results in "about 65% of Indian women still delivering their babies at home" (Dr A Ramadoss, quoted by Reuters, 1 March 2007). As a result we do not have an idea of the number of safe deliveries. No agreed data on Maternal Mortality is available yet. The National Family Health Survey gives one set of figures and the WHO arrives at another. Methods of calculations vary, they say. But both and many others would agree that the figure cannot be better than 400 per 100,000 live births. India accounts for 20% of the world's maternal deaths, with a woman dying every five minutes. Paul Hunt, an official of the UN reportedly said, "If you are about to deliver a baby, they must be the last places you would wish to go", he said, referring to the Indian states he visited.

If lack of access and service is keeping women away from health services, take a look at custodial homes and prisons

Prison Statistics of India, 2006 reported a terrible shortage of space. Occupancy rate in various jails was very high against the available capacity for female inmates. Over 12 states reported prison occupancy of more than 100% over the available capacity. Another insensitive and uncaring gesture (unlawful too?) is to keep undertrials in prisons. Jails exclusively meant to lodge women convicts have women undertrials too: Delhi (383), Maharashtra (345) followed by Punjab, Rajasthan, Tamil Nadu, Bihar and Kerala.

Who account for these large numbers of undertrials among women? In Andhra Pradesh and Tamil Nadu women often are the carriers of sachets/pouches of liquor. It is common knowledge that when the excise department wishes to prove its performance, it fills its fact sheet with the arrests of these women. This is a legal step but distorts the picture of illegal liquor trade. These women are but the last link in a big long chain whose top brass are never brought to book.

After the arrest, these women languish as undtrials most often as families cannot bail them out. Many such women whom I have met had stayed longer in jails as undertrials than their conviction would warrant, if and when proven guilty. Some of them were not acceptable to their families when they returned as 'they had been in jail'.

Women often are the victims of police brutality. They are roughed up, arrested by policemen at ungodly hours, asked to get their witnesses even in prosecution cases. Women prisoners are often reportedly abused and exploited. There are instances of elderly women languishing in the prisons even after their due time, for want of place to go to.

Our criminal justice system needs to be revamped. Cases affecting women such as eve teasing and rape do not reach their logical conclusion. NRI husbands who desert their wives or forcefully take custody of their children rarely respond to the Indian Courts.

Rural India has fewer opportunities for men and women. Agriculture is no longer profitable. Even subsistence agriculture is not sustainable any more. The proportion of population depending on agriculture for subsistence is more than 50% while the share of agriculture in the GDP has dropped considerably

The Census 2001 showed that 28% of all working women are farmers. Not all of these women have land titles. It is relevant here to note that between 1991 and 2001 there was a substantial decrease in the number of male agricultural labourers while simultaneously there was an increase in the numbers of women agricultural labourers. Smt Meena Swaminathan says, "Farming too is getting more feminised, thanks to men's migration, leaving women to take care of the land".

But why should men migrate leaving women to tend to the unyielding land? Women, who most often do not possess land titles, cannot raise credit, and after all cannot do all jobs in the field. The National Rural Employment Guarantee Scheme promising 100 days of work for every rural family in the battle against rural poverty should have kept the men back? The *Wall Street Journal* (Live mint.com) reported on 10 January 2008, "only 3% of households which signed up received employment for 100 days and many got only 2 weeks". It was reported that the internal audit of the Scheme cited, "widespread examples of corruption, inefficiency and misuse of funds for the poor performance."

Men migrating to cities, rising input costs in agriculture and differential wages are factors contributing to the vulnerability of women. When a woman journalist is attacked and killed while returning home from work, or when a woman staff of a BPO is killed the media rightly draws the attention of the nation. The collective consciousness of the nation gets a blow. The risks the rural poor women are exposed to are only stories for Bollywood to show as a feature film.

Women in vulnerable socioeconomic situations were victimised by the proverbial landlords or the *rentier* class. Those days are *passé*. They are now approached by faceless middlemen and touts with great promises and advance cash payments for 'jobs' in large metros. These women actually end up becoming a part of a large international racket in human trafficking. The BBC reported in July 2006 that the number of prostitutes in India has risen by 50% in less than a decade (1997-2006). Many of the women joining the trade are between 12-15 years of age. Dr KK Mookerjee who conducted this study explained the reasons for the growth: "New stimulating factors are a change in attitudes, sex trade, migration, globalisation and increase in hospitality industry".

These very reasons have also driven young women to terror groups. Women are drawn by the aggressive ideology or by the opportunity to fight the system which failed them. However, it is alleged that even in the ideologically proud Naxal groups, women play the role of comfort girls. Young women wielding guns is a romanticised image projected by the Maoists. The Maoists may address these women as *'akka'* (sister) but their role in the non-combat aspects is well known.

We quite often come across reports of illegal immigrants arrested in various parts of our country who are married to Indian women. The attitude of the parents or of the women towards such a marriage in the context of the family-community-nation is worth analysing. This has serious national security and social implications.

The 73rd & 74th Amendments to the Constitution gave one-third of reservation for women at the *panchayat* level elected bodies. Many women that this writer has talked to were given an opportunity to actively plan and execute, alongside men, for their immediate local economies. Nearly two decades after this major step we see there is a shift in the priorities in planning for the betterment of the communities. Clearly, women's participation has brought the focus back to the family, children and environmental matters. Women's participation has ensured that a little more thought went into issues that especially concerned women and children: water connections are nearer households, old schools have toilets and newer schools are no longer in the remote corner causing safety concerns.

Simultaneously, with Self Help Groups spreading to include more and more women, village economies are showing dynamism, enough to propel self-confidence, but insufficient to meet growing aspirations. Moreover, with the devolution of financial powers still awaited, the local *panchayats* are with workable ideas and without the resources.

Today, refreshing our mindset towards our women is essential, particularly because of the impact globalisation is having on our society. Economy, society and culture are each dynamic on their own and have influences on one another in vibrant ways. Attempts at measuring these influences can only touch the tip of an iceberg. Measuring them in their entirety would be a sheer impossibility due to their dimensions and nature of being dynamic. Most importantly, impact on culture cannot be quantified. Are we prepared for the avalanche of influences that is now engulfing us? Before we find an answer to this, it will be useful to understand a few features on how our society has evolved over the centuries.

Like the proverbial spider, we have woven our society from within ourselves —from the eternal Vedas. We welcomed changes and new ideas, proudly declaring: *"Aaa no bhadhraah kratavo yantu visvatah"*— Let noble thoughts come from every side. (Rig Veda I.89) True to this magnificent thought, India continues to be the melting pot of various cultures.

There are inscriptions and literary references to show as how and when changes were necessary, thanks to this open and welcoming culture that we wove for ourselves, we responded to new and fresh ideas. Where necessary, we adapted ourselves to the changes. Our law makers responded, sometimes positively, several other times regressively, to change the laws that governed us to keep our society and culture intact.

I wish to draw your attention to an excellent book written by Shakuntala Rao Shastri, *Women in the Sacred Laws*. In this small book the author effectively brings out in great detail, how in the last nearly three thousand years we have responded to the changes we so welcomed; and carefully weeded out the not so "noble thoughts" which also blew in.

This we did with ease because it was our *sanskruti* – culture to accommodate, to be at peace with oneself and with others. It was our *sanskruti* to do everything that will hold a society and community together. And family is where the society/community begins. Nothing that would break or fragment family-society-community was considered "noble". For example, violence breaks and disintegrates and hence is unacceptable.

All this we did with a certain inner strength — a strength which came out of the fact that man and woman are only two halves of the same whole.

"Sa imamevatmanam dvedha apatayat; tatah patisca patni ca abhavatvam. Tasmaat idam ardha brgalamiva sva iti ha sma aha yagyavalkyah"

Meaning: The Divine person parted one's very body into two: from that came husband and wife. Therefore Yagyavalkya said this body (of husband or wife) is one half of oneself, like one of the two halves of a split pea. (*Brhadaranyaka Upanishad* I.4.3)

Western feminists demand changes in the law from a position of weakness. This weakness springs out of a myth that is ingrained in their religious belief: women came out of the rib of man and hence are inferior to him. From this position of weakness based on a myth they are fighting for another myth: equality.

Over the centuries and even till date, when we failed to protest against the regressive laws made by our ancient or new lawmakers or when we even forgot our strength and joined the fight for the mythical equality, we felt weak and powerless. Our attitude and language was to demand as though from our 'superiors' and not talking to our partners, in addressing our problems. Thus, we alienated our fathers, brothers and husbands. We cannot repeat this mistake. We have to address the issues which arise in the process of economic and cultural globalisation together with our men.

Swami Ranganathananda states "We have no ideological restrictions against women's development, apart from the feudal (add colonial) social stagnation that we have inherited, which is still very powerful, especially in our rural areas". If this is so, then it is the feudal and colonial baggage that we have to throw away first. Together with this, the junk that is blowing in from globalisation should also go out. In accordance with this, Pundit Deen Dayal Upadhyaya says, "The acceptance of new things can be invigorating and conducive to growth of a nation only if it is in keeping with its values, modes of life, ideals and age-long traditions".

Family is the key to our social structure. It is the basic unit on which our nation's strength lies. The importance of family is recognized by the United Nations under article 23(I) of the International Covenant on Civil and political rights, adopted by the General Assembly on 16 December 1966. It declares: "The family is the natural and fundamental group unit of society and is entitled to protection by society and State".

Deliberate efforts should be made to keep the family intact. I go a step further – nuclear or joint family should be nurtured. It will be relevant here to cite *Dharma the Global Ethic*, written by Justice Rama Jois. The author puts forward a coherent case for family life. The *Dharmic* obligation to subordinate personal interests to serve the children and elders of ones family is not prejudiced in favour of the man or the woman. It is an obligation set on both and an obligation that was laid with a foresight to keep a healthy and humane social order.

In a globalised world, care of the sick, disabled and destitute are demanded as human rights from a faceless establishment. We are ready to pay huge taxes for a social security network which will establish homes for the aged, but we are unwilling to share our responsibility of our own parents, particularly, widowed mothers. In the Mahabharata, *Shanti Parva* (108.13, 28-30), it is said that there is nothing more reprehensible than to disregard one's mother. Are we in compliance with this excerpt when looking at the status of a widow vis-à-vis a widower within our households?

On the other hand, nowadays young couples take on professionally demanding jobs. Not only is the money needed to keep the family together but from the woman's point of view, educated and qualified as she is, she too needs to achieve professional excellence. However, in the globalised world, professionals work for a global clock which has a 24-hours 'day' time. It is from this ill of globalisation that through our laws we have to particularly guard our women.

The 24-hours 'day' time clock promotes and perpetuates pure materialism and consumerism. You earn more spend more, earn even more and... so on. This way, the individual is gratified, albeit, only at a material plane. The welfare of the other individuals (elders, sick and dependents) is forgotten. The family has forgotten the *Dharma* and is only focussing on *artha* and *kama*.

This way we neither fulfil our duty to our elders nor do we receive their guidance for our children.

Recently, an Act was passed in the Parliament of India for the protection and upkeep of Parents. The Act is welcome. However, the Act cannot say what Dharmavyadha, a mere meat-seller told Sage Kaushika,'*... go back to them...go and serve your parents...*' with the same passion, can it? (Mahabharata, *Vana Parva* 215.13)

Taking the debate further, Vandana Shiva in *Earth Democracy* gives several specific examples of how the globalised economy makes *'living cultures'* sterile and gradually kills them. "Dying cultures kill themselves, and from their negative identity unleash violence on others...We...have a deep identity of place... we have bonds of family community and country... Living cultures are rooted in life – the life of the earth, the life of the community."

This killing of living cultures can be seen through the changing contents of our television programmes. There are very few programmes with no violence. There is no distilling the good from the unacceptable. Many serials of the West that are downgrade, cheap and canned and are shown regularly — unfortunately these are watched by our young. They start role playing these characters as if they are worthy of our emulation. They dress, eat and speak like them. Gradually they draw on their attitudes too. Irrespective of age or experience, everyone is equal and this belief is manifested in every thought, word and deed.

This is completely at variance with our culture — age and experience is expressly respected. In turn, the aged and experienced were accommodating, encouraging and mentoring the young. Unmindful of this, when we emulate what is alien, the consequence can be disastrous.

The case of the young upcoming artist on the television trying to prove her talents to a ruthless jury was covered by the media. This is the impact of globalisation on our socio-cultural ethos. The girl is now in a hospital luckily, being attended to by her family and not by the faceless welfare institutions. Most of these Indian icon building television programmes are copies of the American aggressive original. They do not identify icons but draw our young to a false world of talent search. During the process, these talent searchers drive the participants to aggressive display of their skills and pressure them to clothe themselves in 'acceptable' attire. They even transform the appearance of the participant – don't we remember *Jassi Jaisi Koi Nahin*.

And now, Jassi should be 'size zero' too. After all is over, the icon, successful or otherwise does not know who she is – should she be the girl she was or the wannabe icon? Is she a puppet or a robot?

How does this impact our women, you may ask? The Indian way to be an icon was through the *guru shishya parampara*: slowly but surely through the rigour of learning and *sadhana/riyaaz* you hone your skills. One is recognised as they are budding and recognised when mature too. Contrary to this is the approach to icon building, which is inherently *vkriti(regressive)* in nature. Families see the quick publicity for their girls through the media. They invest in their clothing, teach a few each of folk, classical, contemporary songs and rush to the competition. Is this sustainable?

There is only big money in all this – the impact of globalised media, energised by the advertising industry for a global audience. All this breed a sense of insecurity in men and women. When insecurity spreads in the society, it is particularly women's freedom which is affected.

The final word on statecraft is given by Bhishma in the *Shanti parva* (12.68.32):

> *"Striyasca-purusa margam sarvalankarabhusitah;*
> *Nirbhaya pratipadyante yada raksati bhumipah."*

Meaning: That is a well governed state, where women are adorned with all dress and ornaments, and unaccompanied by men, can move freely and fearlessly on its roads and lanes.

Women can contribute in building such a society. We need not get carried away to either extreme. Women are not that 'precious object' to be constantly under protection. At the other extreme, she cannot be the 'free-from-man' feminist.

Even Betty Friedan, the pioneering American Feminist had to reconsider her earlier thoughts. Somewhere between the two extremes is the sustainable and true position that she is but a half of a whole. However, she cannot be denied her space in that whole.

Our laws will have to be made with a humanistic world view. We have to periodically refresh our memory with the noble thoughts our ancients have given us on respecting balanced womanhood. Simultaneously newer thoughts should also be welcomed.

(The writer is a member of BJP National Executive)

□

Illegal migrations: The Way Out

—**Prakash Singh**

Migrations have been taking place from the beginning of civilisation. People move across the borders for a variety of reasons: political, ethnic, economic, military or environmental – sometimes, a combination of these. The process of globalisation, the lure of better economic opportunities in developed countries and the ethnic conflicts in certain regions gave fillip to trans-border movements. In the recent past however, there has been a steady growth of anti-immigrant feeling in several countries. The unskilled immigrants are looked upon as a burden on the country's economy. Social tensions also develop between the natives and immigrants because of their different backgrounds. In Europe, the anti-foreigner sentiment in countries like Germany, France and Austria contributed to the emergence of right-wing parties which thrived on anti-immigrant feelings. Several countries have passed legislation to limit immigration.

In the US, particularly after September 11, there was a general feeling that the immigration system needs to be made tighter. In two national polls, at least 80 per cent Americans concluded that the United States had "made it too easy" for foreigners to enter the country. USA therefore enacted the PATRIOT Act which mandated the Justice Department to develop an entry-exit system to control immigration.

Illegal Migrations from Bangladesh

One of the biggest problems facing India and having a direct bearing on the country's economy and security is that of the continuing illegal migration of Bangladeshis into India. After 1947, a large number of Hindus crossed over from East Pakistan to the states of West Bengal, Assam and Tripura. In due course, when the Pak Army started persecuting the Bengalis, a large number of Muslims also crossed the borders into India. After the break-up of Pakistan and the liberation of Bangladesh in 1971, it was expected that the new regime would ensure communal harmony and tackle the social and economic problems of its teeming millions in a manner which would eliminate or at least reduce the factors contributing to migration. However, that did not happen and both Hindus and Muslims continued to pour into India in huge numbers.

The assassination of Sheikh Mujib in August 1975, lifting of the ban on communal parties by General Zia-ur Rehman, and declaration of Islam as State religion in 1988 by General Ershad were accompanied by intensified attacks on the minorities – the Hindus, Buddhists, Christians and the tribals. The demolition of the Babri shrine in India in 1992 had a disastrous fall out: thousands of Hindu houses were destroyed, hundreds of Hindu women raped and innumerable Hindu temples desecrated or destroyed. The Hindu population of Bangladesh has, as a result, been declining. The parliamentary elections of October 2001 in Bangladesh were followed by yet another wave of persecution of the minorities because of their suspected support to the Awami League which lost at the hustings. A British journalist, John Vidal, in an article published in *The Guardian*, commented on the pogrom in Bangladesh in the following words: "In 2001, dozens of people were killed, more than 1,000 women from minority groups were raped and several thousand people lost their land in three months around the election". A Bangladeshi writer, Salam Azad, observed that the Hindus in Bangaldesh appeared to be left with only three options: to embrace Islam, to leave Bangladesh, or to commit suicide. The government of Bangladesh turned a blind eye to these crimes and allowed the culprits, mostly Bangladesh Nationalist Party (BNP) followers and the Jamaat cadres, to go scot-free. The Amnesty International also criticised the government of Bangladesh for the large scale attacks on the country's minority communities, particularly the Hindus.

The Muslims have been moving into India primarily for economic reasons and it is estimated that presently they constitute nearly seventy per cent of the infiltrants. The net result is that Bangladeshis of all hues have been flooding India. According to Sharifa Begum of the Bangladesh Institute of Development Studies in Dhaka, nearly 3.5 million people "disappeared" from East Pakistan between 1951 and 1961, and that another 1.5 million possibly entered India between 1961 and 1974. The records of the Election Commission of Bangladesh also make an interesting study. In 1991, the electoral roll of Bangladesh had 6,21,81,745 voters but, during their revision undertaken in 1995, the Commission had to delete the names of 61,65,567 voters from the electoral rolls, apparently because these people were no more living within Bangladesh. Again, in June 1996, the Commission removed the names of nearly 120 thousand Bangladeshi citizens from the country's electoral rolls. These people were not disappearing in thin air – they were moving towards the contiguous states of India.

The factors which have been encouraging the influx from Bangladesh side are:

- steep rise in population with increasing pressure on land and mounting unemployment,
- recurrent natural disasters like floods and cyclones, uprooting large segments of humanity,
- better economic opportunities in India,
- religious persecution of Hindus and discrimination of tribals,
- Islamic interests encouraging expansion of territory,
- organised immigration by touts and anti-social elements, and
- porous and easily negotiable international borders.

The bulk of the Bangladeshi immigrants are in the states of Assam, West Bengal, Bihar, Delhi and the North-Eastern states. An estimate of Bangladeshi immigrants in India was provided by Madhav Godbole, who headed the Task Force on Border Management. In his report, submitted to the Government of India in August 2000, he placed the figure at 15 million with about 300 thousand Bangladeshi nationals entering India illegally every year.

Lebensraum

Bangladesh is one of the most densely populated countries of the world. The pressure on land is immense. The Bangladesh government, therefore, hardly makes any efforts to stop the exfiltrations. On the contrary, it is perhaps happy that it would have that many less persons to feed and take care of. A section of intellectuals in Bangladesh have even been legitimising the theory of *lebensraum* - living space for the people of Bangladesh. In early nineties, Sadiq Khan, a former diplomat, publicised the following views:

"There is no reason why Bangladesh should not raise, in any appropriate UN forum, the question of a world demographic order. There is no reason why regional and international cooperation could not be worked out to plan and execute population movements and settlements to avoid critical demographic pressures in pockets of high concentration. There is no reason why under-populated regions in the developed world cannot make room for planned colonies to relieve build up of demographic disasters in countries like Bangladesh."

Several other thinkers, economists and former diplomats of Bangladesh have also been articulating the idea of free movement of people across the international borders. Prof. Amena Mohsin of Dhaka University asserted that "migration is a normal and natural phenomenon and cannot be stopped, the need today is to evolve ways to legalise it". Abdul Momin, former Foreign Secretary of Bangladesh, suggested that "our bulging population might find a welcome in adjacent lands inhabited by kindred peoples".

The concept of *lebensraum* has been vehemently attacked by Indian thinkers. Baljit Rai considers the formulations of Sadiq Khan "an astute attempt at international banditry, gangsterism, land-grabbing and squatting".

Assam

During the period 1991-2001, the bordering districts of Assam witnessed very high increase in the growth of Muslim population. It was 29.5% in Dhubri, 31.7% in Goalpara, 27.2% in Hailakandi, 29.4% in Karimganj and 24.6% in Cachar. The growth of non-Muslim population was much lower. The Assamese are greatly worried over the prospect of immigrants gradually acquiring voting rights and thereby exercising undue political influence in the state legislature. Bezboruah is of the view that there should be "some kind of legislative safeguard by assuring a certain number of seats to the indigenous people". Sanjoy Hazarika's recommendation is that "not less than 60% (seats) should be reserved for the local communities".

West Bengal

The Task Force on Border Management recorded that "due to large scale immigration, the border belt of the West Bengal has become predominantly Muslim". According to a study done by the Centre for the State and South-East Asia Studies, out of the 292 assembly constituencies of West Bengal, Bangladeshi immigrants can determine the poll outcome in 52 assembly constituencies while in another 100 constituencies they can significantly influence it.

North-Eastern States

The sparsely populated states of the North-East are being overwhelmed with the arrival of Bangladeshis. In Nagaland, the Bangladeshis are mostly concentrated in and around Dimapur. A couple of thousand Bangladeshis have reached Manipur also. There is a sprinkling of Bangladeshis in Arunachal Pradesh and Mizoram as well. Meghalaya has received a larger share of Bangladeshis because of its contiguity with Bangladesh. In Tripura, the tribals are in a state of rebellion because from being a majority in the State they have been reduced to the status of minority on account of the large scale influx of Bangladeshis.

Other States

Most of the other states of India also have sizeable Bangladeshi population.

In Bihar, Bangladeshi immigrants are conspicuous by their presence in the eastern districts of Purnea, Araria, Katihar and Kishanganj. The growth in their population has generated a sense of insecurity among the local Hindus, many of whom have sold their land to the Muslims and moved to other places.

In Delhi, several residential colonies in Seelampur, Jama Masjid area and Yamuna Bazaar of Old Delhi are currently dominated by Bangladeshi immigrants. They are now moving to the satellite towns of Gurgaon, Faridabad and Noida also.

Judicial Intervention

The Supreme Court of India, in a landmark judgement (July 2005), while repealing the notorious IMDT Act, observed that "there can be no manner of doubt that the State of Assam is facing 'external aggression and internal disturbance' on account of large scale illegal migration of Bangladeshi nationals" and therefore directed the Union of India "to take all measures for protection of the State of Assam from such external aggression and internal disturbance as enjoined in Article 355 of the Constitution".

The illegal Migrants (Determination by Tribunals) Act was passed in 1983 ostensibly to expel the illegal migrants, but it was heavily tilted in their favour and proved to be a toothless legislation. The Assamese intellectuals considered it a 'black law' because it discriminated Assam, which was saddled with this law, while all other States were governed by the Foreigners Act of 1946. No civilised country, as DN Bezbourah said, had two immigration laws. The Government of India, however, even after the Court's directions, instead of taking steps to evict the illegal Bangladeshi migrants, issued two State-specific notifications reintroducing the IMDT Act by the backdoor and negating the key provisions of the Foreigners Act.

The Apex Court, in a rebuke to the Union Government, in December 2006 scrapped the notifications on the ground that they were a cover up for non-implementation of Court's 2005 directions and that they failed to serve the purpose of detecting illegal migrants. It also said that subordinate legislation could not violate substantive law and that the government was duty bound to protect the State from aggression.

Recently, a parliamentary panel also expressed the view in April 2008 that "the large presence of illegal Bangladeshi immigrants poses a grave threat to the internal security and it should be viewed strongly". The Government of India unfortunately continues to drag its feet in the matter and has not initiated any definite measures to throw out the illegal migrants.

Threat to National Security

It is a matter of serious concern that the fundamentalist elements in Bangladesh have been propagating that the borders defined at the time of Partition are no longer relevant and need to be changed, taking into account the recent demographic changes. The Jamaat-e-Islami of Bangladesh has been talking of *Swadhin Muslim Bangabhumi* (Independent Muslim Bengal) in India.

Lt. Gen. (retd) SK Sinha, the then Governor of Assam, in a communication to the President of India sent on November 8, 1998, observed that the illegal migration into Assam was the "core issue" behind the Assam student agitation and was also the "prime contributory factor" behind the separatist movement in the State. Giving a grim assessment, he said:

"As a result of population movement from Bangladesh, the spectre looms large of the indigenous people of Assam being reduced to a minority in their home state. Their cultural survival will be in jeopardy, their political control will be weakened and their employment opportunities will be undermined. This silent and invidious demographic invasion of Assam may result in the loss of the geostrategically vital districts of Lower Assam [on the border with Bangladesh]. The influx of these illegal migrants is turning these districts into a Muslim majority region.

It will then only be a matter of time when a demand for their merger with Bangladesh may be made. The rapid growth of international Islamic fundamentalism may provide the driving force for this demand.... Loss of Lower Assam [the area close to the Bangladesh border will sever the entire land mass of the North-East from the rest of India and the rich natural resources of that region will be lost to the Nation".

The Task Force on Border Management constituted by the Government of India, in its report submitted in August 2000, severely criticised the political establishment for its failure to tackle the problem:

"There is an alls round failure in India to come to grips with the problem of illegal immigration. Facts are well known, opinions are firmed up, and operating system is in position. But the tragedy is that despite this, nothing substantial happens due to catharsis of arriving at a decision in this regard due to sharp division of interest among the political class."

The Group of Ministers also, in their Recommendations on the *National Security System* (February 2001), while taking care of Bangladesh's sensitivity in the matter, reiterated that "the massive illegal immigration poses a grave danger to our security, social harmony and economic well being".

Suggestions

The Government of India should take a tough stance in the matter with the Government of Bangladesh. The latter have been denying any illegal migrations. This is unacceptable in the face of incontrovertible evidence to the contrary. They should be made to accept a sizeable chunk of Bangladeshis back even if we accommodate some Bangladeshis in the country. Coercive diplomacy is the only option left. Economic sanctions could be considered and, as a last resort, armed intervention may not be ruled out.

There is a school of thought that India should contribute to raising the standard of living of the people of Bangladesh. The idea is that once their economic condition improves, the temptation to migrate would be comparatively less.

Government has been offering generous economic package to Bangladesh. Private sector from India has also shown keenness to make heavy investments in Bangladesh. Unfortunately, however, there are no reciprocal gestures. The Tatas of India recently decided to pull out from Bangladesh.

Meanwhile the Government of India has embarked on a comprehensive programme to strengthen its border control by fencing the Indo-Bangladesh border. Out of the total length of 4,095.7 km of the international border, it is proposed to fence 3,286.8 km. So far 2535.80 km has been fenced. Besides, border roads over a stretch of 3250.60 km has also been laid.

The following suggestions also merit serious consideration:

- The National Register of Citizens of 1951 should be reviewed, computerised and updated.
- The government should appoint a National Immigration Commission to frame a National Migration Policy and a National Refugee Policy.
- The Foreigners Act, 1946 should apply to the entire country uniformly.
- The existing Border Security Force posts and the BSF water wing should be strengthened and work on border fencing expedited.
- All Indian citizens should be issued a multi-purpose ID card. The non-citizens should also be issued cards but these should be of a different colour.

The matter is much too serious to be deferred any longer. As Weiner has said, it is important to take "perceptions and fears seriously and not dismiss them as irrational, xenophobic, or paranoid". India will be ignoring the dangers to its communal harmony, economic well being and, above all, security at its own peril.

(The writer is a former Director General of Police, Assam)

□

Himachal on the path of Progress and Prosperity

—Prof Prem Kumar Dhumal

25th January is an important and historic day for the people of Himachal Pradesh. It was on this auspicious day in 1971 that Himachal Pradesh attained Statehood and became the 18th State of the Indian Union.

Himachal Pradesh, which started its development journey in 1971, has not only emerged as a benchmark in the development of hill areas in the country but has also shown the way to big states by becoming a pioneer in various fields. Today, it is reckoned as the Best State in the country, a fact which has been underscored in various surveys conducted by prestigious agencies from time to time.

Proud Achievements

A comparison between the figures for various indicators of development in 1971 and today, bears out the speedy progress the State has made during all these years. The per capita income has gone up from Rs 651 in 1971 to Rs. 44803 in 2008, and is likely to cross Rs 46,000 in 2009. The Gross Domestic Product at current prices has shot up from Rs 223 crore to Rs 36,940 crore. The Annual Plan expenditure which was only Rs. 2.11 crore in 1971, went up to Rs 2,700 crore in 2009-10 and has been pegged at Rs 3,000 crore for 2010-11. Food production has increased from 9.36 lakh metric tonne to more than 15 lakh metric tonne, and fruit production from 1.49 lakh metric tonne to 6.28 lakh metric tonne.

Himachal Pradesh today has road length of more than 31,000 kms against only 7,740 kms in 1971. All census villages in the State enjoy the facility of electricity and water. Having attained the status of Apple State of the country, Himachal Pradesh is now being recognised as Fruit State and is poised to become the Power State of the country.

People - Hardworking, Honest

The credit for whatever the State has achieved goes to the hardworking, honest and sincere people of Himachal Pradesh who have exploded the myth that hills are destined to be poor. Credit also goes to the leadership the State got from time to time. We cannot forget to remember on this day, Dr. YS Parmar, the first Chief Minister of the State who laid a sound foundation for its overall development.

The people of the State have given me the opportunity to serve as Chief Minister twice, first from 1998 to 2003, and now, from 2007 onwards. The endeavour of the government all these years has been to ensure that the state makes rapid progress; public welfare, especially of the weaker sections and the downtrodden, is ensured; and the common man gets the benefits of development. We have set our priorities keeping in view all these facts. Roads, education and health are the three vital areas which top the list of our priorities as these concern the common man whose welfare dictates all our policies.

Revolution in Roads

We have given priority to the construction of roads and are working on a plan to provide road connectivity to all such villages having a population of 250 or above, by 2012. In the last two years, 1,715 km length of roads have been constructed and 1,600 km length of roads have been metalled. 98 bridges have been constructed to strengthen connectivity. Two new National Highways have been got sanctioned for the State. These are Nagrota Bagwan-Ranital-Mubarakpur and Paonta Sahib-Shillai-Hatkoti Road.

The State Government has taken up the matter with Central Government for four-laning of the Parwanoo-Solan stretch of the Kalka-Shimla National Highway. Central Government has sanctioned Rs 549 crore for the purpose. The State Government is also working on a plan to convert some National highways and State highways into Express highways to improve road connectivity.

Himachal - an Education Hub

Efforts are being made to make Himachal Pradesh an 'Education Hub' of the country. For this, educational institutions of standard and repute are being opened in the State. Special thrust is being given to skill-upgradation of our unemployed youth and promote vocational education. Approval has been given for opening one Technical Education University in the government sector besides 16 other universities in the private sector in the State. Atal Shiksha Kunj is being developed at Kalu Jhanda in Baddi area of Solan District where reputed institutions are being encouraged to open educational institutions to develop it as a world class 'Education Hub'. One Central University has been sanctioned for the State. The classes in the Indian Institute of Technology (IIT) at Kamand in Mandi District have already started and the Institute of Fashion Technology at Cheb in Kangra District has also been inaugurated.

Specialised and better healthcare facilities are being ensured at the doorsteps of the people. The 'Mahila Gram Panchayat Swasthya Sahayika Yojna' has been started to strengthen healthcare services at the *panchayat* level. The existing health institutions and medical colleges are being strengthened with latest equipment and specialised services. The Government plans to open medical colleges in Mandi, Hamirpur and Una Districts in the public-private-participation mode. As many as 449 allopathic doctors and 182 ayurvedic doctors and hundreds of nurses and para-medical staff have been appointed in the last two years. The National Health Insurance Scheme is being implemented throughout the State, after its successful implementation in the two districts earlier. Under this scheme, more than 2,98,000 families living below the poverty line, would get health insurance cover of Rs 30,000 each. They will not pay any premium for this cover and Government will bear this cost.

Emphasis on Agriculture

In Himachal Pradesh, more than 90 per cent population lives in rural areas and out of them about 70 per cent is dependent on agriculture allied sectors for their livelihood. State Government is taking effective steps to improve the economy of the farmers. Two ambitious schemes: Rs 353-crore Pandit Deen Dayal Kisan-Bagwan Samaridhi Yojna and Rs 300-crore Doodh Ganga Yojna have been started last year. The farmers are being provided 80 per cent subsidy for poly-houses and micro irrigation. Up to December, 2009, more than 4000 poly houses were sanctioned out of which 1223 have been completed and 1100 are under construction.

To accelerate the pace of development, we have been ensuring effective implementation of the plan and other schemes by taking up frequent review at various level. Annual Plan of Rs. 3000 crore has been proposed for the year 2010-11 as against Annual Plan of Rs. 2700 crores approved for 2009-10.

Women Empowerment Accelerated

Women empowerment has been given added attention by the State Government in the last two years. Himachal Pradesh is the first state in the country to have reserved 50 per cent seats for women in the Panchayati Raj Institutions (PRIs) and urban local bodies. Insurance benefits under the Matri Shakti Bima Yojna have been increased by four times and Rs 1 lakh is being given in case of death of a woman beneficiary or her spouse; and Rs 50,000 in case of injury. The Jiwan Shree Bima Yojna is being implemented for Anganbari workers and helpers. A sum of Rs 11,001 is being given to eligible girls as marriage grant under the Mukhya Mantri Kanyadan Yojna. The income limit for eligibility under the scheme has been increased from Rs 7,500 to Rs 15,000 per annum.

More Employment & Housing

The National Rural Employment Guarantee Act is being implemented throughout the State. During the last two years, 379.26 lakh man days were generated by providing employment to 8,56,520 families by spending Rs 646.28 crore. Such ambitious schemes as Indira Awas Yojna and Atal Awas Yojna are being implemented to provide housing facility to the rural houseless families. More than 10,000 houses have been constructed under both these schemes in the last two years.

The basic unit of democracy *the Panchayati Raj Institutions* (PRIs) are being strengthened. Every Panchayat in the State has been provided Panchayat Secretary and Panchayat Sahayak. The Government has given direction to keep every Panchayat Office open on every working day from 10 am to 5 pm so that people do not face any inconvenience for getting their works done from the Panchayats. With a view to involving these institutions in the development process, they have been granted financial and supervisory powers. The honorarium of elected PRI representatives has been enhanced.

Efforts are being made to generate additional resources through the hydel, industrial and tourism potential of the State to make it self-sufficient.

Power State

Hydel power generation has been accorded top priority. A target to harness 12,000 MW of power by 2012 has been fixed. In this effort, private, joint and state sectors have been involved. 70 per cent employment is being ensured to Himachalis in hydro power projects being executed in the private and joint sectors. To ensure transparency in the allotment of power projects, the State Government has decided to adopt open bidding system for allotment of projects of more than 5 MW capacity.

Industrial development has been given a big boost. Himachal Pradesh offers industrial peace, pollution-free environment, uninterrupted power supply, a responsive administration and an attractive package of incentives to entrepreneurs for setting up units in the State. In the last two years, 2,051 industrial units involving an investment of Rs 10,640 crore, and employment potential of 90,000 persons, have been given approval. Out of these, 1,616 new industrial units have been established with an investment of Rs 2,547 crore. A land bank of 8,000 bighas has also been created for the entrepreneurs interested to set up their units in various parts of the State.

Nature has blessed Himachal Pradesh with immense natural beauty and grandeur which offers vast scope for development of tourism in the State. Emphasis has been laid on the promotion of Nature, historic, religious and adventure tourism. The 'Home Stay Scheme' has been introduced to take tourism-related activities to the rural areas.

152 Home Stay units have been registered so far. In order to preserve the old grandeur of Shimla town, the 'Shimla Heritage Tourism Scheme' has been launched. Himachal Pradesh has emerged as the 'Best Tourist Destination' and Shimla town the 'Best Mountain Town' in a survey conducted by CNBC Awaaz. A 20-year master plan for integrated tourism development of the State is being formulated.

Swarojgar, Swavalamban, Swabhiman

Swarojgar, Swavalamban and *Swabhiman* (self-employment, self-reliance and self-respect) are the objectives on which Government is working. We are moving forward to achieving this by laying special emphasis on resource mobilisation.

We are committed to providing a clean, transparent and responsive administration to the people. The Prashasan Janta Ke Dwar programme has been restarted and Public Grievances Redressal Cells have been set up in all departments to ensure speedy redressal of public grievances. Public grievances are also being solved online under 'e-Samadhan'. With a view to providing better Information Technology services to the people, 3,366 Lokmitra Kendras are being set up at the *panchayat level.* Revenue and welfare-related information is being provided through 'e-governance' to make public service information available at the click of the mouse.

Whatever we have been able to do, has been possible due to the unstinted cooperation and support the Government got from the people.

I hope and look forward to similar cooperation in the times to come. We will spare no effort to ensure speedy development of the State and welfare of the people. Let us, join hands to make Himachal Pradesh a self-sufficient and ideal State.

(The writer is the Chief Minister of Himachal Pradesh)

□

A Case Study of Conversions in North-Eastern India

Conversions—a threat to National Unity

—R K Ohri, IPS (Retd)

Some time ago there was a furious debate about the reaction of some Hindu groups to the conversion campaign by evangelists in Orissa and some other States. While violence against any community must be condemned and contained with a heavy hand, the impact of large-scale conversions on the unity of Indian nation needs to be analysed and understood. Therefore, time has come to undertake a holistic analysis of large-scale conversions by evangelists in North-Eastern States in pre-independence and post-independence India. This case study attempts to highlight the impact of large-scale evangelist activity on the unity and integrity of the Indian nation.

Immediately after the British decamped from the sub-continent in 1947, India had its first brush with armed insurgency in Nagaland, a strategic and picturesque part of the sensitive north-eastern region. Geographically, Nagaland is bound by the plains of Assam to its west and north, Manipur in the south and Tirap division of Arunachal Pradesh and Myanmar to its east. This small state comprising a population of 2 million people has lush green forests and a difficult terrain with hills rising from 3000 to 9000 feet. For centuries, it had remained inhabited by more than a dozen hardy Naga tribes of whom Angami, Sema, Ao, Chakosang, Rengma, Sangatam, Teliang, Konyaks and Kukis are the prominent ones. Traditionally, Nagas have been head-hunters and there were frequent wars between different tribes. Before the advent of British rule, the Nagas had maintained their tribal way of life and preserved their rustic ancient culture. As references in various epics showed, warring Naga tribes had been part of the Indian civilisation. The arrival of Christian missionaries in the nineteenth century changed the scene drastically. The process of evangelisation was started under British tutelage and by the year 1931 nearly 13 per cent of the total population of Nagaland had been converted to Christianity. A quantum jump in conversions was, however, witnessed during the years 1941-51 and by 1951 the percentage of Christians rose to 46. Since then the evangelists have not looked back and now the Christians comprise nearly 90 percent of the State's population. It needs to be understood that large scale conversions took place after India gained freedom. A similar drive for religious conversion of tribals by Christian missionaries had started unfolding in another inadequately administered district of Assam, i.e. Lushai Hills district, now known as Mizoram. And by 1921 more than 28 per cent population was converted to Christianity. In fact, during one single decade of 1941-1951 there was a quantum jump in conversions in Lushai Hils district and the 1951 census recorded the Christian percentage at 90.5 per cent in this sensitive tribal district of Assam.

This brief introduction about activities of Christian missionaries is necessary to comprehend the phenomenon of armed militancy breaking out in north-eastern India within a few years of independence. It was openly aided and abetted by the multiple groups of evangelists operating in the sensitive region. Apart from poor and ineffective governance, the major cause of insurgency was the alienation of the tribals from their indigenous roots due to large-scale conversions in these two strategic areas of the North-East (now full-fledged States). That explains how Nagaland and Mizoram became the storm centres of aggressive militancy which erupted in the region in 1950s and 1960s and thereafter set the pace for subsequent outbreak of multiple insurgencies which continue to bedevil the region, especially Nagaland, till date.

Before the outbreak of large-scale militancy in 1955, the area now known as Nagaland consisted of Naga Hill district and Tuensang Frontier division of NEFA. (North Eastern Frontier Agency). The Naga Hill district, made up of Kohima and Mokokchung sub-divisions, was administered by a Deputy Commissioner who reported to the Government of Assam, while Tuensang division was controlled by a

Political Officer belonging to Indian Frontier Service. The latter reported to the head of the North East Frontier Agency. Due to myopic vision of the then government led by Pandit Nehru influenced by the philosophy of Verrier Ellwyn, in which *Gaon Burrahs* (elderly villagers) and *Dubhashis* (interpretators) played a key role as intermediaries between the government and the tribal population. For that reason Nagaland, an important border region of Indian Union, remained loosely administered which facilitated the growth of secessionism and insurgency. Similarly the Mizoram district of Assam, bound in the north by Manipur, in the south by Myanmar, and in the west by Bangladesh and Tripura was administered quite loosely and ineffectively in deference to the Nehruvian policy of non-interference with the lifestyle and culture of tribal people. Significantly, no attempt was made at any stage after independence, to prevent Christian missionaries from disrupting and destroying the cultural ethos of the local populace. Though the British rulers had placed the tribal territories of Naga Hills, North East Frontier Agency (NEFA) and the Lushai Hills (present Mizoram) under the Inner Line Regulations of 1872-73 to restrict the entry of non-tribals into these areas, Christian missionaries were always given free run in the region for preaching the gospel to tribal population. It was a peculiar arrangement under which all Indian citizens, excepting government officials, were required to get an Inner Line Permit before entering the sensitive region. Unfortunately post-independence, too, the Government of India continued with the same suicidal policy.

Immediately after independence AZ Phizo, a former lower level functionary of the Indian National Army of Subhash Chandra Bose, managed to wrest control of the NNC (Naga National Council) and started seeing the vision of an independent Christian state of Nagaland. Even before India gained freedom he had led a delegation to see Mahatma Gandhi in 1947 to press for the creation of an independent Nagaland. Due to utter lack of strategic vision, or some other inexplicable reason, shortly before independence the then Governor of Assam, Sir Akbar Hayadri, signed a nine-point agreement with the Naga National Council which permitted the Naga Council "to develop themselves according to their freely expressed wishes". The agreement included a clause which stipulated that after ten years "the Naga Council will be asked whether they require the above agreement to be extended for a further period, or a new agreement regarding the future of the

Naga people arrived at". Phizo claimed that this clause was tantamount to acceptance of the Naga demand for total independence. Interestingly, just a day before India attained independence, the NNC, under the leadership of Phizo, declared independence for the Naga Hills on August 14, 1947. He started a militant campaign against the Indian state. For indulging in subversive activities Phizo was arrested on July 9, 1948, but was released after some time when his son was killed and his wife was seriously injured in a car accident. He was able to muster support for the cause of Naga independence from most Christian missionaries and the Baptist Church, headed by the highly influential and well-known evangelist, Rev. Michael Scott. The demand for an independent Nagaland was propagated on the ground that the Nagas needed a separate independent homeland because of their Christian identity. As a result of prolonged evangelisation and close contact with the British missionaries, a large number of educated Naga elite had started viewing themselves as a people with a different cultural identity, far removed from the Indian nation, but close to their erstwhile British masters. Many of them thus started subscribing to Phizo's ideology of a separate Christian State of Nagaland. Several office-bearers and members of the Nagaland Baptist Church Council openly supported Phizo and his secessionist ideology. When Government of India turned down his demand for granting independence to Nagaland, in 1951, Phizo threatened to raise the issue in the United Nations. Taking cue from the bungling of the Indian government over accession of Jammu & Kashmir State, Phizo started articulating the demand for a plebiscite to ascertain the wishes of Nagas. Unfortunately, the weak-kneed policy of the Central government gave a big boost to secessionist activities of Phizo. Soon they were able to extend their influence among Naga masses and successfully sowed the seeds of secessionist militancy right up to Indo-Myanmar border. In 1952, Phizo was arrested once again, this time in Myanmar (then known as Burma) but was released in 1953. Soon thereafter he went underground. In the first week of May 1953 a massive raid was organised by the Assam Rifles and security forces at Khonoma, Phizo's native village, but Phizo could not be arrested. By the end of 1954, he managed to set up a ragtag underground government in Tuensang sub-division and succeeded in drawing a large number of Naga youth into his network which ultimately took the shape of an armed rebellion against the State. Interestingly, a small minority group of non-Christian Nagas were the followers of Rani Gaidiliu who had sporadically opposed the British rule and resisted the attempts of evangelists to convert them. They did not subscribe to the secessionist movement launched by A.Z. Phizo and chose to remain loyal to India. By February 1956 Phizo and his rebel group were able to frame a separate constitution for Nagaland and in March 1956 once again they declared independence. Soon thereafter army was inducted into Nagaland to put down the raging insurgency.

Meanwhile, after receiving arms from the government of East Pakistan (now Bangladesh) the insurgents managed to set up a parallel government styled as the Federal Government of Nagaland (FGN) which claimed to have a Naga army of eight thousand guerillas divided into 3 army commands with 27 battalions — the battalion size varying from 300 to 500 armed men. After some time Phizo managed to escape to East Pakistan (Bangladesh) in 1957 and from there he migrated to the U.K., never to return to India. But he continued to direct the secessionist insurgency from abroad and even tried to plead the cause of Naga independence at international fora till his death in 1990. Meanwhile, a sixteen-point agreement was reached between the Government of India and Naga Peoples Convention in July 1960 under which Nagaland was created as a separate State within the Indian Union. On December 1, 1963, Nagaland was formally constituted as sixteenth State of Indian Union, and in the first election to Nagaland State assembly nearly 70 per cent voters participated.

Even after 1964, the Naga militancy continued to ravage the countryside, with alternating spells of amnesty and peace parleys. In April 1964 a Peace Mission was constituted consisting, among others, of the well known Socialist freedom fighter, Jai Prakash Narayan, BP Chaliha (the then Chief Minister of Assam) and Rev. Michael Scott, a highly influential Baptist missionary. In the first week of September 1964, the Peace Mission was able to put in place a ceasefire agreement, because slowly a viewpoint had emerged that the Naga people were yearning for peace and were keen to negotiate a political settlement, hoping that the proposal will be backed by the "public opinion as a whole and influential Church leaders". But soon thereafter the Peace Mission became dysfunctional because of anti-national activities of Rev. Michael Scott who had all along been suspected of fomenting trouble in the region. He was, therefore, asked to leave the country in May 1966. It may be recalled that after death of Pandit Nehru in May 1964 there was a change in the political perception about activities of Rev. Michael Scott. On his return to the United Kingdom, Rev. Scott showed his true colours by taking up the cause of Naga independence and made an open attempt to carry the brief of Naga independence right up to the United Nations. Luckily he could not succeed in his nefarious design.

The peace brokered in 1964 by Jai Prakash Narayan did not last beyond February 1967 when hostilities broke out once again with full force. For a change, this time, the Indian security forces came down heavily on the insurgents.

It may be recalled that after the serious debacle of 1962 Indo-China war, some Naga insurgents managed to cross over into China to equip themselves with modern weapons, ostensibly with the blessings of Phizo from abroad. But that ill-advised attempt to join hands with Communist regime in China led to a split in the ranks of insurgents because of strong commitment of the rank and file of Naga insurgents to Christian faith. Despite Phizo's advice, the local Naga leadership decided not to have anything to do with the "Godless" Communist ideology which they felt was repugnant to the Christian ethos of Naga community. Thus, the split between the pro-China leader Tatar Hoho and the anti-Communist group led by Mhassieu helped the government in strengthening the administrative structure at the grassroots level.

For the last 62 years insurgency has continued to erupt across the region at regular intervals. Even though Nagaland has now a democratically elected government, militancy continues to break out at regular intervals. Presently the Naga militants are divided into two opposing groups known as NSCN (Isaac-Muivah) and NSCN (Khaplang). The former group has been running an underground Government of the Peoples Republic of Nagalim. To emphasise their Christian identity the letterheads of the militant outfit are superscribed with the legend "Nagalim for Christ".

In the last week of February 1966 a similar outbreak of armed insurgency shook Mizoram, formerly known as the Lushai Hills district of Assam, which area was formally annexed and included in the British India on September 6, 1885. A new Lushai Hills district was formed in April 1888 with Aizwal as its headquarters. In April 1946 a political party, known as the Mizo Common Peoples Union came into existence. On the eve of independence it issued a statement emphasising that the Mizo people were opposed to the retention of their district as a political unit under independent India but were agreeable to join the Provincial legislature. They demanded that excepting the current subjects no legislation passed by the Provincial Assembly (of Assam) should apply to the Lushai Hills and that all rights and privileges about their internal administration will remain vested in them. A demand was voiced that the Mizo district should include all neighbouring areas of Manipur, Tripura and Chittagong Hills which had sizeable Mizo population. Soon a dissident group was born which demanded that the Lushai Hills should join Burma because they were ethnically closer to the tribes of northern Burma (now Myanmar). Shortly thereafter, another party, known as the United Mizo Freedom Organisation (UMFO) came into being with the help of the chiefs of various Mizo tribes who felt uncomfortable in the Mizo Union. In fact, due to fierce hostility towards each other and opposition by various groups towards the Indian State, no flag hoisting ceremony could be held in Aizwal on August 15, 1947 when India attained independence.

The initial provocation for Mizo rebellion came from one of the worst famines (called "Mautam" in the local dialect) in 1959 which caused widespread distress to Mizo people. Unfortunately, due to administrative inefficiency and inadequacy of relief, there was widespread discontent which caused the Mizo Union MLAs to resign from the Congress legislature party and a new party, Mizo National Famine Front, was formed by some hot heads. The new outfit was able to get strong support from the local populace and in October 1961 it converted itself into a political party and dropped the word "Famine" from its nomenclature and came to be known as Mizo National Front (MNF). Its leadership was assumed by Laldenga, a former havildar of Indian army, then working as a clerk in the District Council, who set up an armed wing called Mizo National Army (MNA), with the avowed aim of seeking independence. This group had drawn inspiration from Naga insurgents and its members were imbued with the zeal of their new found love for Christian faith. They took recourse to frequent violence and intimidation due to which Laldenga was arrested in 1963. But later on, the then Assam Chief Minister BP Chaliha, ordered his release in the hope that sooner or later, he would be able to win Laldenga to his side. But things went wrong and during the next two years M.N.F. was able to consolidate its hold on the people. An armed wing, known as Mizo National Army, was organised. Its core group comprised disbanded soldiers of 2nd Assam Battalion who had rebelled while on duty in Jammu & Kashmir. These trained disgruntled ex-soldiers were able to induce many deserters and ex-servicemen from Assam Rifles and Assam Regiment to join them. Initially they had only 303 rifles and some Japanese weapons of World War II vintage, but soon managed to get weapons from the neighbouring East Pakistan (now Bangladesh). Thanks to the endeavours of Christian missionaries Mizos had acquired a high level of education which promoted religious consciousness and political ambition among them. Laldenga was therefore able to organise a dedicated underground movement.

The government was caught virtually napping when on February 28, 1966, trained MNF insurgents rose in rebellion simultaneously in Aizwal, Lunglei, Vairangate and Chhimluang. They attacked and virtually overran the Assam Rifles post at Lunglei and killed some jawans of Assam Rifles and kidnapped the Sub-Divisional Officer, Shri Pillai. They also plundered the sub-treasury at Lunglei and seized the treasury at Aizwal in a well coordinated surprise attack. On March 1, 1966, the MNF made a formal announcement declaring Mizoram as an independent State. The rebels took complete control of the Aizwal district headquarters. In another swift move, the rebels overran the security checkpost at Vairengate and cut off the main border road connecting Mizo Hills with the rest of the country. It took the Assam government and the Central government quite some time to gather their wits. On March 2, 1966, Mizoram district was declared a disturbed area by Assam government and a contingent of 61st Mountain Brigade set out to restore peace in the trouble zone. The army contingent reached Kolasib on March 4 and managed to free from the captivity of the rebels a large number of government employees. But the situation was so bad that ultimately IAF had to be requisitioned to bomb the fortified positions of the rebels which caused considerable loss to property. It was only on March 12, 1966, that the authority of the Assam government could be re-established in and around Aizwal. Ultimately a brigade of Indian army was stationed in Aizwal. Widespread insurgency, however, continued in the rural areas. Meanwhile, the new state of Bangaldesh came into being due to which Mizo rebels found it difficult to get weapons and logistic support from there. Ultimately the MNF shifted its armed units to Arakans in Myanmar (i.e. Burma). Mizoram was finally constituted into a Union Territory on January 21, 1972. Due to intervention by some intermediaries, negotiations between the rebels and the government started which only enabled the MNF to consolidate its position and recruit and train more rebels.

After a short spell of lull the MNF started its depredations almost with a vengeance. In April 1973 Superintendent of Police (Special Branch) AK Roy was shot at thrice in Aizwal city. Within the next three months a number of government functionaries were targeted and killed. In the middle of 1974 the then Lt. Governor of Mizoram, Shri Mookerjee, was ambushed and wounded.

In December 1974, the rebels issued "QUIT MIZORAM" notices ordering all non-Mizos to leave the Union Territory failing which they might face death. The threatening notices were pasted at prominent place in Aizwal town and several smaller towns by the secessionist MNF activists. These threatening notices created quite a scare. A diabolical plan was drawn up to further terrorise the non-Mizo government officials by targeting senior police and security officers. In furtherance of their plans, a self-styled Col. Baikvela of Mizo National Army, visited Aizwal and deputed a handpicked MNF officer, Capt. Lalhliea, to execute certain secret plans under the guidance of Major Kapchhunga of Mizo National Army. The whole MNA garrison of Aizwal town was placed at his disposal. Capt. Lalhliea and his armed gang equipped with automatic weapons set themselves up in the house of Miss Zari, a lady clerk in the office of Inspector General of Police. On January 13, 1975 around 1600 hrs when the then IGP of Mizoram, late Shri Arya was holding a meeting with his DIG Police, LB Sewa and SP CID (Spl. Branch) K Panchpagesan, five insurgents led by aforesaid Capt. Lalhliea of MNF drove into the Police Headquarters wearing police uniforms. Facing no resistance from the armed guards (who happened to be Mizos), they barged into I.G.P.'s office and shot dead the 3 senior police officers in cold blood. Surprisingly, they were able to escape without being engaged in fire by the armed contingent of Mizoram Armed Police stationed outside the IGP's office. It was a shocking incident which greatly demoralised the entire administration.

Soon thereafter for tackling the growing insurgency the Government of India handpicked Brig. GS Randhawa, as the new Inspector General of Police. He organised extensive anti-insurgency operations in which Major Kapchhunga of MNA, who was privy to the murder of three senior police officers and had been functioning as Town Commander of Aizwal, was arrested. Soon thereafter Capt. Lalhlie was killed in an encounter by the BSF outside Aizwal town, while his another accomplice in the crime, Capt. Ronuna, was shot dead by the brave jawans of 55 Battalion of Central Reserve Police Force. Subsequently Miss Zari and MNA's Aizwal Town Commander, Major Kapchhunga, were arrested and tried in court. Finally they were awarded life imprisonment for cold blooded assassination of three senior police officers.

The insurgency continued for a number of years and heat was turned by the rebels against non-Christians quite often. In the process thousands of Reangs (an ethnic Hindu tribe) and Chakmas, who are Buddhists, were forced to migrate out of the State. The menacing "Quit Mizoram" notices kept on appearing from time to time. The main targets were non-Mizo and non-Christians, mostly government employees. For instance, on June 1, 1979 an order was issued which read as follows:

"GOVERNMENT OF MIZORAM — QUIT MIZORAM ORDER"

"It is hereby ordered that all non-Mizos who are degrading Mizo nationalism, should leave Mizoram before lst July 1979. Government of Mizoram will take action against those who violate this order and still remain in Mizoram.

This order does not concern/apply to those who are born in Mizoram and are Christians involved in the Chruch activities."

To sum up, after several decades of extensive operations the evangelist-inspired insurgency in Mizoram was effectively put down. After a long spell of civil strife, now Mizos are steadily joining the national mainstream. But the problem in Nagaland remains unresolved. In Tripura, too, an ISI-aided terrorist organisation, National Liberation Front of Tripura and some other militant outfits have been spearheading anti-national and anti-Hindu campaigns of militancy.

Though Mizoram is now more or less peaceful, there has been a systematic ethnic cleansing of Reangs who are 'Adivasi' Hindus, originally from Tripura, but had settled down in Mizo Hils area for several generations. They are contemptuously referred to as 'Bru' by Mizo Christians and their villages and habitats are regularly targeted by Mizos. Though some Reangs have converted to Christianity, the majority of them have retained their Hindu roots. In addition to nearly 30,00 Reangs uprooted earlier, nearly 5,000 Reangs were recently pushed out from their ancestral homes in October-November 2009. There were allegations that a concerted effort was being made to convert them to Christianity. In view of religious and cultural differences between Mizos and Reangs the latter have been demanding an autonomous council to safeguard their interests. Originally, there were nearly 80,000 Reangs in Mizoram, but now nearly 35,000 of them are living in Refugee Camps under sub-human conditions in Tripura State.

In another alarming development, the ruling Nagaland government led by Neiphiu Rio is reported to have drawn up a proposal to replace the national emblem, i.e., the Ashoka Chakra, with Naga motifs. A suggested motif for the State emblem of Nagaland depicts "Mithun" (a species of bison) along with the words "Unity Nagalim", or the words "Greater Sovereign Nagaland" inscribed thereunder. The militant rebels of NSCN (Muivah-Isaac) have been using letterheads with the inscription "Nagalim for Christ" right on top to emphasise their Christian identity. Thus, secessionist militancy continues to erupt across Nagaland off and on, despite sustained efforts to secure a peaceful settlement.

The foregoing case study reveals the seamy side of the evangelist campaign in the North East. It shows the damage which the conversion politics, has inflicted on the unity of our motherland in that sensitive region. The sordid role which evangelists have played in Nagaland and Mizoram, two important North-Eastern States, is a classic example of subversion and secessionist movement. The long spell of militancy in the North-East is a direct consequence of the activities of Christian missionaries, who successfully poisoned the minds of gullible masses against the Indian State.

It may be pointed out that the evangelists have openly declared their intention to convert to their faith the 'heathen' Hindus of India. Under 'Project Joshua' billions of dollars are pouring into India and some other countries of Asia to carry forward the agenda of mass conversions. Late Pope John Paul II while speaking to a congregation in November 1991, the day of Diwali, had declared: "Just as the first millennium saw the Cross firmly planted in the soil of Europe and the Second in that of America and Africa, so may the Third Christian Millenium witness a great harvest of faith on this vast and vital continent."

In this context it may be pertinent to highlight the dangerously disruptive effects of evangelisation experienced in Kandhamal district of Orissa in the year 2008 after the dastardly assassination of Swami Laxmanananda Saraswati on August 23, 2008, on the day of Sri Krishna Janamashtami. Swamiji had a huge following among Hindu tribals of Kandhamal and was leading the anti-conversion campaign from the front. It is widely believed that he was got killed by a group of hot-headed evangelists, though the police claim that Swamiji was killed by Maoists. Soon Kandhamal erupted into anti-conversion riots which ravaged the district for several weeks in which 38 persons were killed and more than 100 injured. The dimensions of the human tragedy unleashed can be gauged from the fact that the number of cases of rioting and allied crimes registered rose to 1004, while nearly 1218 persons were arrested. The government appointed a single judge Inquiry Commission to identify the factors which led to the massive break down of law and order, though it was widely known that the single most important reason for trouble in the sensitive district was the conversion campaign launched by evangelists which was greatly resented by Kandhas, a predominant Hindu tribe of the area, who held Swami Laxmananda Saraswati in high esteem. Recently in July 2009. Justice SC Mohapatra wrote his 28 page interim report in which he blamed the conversions, re-conversions and land disputes between Kandha Hindus and Pana Christians (who were converts from Scheduled Caste Hindus).

The one single message conveyed by this study of insurgency in the North-East and large-scale social strife in Kandhamal district of Orissa is that attempts of evangelists to convert the Hindu masses have the potential to undermine the unity of the Indian nation and destabilise the societal fabric of fraternity across the country.

(The writer is a former Inspector General of Police. He has authored two books and contributed several articles to various publications.)

□

Making Agriculture Play a Greater Role in Indian Economy

—JC Jetli, IAS (Retd)

General

There is an urgent need that Agriculture should play a greater role in Indian Economy than it is playing at the moment. This will be possible only if the crisis facing Indian agriculture is tackled on a war footing and solid and new initiatives are taken to deal with the crises facing this important sector. The agrarian crisis in India has been caused by several factors, such as the decline in the share of agriculture in the Gross Domestic Product (GDP), decline in the real growth rate of agriculture leading to virtual stagnation, dependence of a large population on agriculture including working population on land, declining relative productivity of agriculture, steep decline in per capita availability of land, marginalisation of ownership and operational holdings, higher input costs, low return on investment leading to monthly income not covering costs, feminisation of agriculture, severe stress on the availability of water, marketing problems, absence of adequate infrastructure particularly post-harvest infrastructure, increase in indebtedness particularly from non-institutional sources, rapid environmental degradation, decline in support system, neglect of extension services, and of agricultural research and development.

Large Population Dependent on Agriculture

Farming is the largest private sector enterprise. India's population in 2004-05 was 1092 millions of which the rural population is 71.4 per cent. Out of this about 60 per cent is dependent on agriculture. The estimated labour force in 2004-05 was 467 million and out of this, 348 million (71.61 per cent) lived in rural areas. Of the total workers 56.5 per cent worked in agriculture. Of the rural work force of 348 millions as many as 247 million (72.5 per cent) worked in agriculture. The dependence of a large population and labour force on agriculture puts great pressure on this sector.

Share of Agriculture in GDP and Employment

There has been a shift in terms of sectoral distribution of GDP. This is not accompanied by the corresponding shift of labour force. The share of agriculture in GDP declined from 41.0 per cent in 1972-73 to 19.5 per cent in 2005-06. (See table see the next page)

The figures above show the large and increasing gap in per worker earning in agriculture and non-agriculture sectors — 56.5 per cent of the national workforce produces only one-fifth of the GDP i.e. 19.7 per cent. Besides, there is also decline in the ratio of workers productivity in agriculture to non-agriculture. Increasing population and labour force continues to depend on limited and non-expanding land resources. As a result there is a continuous decline in availability of land per agriculture worker.

Increasing Marginalisation

The increase in labour force and decrease in cultivable area has led to increase in the number of holdings with lower size. From 1960-61 the number of holdings doubled from 50.77 million to 100.27 million, while the area operated declined from 133.48 million hectares to 107.65 hectares. As a result, the average size of holdings has declined leading to marginalisation. About 87.6 per cent of farmers belonged to marginal and small category and operated only 43.5 per cent of area — the medium and large farmers operating the remaining area.

Share of Agriculture in GDP and Employment

Year	Share of Agriculture in GDP at 1999-2000 prices (%)	Share of Agriculture in Employment-UPSS (%)	Ratio of Worker Productivity in Agriculture to Non-Agriculture	Ratio of Worker Productivity in Non-agriculture to Agriculture
1972-73	**41.0**	**73.9**	**0.287**	**3.49**
1993-94	**30.0**	**63.9**	**0.285**	**3.51**

1999-00	25.0	60.2	0.252	3.97
2004-05	20.2	56.5	0.199	4.94
2005-06	19.7	-	-	-

Note: GDP denotes Gross Domestic Product and UPSS denotes Usual Principal and Subsidiary Status.

Source: Central Statistical Organisation (CSO), National Accounts Statistics, Various Years and National Sample Survey Organisation (NSSO), Employment and Unemployment Situation in India, Various Rounds.

Higher Input Costs

Non-availability of agricultural inputs at reasonable costs and in time is another problem facing farmers. There is also need for proper information regarding the inputs required taking into account the soil health. Lack of proper, reliable and independent information places the farmers at the mercy of sales agents of companies selling inputs who are motivated by profit motive rather than the interest of the farmers. Lack of credit also pushes farmers to purchase inputs from local suppliers who often provide sub-standard inputs. All this adds to the cost of farming. There is need for an effective delivery system with introduction of soil health card and efficient extension services.

Irrigation Resources

Agriculture in India is still predominantly dependant on rainfall. Rain-fed areas account for about 60 per cent of the total 142 million hectares of net sown area assessed in the country. Only about 43 per cent of the net sown area is estimated to be irrigated.

Ground water has become the largest source of irrigation and is facing the problems of over-exploitation and depletion. The rain-fed agriculture has low productivity and low input use. A large population of poor resides in rain-fed areas. Traditional water harvesting systems have become defunct because of neglect and watershed development has not made much headway. Full exploitable potential of irrigation in the country has not been tapped. A substantial irrigation potential is locked up in projects which are in pipeline. Where irrigation projects have been completed there is the problem of under-utilisation because of lack of field channels, etc.

Environmental Stress and Degradation of Land

There is growing pollution of river and canal water caused by industrial effluents and agricultural run off with toxic chemicals and heavy metal. Soil erosion is another serious cause of land degradation. Estimates show that around 130 million hectares of land (45 per cent of total geographical area) is affected through ravine and gully formation, water-logging and shifting cultivation. The accumulation of salt and alkalinity affects the productivity of agriculture. There is water-logging in irrigated command areas to the extent of 2.46 per cent as per recent estimates. Besides, 3.4 million hectares suffer from surface water stagnation. The drainage aspect has not been given adequate attention in major and medium irrigation projects. The excessive and unbalanced use of fertilisers and pesticides has led to depletion of soil nutrition and nitrate contamination of ground water.

Technology Fatigue

Since 1990 there is gradual deceleration in the growth rate of most crops, especially rice and wheat despite increase in use of inputs such as fertilisers, indicating inefficiency in input use and decreasing profitability of crop production. The seed-fertiliser technology seems to have exhausted its potential and is no longer efficient. A major reason for this is reduced public investment in agricultural research and development, increasing reliance on technology import rather than the development of indigenous technology.

Decline in Living Standard of Farmers

The nominal farm business income per hectare of gross cropped area deflated as consumer price index has registered a slowly declining trend. The income from agriculture is becoming inadequate to meet the basic consumption requirements of not only marginal farm households but also medium-sized farm households with two to four hectares of holdings. As per recent estimates, the average monthly income per farmer household is Rs. 2115/- and the monthly consumption expenditure is Rs. 2770/- . Only farmers with holding of 4 hectares and above have a surplus income over expenditure.

Decline in Growth Rate

The growth of agriculture, both in terms of gross product (GDP) and in terms of output, shows a declining trend. The growth rate of

GDP from agriculture decelerated from 3.08 per cent in 1980-81 to 2.57 per cent in 2005-06, at 1999-91 prices. The annual growth rate for all crops taken together decelerated to 1.58 per cent from 3.19 per cent during 1980-81 to 1990-91.

Decline in Production of Foodgrains

It is significant that food grain growth also recorded a fall from 2.58 per cent in 1980-81 to 1990-91 to about 1 per cent which is lower than the growth rate of population of 1.9 percent. This is due to gradual decline of yield levels of almost all crops. The decline of effectiveness of pesticides and spurious pesticides have largely contributed to this. Thus the per capita availability of food grains has declined.

Deceleration in the Overall Employment Growth

Deceleration in Agricultural growth is accompanied by deceleration in employment growth in the economy. In view of this, it is becoming difficult to absorb labour from agriculture into other activities. Because of the sharp increase of the labour force open unemployment has gone up and the number of unemployed has increased substantially.

Gross Capital Formation (GCF)

The Share of Gross Capital Formation declined from 16.1 per cent during 1980-81 to 7.3 per cent in 2005-2006. The share of public sector GCF also declined from 43.2 per cent in 1980-81 to 19.2 per cent in 2004 -05. This low level of GCF is also indicative of decline of agriculture.

Agriculture Credit

The main vehicle for reaching agriculture credit to farmers was the cooperatives. After nationalisation of Banks in 1969 the commercial Banks were also assigned the role of providing agricultural credit to supplement credit by cooperatives. The cooperative structure has virtually collapsed over time. The share of cooperative credit in total agriculture credit has gone down from 70.8 per cent in 1975-76 to only 21.8 per cent in 2005-06. This has adversely affected the small and marginal farmers as cooperative societies had greater reach to them as compared to commercial banks. Though the small and marginal farmers constitute over 87 per cent of the farmers, their share of institutional credit is less than 25 per cent. Over the years the share of credit of larger farmers has gone up although their share in area has remained the same. The small and marginal farmers in particular are being driven to non-institutional sources for obtaining credit involving higher interest burden.

Increase in Malnutrition

Various studies have brought out the increasing food insecurity and malnutrition amongst farmers and other rural poor. This is because agriculture has ceased to be profitable for a large number of farmers, particularly for small and marginal farmers. The higher cost of agriculture and low return is leading to distress for the producers of food grains. Because of the less income compared to the consumption expenditure, the producers of food grains lack purchasing power to meet their needs. Social protection programmes and safety net are not adequate.

Farmer Suicides

All these factors leading to stagnation in agriculture have resulted in farmer suicides. Various estimates have been made which indicate that more than one lakh farmers have committed suicides in recent years. According to the National Crime Record Bureau 17,060 farmers committed suicide in the country during 2006 with Maharashtra having the highest number of 4453 suicide deaths. Punjab is the latest in the list of States having farmers' suicides. In Vidharbha region alone, more than 1200 farmers have committed suicides since April 2008. In the first 37 days of 2009, 92 farmers lost their lives in Vidharbha region.

Right to Live

Agriculture is vital for the national economy. Some of the important factors mentioned above which are causing distress in this sector raise another important issue of 'Right to Live with dignity', guaranteed by the Constitution to every citizen of the country. The vast majority of farmers, who are performing the important function of feeding the nation are themselves deprived of the 'Right to Live with dignity' and are being led to commit suicides. This is a pointer to the need for reorienting policies to ensure that agriculture plays a greater role in the national economy. The delay in doing so has important implications for the country and will lead to the worsening of the agrarian crises.

Interventions Urgently Needed

The problems of the agriculture sector have been studied in depth by the 'National Commission on Farmers' constituted by the NDA Government and headed by renowned agricultural scientist Dr MS Swaminathan. There is urgent need to implement the recommendation of this commission in a time- bound frame-work. Some of the measures which call for urgent action are mentioned below:

(i) Need for larger Public Investment

There is need for larger public investment in rural infrastructure in general and the infrastructure needed for agriculture in particular. Public-private investment is welcome in this sector. It has, however, been the experience that while public investment reaches larger sections of the population, including small and marginal farmers, private sector investment benefits only the richer sections of the population, including big and well-to-do farmers. The major problem in agriculture sector has been diminishing public sector investment. The percentage of investment in rural sector and in agriculture should have some bearing to the large percentage of population residing in rural areas and the large percentage of workers involved in agriculture.

(ii) Infrastructure in Rural Areas

There is need to focus on the Infrastructure required in rural areas and in agriculture. It must be realised that agriculture is the backbone of the Indian economy. Thus, the investment in irrigation, power, roads, health, education, IT services in rural areas should get priority and the public investment in rural infrastructure should be in proportion to the rural population. Special consideration should be given to post-harvest infrastructure for agriculture, such as food grain storage facility, cold storage, transport facilities including air-conditioned transport and to minimise post-harvest losses.

(iii) Marketing

There is a need to improve marketing so that farmers get proper and adequate return for the produce. This will call for making available timely marketing intelligence, promotion of grading, branding, packaging and development of markets for local produce. Efforts are called for to review and abolish all controls and regulations and for relaxation of internal restrictions which are hindering increase in farmers' income. The marketing strategy should aim at developing a single national market. The farmers must be provided an assured and remunerative marketing facilities and opportunities.

(iv) Conservation of Prime Farm land for Agriculture

There is a need to ensure that prime farm land is conserved for agriculture. As per Special Economic Act of 2005, the Government has notified 400 such zones in the country. 'These special economic zones are designed to enhance trade and export income. The land acquired for these zones is far in excess of need. According to one study, more than fifty per cent of land acquired is fertile land. This has an adverse effect on agriculture. The establishment of these economic zones should not be at the cost of conservation of prime farm land for agriculture. This policy needs an urgent review and calls for evaluating the success of these economic zones in promoting trade and export before the setting up of more zones. In any case, there should be complete ban on acquisition of fertile and irrigated land for the zones. More emphasis should be laid on Special Agricultural Zones (SAZ). In these Special Agricultural Zones. Integrated attention should be paid to natural resources, conservation and enhancement, eco-farming, improved local level consumption to overcome malnutrition and promotion of pro-small farmer commerce. In these special agricultural zones, agricultural scientist extension agencies, mass media and Ministries and Government Departments dealing with agriculture, animal husbandry, fisheries, forestry, environment, agro-processing and agri-business, irrigation, commerce, rural development, IT, finance and banking work on the principles of convergence and synergy to find solutions for small and marginal farmers. The promotion of and smooth functioning of these Special Agricultural Zone in the entire country should receive special priority as agriculture is more vital for the economy.

(v) Preservation and Economic use of Water

While there is need for more public investment in developing the full potential of irrigation in the country, completion of projects in the pipeline and to improve the utilisation of completed projects, there is also the need for enhancing water use efficiency. As major part of agriculture in the country is dependent on rain, rain water harvesting and aquifer recharge and treated effluent water and water quality should receive priority. Sustained effort is needed to ensure water for every field.

(vi) Issue of Soil Health Cards

In order to enhance agricultural production, there is an urgent need to set up a mechanism which can study the soil status and provide every farmer a 'Soils Health Card' indicating the organic matter and macro and micro-nutrient status of the soil. This will enable the farmer to plan crops and work out necessary inputs needed to get higher production.

(vii) Agriculture Credit

The problem of indebtedness of farmers needs urgent attention. The cost of inputs for majority of the farmers is more than the income from agricultural production. This has placed most of the farmers in debt trap and is the main cause of suicides by farmers. Besides the credit for agriculture, the farmer is compelled to take loans for meeting expenses on health and social functions. Majority of small and marginal farmers have no access to institutional credit and have to depend on non-institutional credit which is at a very high cost. There is need to deal with this problem on a realistic basis as it is linked to the farmers' right to life guaranteed by the Constitution. The loan waiver scheme announced by Government has benefitted only a small section of farmers who had taken institutional credit. Even in their case, the loan waiver scheme had several conditions which drastically reduced the number of farmers who got the benefits. The vast number of farmers who had no access to institutional credit was left out of this scheme. The scheme of loan waiver should have provided relief to all farmers keeping in view the agricultural distress affecting this sector.

It is, therefore, essential to freeze the loan recovery in respect of loans taken up to a cut-off date for five years in respect of all farmers and to work out a scheme for taking over of non-institutional credit of all farmers by financial institutions. The Government should provide subsidy to the financial institutions to cover the interest for these five years during which the moratorium on recovery remains in force.

As regards fresh loans, it should be ensured that institutional credit reaches small and marginal farmers in proportion to their number and land holdings. A large number of farmers, household are headed by women who do not possess clear title over land. This is true in regard to many small and marginal farmers also. A way should be found to ensure that these farmers are also able to get credit. The farmers should also be enabled to get credit for meeting health and social expenses.

(viii) Technology and Provision of Inputs

There is need to work out 'low risk and environmental friendly technology', particularly for rain-fed agriculture for integrated pest and nutrient management. An effective and independent extension system linked with Agricultural Universities and Research Institutions needs to be developed to reach the technology to farmers. It should also be ensured that the inputs are available to farmers timely and at reasonable low cost.

(ix) Assured and Remunerative Prices

Remunerative prices need to be ensured to farmers. It is, therefore, necessary to fix Minimum Support Price for all crops to cover the cost of production and provide, in addition, a reasonable surplus to the farmers so that they can lead a life with dignity. The Minimum Support Price should be announced well in advance and procurement should be by public agencies. The corporate houses should not be permitted to corner production at lower costs and make profits by hoarding and selling at high prices. The purchases by the corporate houses should be regulated.

(x) Support System

Agriculture, particularly rain-fed, is subject to uncertainty and is also subject to natural calamities. It is, therefore, necessary to evolve a support system for farmers in the form of comprehensive insurance which covers not only the crops of the farmers, but also income from crops, health expenses and old age pension.

To Sum Up

The development of Agriculture is vital for Indian economy. As the largest percentage of population of the country is dependent on agriculture, the well-being of the population cannot be achieved without tackling the present agrarian crisis with a sense of urgency. Measures need to be taken to reduce the pressure of population dependent on agriculture and shifting the workers engaged in agriculture to other vocations. This is possible only if the focus of policy makers shifts to rural areas and development of rural infrastructure receives the resources and attention in proportion to the rural population. The development of infrastructure in rural areas can enable development of rural industry and rural service sector and lead to greater employment opportunities.

Prosperous agriculture is of great importance not only for national economy but also for assuring a life with dignity to a majority of the population of the country.

(The writer is an IAS (Retd) & former Chairman of Damodar Valley Corporation)

□

Plight of Hindu Civil Servants & Youth under Rangnath Mishra Commission Report

—OP Gupta (IFS Retd)

It is painful to see how politicians right from the days of the 1916 Congress-Muslim League Lucknow Pact till date in the form of the Sachar Committee Report, Rangnath Misra Commission Report, the 15-Point Programme etc has been systematically harming all Hindus by concocting false justifications to reduce, bit by bit, promotional avenues of all Hindu civil servants and the educational, employment and economic (E3) opportunities of all Hindu public servants, Hindu boys and girls, including SC, ST, OBC and leftist Hindu boys and girls, North Indian or South Indian Hindus, all Hindu members of NSUI, ABVP, SFI etc pushing them to second and third class status vis-à-vis minority boys and girls.

Reduction in job opportunities and college seats for Hindus has been happening because Hindus have been voting for such political parties which openly say that they will give first preference to minorities i.e. they will accord second class treatment to Hindus.

The *Hindustan Times* of December 24, 2008 [New Delhi edition] reported that in reply to a question the Parliament was informed that as a result of special efforts made by the UPA Government such as the Sachar Committee, PM's 15-Point Programme etc the share of minorities in central sector jobs increased from 6.9 per cent in 2006-07 to 8.7 per cent in 2007-08. It increased from 7.6 per cent in 2006-07 in the financial sector [Banks. FIs, RBI] to 10.2 per cent; in the

Armed Forces from 5.5 to 8.9 per cant and in the Railways from 2.7 per cant to 6.3 per cant during the same one year period.

Consequently, as per common sense it is obvious that the percentage of Hindus in these sectors has been made to decline by the Manmohan Singh Government which has traditionally been above 95%. Riding on the shoulders of its Hindu voters the Congress Party wants to reduce percentage of Hindus in job sector below 85% in terms of Rangnath Misra Commission.

Right from 1954 the Congress Party Prime Ministers at the Centre have been issuing instructions to all Central Ministries as well as to all State Governments to give special considerations to recruitment of religious minority candidates in public services with obvious implication to reduce percentage of Hindus in public services by hook or crook. In 1983, Prime Minister Indira Gandhi vide her 15-Point Programme for minorities became the first Prime Minister to have issued instructions to include minority members in all the Selection Boards and departmental promotion committees. The circular to induct religious minority members in Selection Boards was again issued by the Rajiv Gandhi Government and the Vishwanath Pratap Singh Government. The Manmohan Singh Govt reiterated it in January 2007 with added condition of making quarterly reports on progress of minority cadidates actually recruited and/or promoted. After all the 'communally appointed members' of the Selection Boards, Departmental Promotion Committees (DPCs) will have to show some result of their being added to Boards and, thus, the intake of minority candidates will go up and percentage of Hindu's intake, whether leftist or rightist, whether forward or backward, whether upper caste or scheduled caste Hindus, whether tribal Hindu or non-tribal Hindu, whether North Indian Hindu or South Indian Hindu, whether Marathi speaking Hindu or Malayali speaking Hindu in utter disregard of their merit, will automatically come down as the total number of vacancies to be filled by any Selection Board is fixed in advance before the meeting. This is happening when the unemployment situation is worsening in India day by day.

I place below seven [A to H] bare facts which show that Hindu voters have been lacking in parental care and have contributed to reducing our own children and grand children to second class status by being careless and casual at times of voting.

Startling Facts

When I bring these facts to the notice of educated Hindus, most of them express shock on their being ignorant of these facts, and, blame media and politicians for this betrayal. But in my humble opinion Hindu voters are themselves responsible for this plight of their children who either abstain from voting or vote to anti-Hindu political parties.

[A] First, let us look into harm which the Rangnath Misra Commission report would inflict upon all Hindu civil servants and all Hindu students and all Hindu job seekers.

On December 18, 2009 the UPA Government tabled the Rangnath Misra Commission Report on the table of the Parliament. It has recommended reducing job opportunities of all Hindu officials and Hindu youth at least by 15%, reducing availability of college seats to all sections of Hindu students by at least 15%; and disadvantaging SC and ST Hindus by yoking them within their reservation quotas with Muslims and Christians who enjoy better literacy rate.

Para 16.2.16 of Misra Commission reads: "Since the minorities — especially the Muslims — are very much under-represented, and sometimes wholly unrepresented, in government employment, we recommend that they should be regarded as backward in this respect within the meaning of that term as used in Article 16 (4) of the Constitution— notably without qualifying the word 'backward' with the words "socially and educationally" — and that 15 percent of posts in all cadres and grades under the Central and State Governments should be earmarked for them."

In the Indira Sawheny case, the Supreme Court had observed— "It is, therefore, clear that economic criterion by itself will not identify the backward classes under Article 16(4). The economic backwardness of the backward classes under Article 16(4) has to be on account of their social and educational backwardness. Hence, no reservation of posts in services under the State, based exclusively on economic criterion, would be valid under clause (1) of Article 16 of the Constitution."

So the Misra Commission recommendation is totally unconstitutional as it suggests giving reservations to Muslims by ignoring the requirements of the Constitution and the Indira Sawhney case law.

All the Hindu officers serving under the Central Government or any State Government should take note that the Misra Commission has recommended reservation of 15 per cent of posts for religious minorities in all cadres and grades under the Central and the State Governments. Ten per cent will be solely for Muslim officials/candidates and five per cent for other minorities.

It means that from the date of implementation 15% posts in the grade of Secretary to Govt of India, and other grades of Additional Secretary, Joint Secretary etc shall get reserved for minority officers which will block or retard career prospect of many Hindu officers and may result into many Hindu officers serving under their own junior minority religion officers. This would be happening all over India in all departments, central as well as provincial, whether school teachers, lecturers, deputy superintendents of police, engineers, deputy collectors, inspectors of police, customs, income tax, public sector undertakings etc.

So it is high time that all Hindu officials and all those Hindus who aspire to join public services should come out of their secular slumber and open their eyes to see that it is Congress Party aided by Communists and various parties [Mulayam Singh, Mayawati, Karunanidhi, Sharad Pawar, Chandrababu Naidu etc] that it is going to harm their career interests permanently and irreversibly.

The Misra Commission has made a false claim that Muslims are under-represented in services. Supporters of Muslim reservation often say that Muslims are about 13 per cent of population but in IAS etc their representation is much less at about 4% so they are under-represented in services and there should be reservation for them to boost their per cent to 13%. For getting into class one services one has to be a graduate. Vide its table 3.6 Misra Commission reports that graduation percentage of Muslims is only 3.6%. As only graduates can aspire for public services percentage of Muslims in services at 4% is fair and already more than commensurate to their graduation percentage.

Further Muslims are about 4 per cent in services but 10 per cent jobs in all cadres and grades are proposed to be reserved for them by Congress. It means that Muslim officers will have much faster pace of promotions vis-à-vis Hindu officers and will also occupy senior positions for longer periods than Hindu officers.

Shri Arif Mohammed Khan, a former Union Minister in the Rajiv Gandhi Government has pointed out that 10 Muslim communities are already part of the Scheduled Tribes and another 83 Muslim communities are included in the OBC list. "Together," he maintains, "they constitute more than 70 per cent of total Muslim population leaving out only the Muslim creamy layer." Similarly, a good chunk of Christians are already included in the Scheduled tribe and the OBC category.

Muslims Literacy Higher

The Constitution of India as well as the Supreme Court has laid down that social and educational backwardness are essential to become eligible for getting reservation under Art 16(4). But Muslims as a community enjoy better literacy rate than Hindus in eleven states and better literacy rate than SC Hindus and ST Hindus on national level so they are not entitled for any reservation as they are not educationally backward.

In its para 12.3 the Misra Commission itself states: "Analysis of literacy rate reveals that Muslims were better off than Scheduled Castes and Scheduled Tribes."

According to the 2001 Census, the Sachar Committee and the Misra Commission [table 3.5, paras12.3, 18.5 etc] Christians have higher literacy rate [80%] as compared to other religious minorities as well as the national percentage of 65%. Christians have higher literacy rate than Hindus. Christians have higher per capita income too. So Christians too cannot claim to be backward in any sense.

In eleven states, Muslim males have higher literacy rate than Hindu males. These states are Andhra Pradesh, Andaman & Nicobar, Chhattisgarh, Gujarat, Kerala, Karnataka, Madhya Pradesh, Maharashtra, Orissa, Pondicherry and Tamil Nadu.

In thirteen states, Muslim women enjoy higher literacy rate than Hindu women; these are Andhra Pradesh, Andaman & Nicobar, Chhattisgarh, Daman & Diu, Dadra & Nagarhaveli, Gujarat, Jharkhand, Karnataka, Madhya Pradesh, Maharashtra, Orissa, Pondicherry and Tamil Nadu.[Statements 8a and 8b, Census Report 2001].

The Sachar Committee [page 53] also admits that in ten states literacy rate among Muslims are higher than even that of the upper caste Hindus and also higher than SC/ST Hindus.

Let us examine how many jobs Hindus are going to lose in terms of Misra Report. Till 2009, SC Hindus were entitled to get 1500 posts out of every 10000 posts in Government sector, OBC Hindus were entitled to 2700 posts and ST Hindus were entitled for 750 posts.

The UPA Government in terms of Rangnath Misra Commission is planning to reserve 15% posts for minorities, and as Manmohan Singh has publicly asserted in December 2006 that minorities have first claim over government resources so SC Hindus will get 15% of remaining 8500 posts i.e. 1270 posts, OBC Hindus [including OBC Muslims and Christians] will get 27% of 8500 i.e. 2290 posts, and, ST Hindus [including ST Christians] will get 7.5% of 8500 i.e. 630 posts.

The upper caste Hindu candidates till 2009 were eligible to compete for 5050 posts out of every 10000 posts but now under Manmohan formula they can compete only for 4310 seats. And wonder of wonder is that this reduction in E3 space of all categories of Hindu applicants will be achieved on strength of those Hindus who gave their notes and votes to Congress Party which is pursuing such politics.

The Misra Report para 16.2.7 reads: "As by the force of judicial decisions the minority intake in minority educational institutions has, in the interest of national integration, been restricted to about 50 per cent, thus virtually earmarking the remaining 50 per cent or so for the majority community — we strongly recommend that, by the same analogy and for the same purpose, at least 15 per cent seats in all non-minority educational institutions should be earmarked by law for the minorities as follows:

(a) The break up within the recommended 15 per cent earmarked seats in institutions shall be 10 per cent for the Muslims (commensurate with their 73 per cent share of the former in the total minority population at the national level) and the remaining 5 per cent for the other minorities.

(b) Minor adjustments *inter se* can be made in the 15 per cent earmarked seats. In the case of non-availability of Muslim candidates to fill 10 per cent earmarked seats, the remaining vacancies may be given to the other minorities if their members are available over and above their share of 5 per cent; but in no case shall any seat within the recommended 15 per cent go to the majority community. [This anti-Hindu proviso is similar to a 1937 instruction of British India]

(c) As is the case with the Scheduled Castes and Scheduled Tribes at present, those minority community candidates who can compete with others and secure admission on their own merit shall not be included in these 15 per cent earmarked seats".

As and when it is implemented, Hindu students with marks better than minority candidates may start getting admissions refused even in non-minority institutions managed by Hindu organisations such as Vidya Bharati, DAV Colleges etc. At present out of every 10,000 engineering seats in non-minority institutions OBC Hindu students get 2700 seats reserved for them, 1500 seats for SC Hindus and 750 for ST Hindus. After Misra Report is implemented 1500 seats would first get reserved for minority students, 27% of remaining 8500 seats i.e. 1250 for OBCs and 630 for STs. So mathematically it is proved that there shall be reduction of seats for all Hindu students.

Marxist Hindus, NSUI Hindu students shall also suffer forced secular shrinkage of their E3 space.

Merit Ignored

[B] Hindu students with better marks are being denied admissions into nurseries, schools, colleges and universities run by minorities, whether aided out of taxes collected from we Hindus or unaided. For example, cut-off marks for Christian students for admission into St Stephen's College, Delhi University and cut-off marks for Sikh students into the Khalsa College DU and cut-off marks for Muslims in Jamia Hamdard University is lower than those for Hindu students. Same is the case all over India in all districts.

Hindus are generally under-represented in the staff of minority institutions, and, posts of principals etc are generally reserved for non-Hindus. For example the rule of St Stephen's College Delhi stipulates that a Hindu cannot be its principal and vice-principal though it receives annual grant of Crores of rupees from the Government out of taxes collected from Hindus. Hindu candidates with better CVs are generally denied jobs in these institutions. More than 90 % teaching staff of the Aligarh Muslim University are non-Hindus.

Hindustan Times [July 10, 2008] and the *Indian Express* [July 18, 2008] reported that St. Stephen's College, Delhi gives preference to Christian candidates in appointments. MS Frank, the then acting Principal insisted appointing only Christians. The Supreme Council of this college clarified that a Christian candidate who met the minimum qualifications shall be given preference over non-Christian candidates in matters of appointments. Similar ill-treatment is handed down to Hindus all over India by all other minority institutions.

These institutions quote Supreme Court decisions to justify the second class treatment to all Hindus in matters of admission and employment. In a nut-shell the Supreme Court has ruled that Hindus do not enjoy equality rights guaranteed by the Article 14 of the Constitution in the minority institutions, whether aided or unaided. In other words, according to the Supreme Court Article 14 of the Constitution is not uniformly applicable everywhere and to everyone. This is a flawed interpretation of Constitution by Supreme Court.

[C] The Constitution of India [Articles 15 and 16] guarantees 15% reservations for SC Hindus and 7.5% reservations for ST Hindus but they are denied these constitutionally guaranteed rights in admissions as well as in employment in minority institutions

The OBC Hindus have been given 27% reservations in academic institutions but the Manmohan Singh Government has framed rules in such a way that OBC Hindus are denied this constitutionally guaranteed reservation all over India in all minority institutions.

The point is that as the Constitution is in force on every square inch of India so these reservations must be available to SC, ST and OBC Hindus in all minority institutions all over India. At present some Articles of Constitution are applicable at one place but not at other places. The selective application of the Constitution is flawed and has to be opposed.

The National Commission for Scheduled Castes headed by Congressman Shri Buta Singh also favours giving 'reserved' status to Dalit converts to Christianity and Islam but does not want them to be included in the 15% SC quota and wants to further reduce seats available to general class Hindus so as to create a new quota for Dalit converts. [*Times of India*, July 14, 2007]. So general category Hindus will get size of their cake further reduced.

[D] Hindu students get student loans at higher interest rate of about 10% to 12% per annum but minority students get student loan at 3% per annum from the National Minority Development & Finance Corporation under the Union Ministry of Finance. For confirmation please visit www.nmdfc.org.

Hindus discriminated

On August 27, 2009 the Manmohan Singh government decided that any student whose parents' income is below Rs 4.5 lakh per annum will get full interest subsidy on his student loan for professional course during the course period. But after the course is over a Hindu student has to pay interest at same higher rate of 10 to 12% whereas a minority student will pay at 3%.

[E] Hindu youth gets loans from commercial banks to start a new business at 15% to 18% interest and has to arrange 'margin money' of 15% to 40% of project cost from his private sources, balance comes from the bank. But a minority youth has to put in only 5% of project cost as margin money from his private source, other 35% is given by the National Minority Development & Finance Corporation at 3% interest, and remaining 60% of finance is given by commercial banks at two percentage points less than general lending rate for Hindus.

On March13, 2007 the then Finance Minister Chidambaram had told the Rajya Sabha that of the total priority sector lending, loans to minorities had increased by 33 per cent to Rs 45,490 crores on March 31, 2006 as against Rs 34,654 crores when the UPA Government took office in May 2004.

So, Hindu businessmen will increase their own difficulties in getting bank loans by financing the elections of Congress Party and other UPA parties.

[F] The Manmohan Singh Government has directed that all minority students admitted to 70 top institutions of India like IIMs, IITs etc will get their total fees paid by the Government but Hindu students, whether Leftist or Rightist, whether North Indian or South Indian, whether member of NSUI or SFI have to pay their fees.

If a minority student decides to join any coaching centre to prepare for admission into colleges or public service examinations or jobs in government and private sectors he gets total fees of coaching centre paid by the Government but a Hindu student or his parent has to pay the fees of coaching centre. Details may be seen at www.minorityaffairs.gov.in

At pre-matric and at post-matric level a minority student will get scholarship from class I onwards if he has secured not less than 50% marks in the previous year examination but such facility is not there for all Hindu students. The SC, ST and OBC Hindu students have to have more than 60% marks for being eligible for any scholarship though Muslims, Christians etc enjoy higher literacy rates. Further SC, ST and OBC Hindu students get scholarships from class VI onwards.

[G] It may come as total surprise to many Hindus that there are many posts under the Government which are paid out of taxes collected from we Hindus but a Hindu howsoever liberal or Marxist he may be, he is legally debarred from holding such posts such as posts of the Chairman of National and Provincial Minority Commissions, principals of St Stephen's Delhi [and similar minority institutions running into thousands and thousands all over India] etc.

Under section 3 of the National Minority Commission Act, a Hindu cannot be its Chairman and at least five of its seven members including Chairman shall have to be from amongst the minority communities. This law was enacted by PV Narasimha Rao Government.

Section 4 of the National Commission for Minority Educational Institutions Act 2004 passed by the Man Mohan Singh Government stipulates that only persons from minority communities shall be eligible to be appointed as Chairman and members of this Commission. Hindus have been totally excluded from this Commission.

As representation of Hindus in Sachar Committee, Rangnath Commission etc have been below their demographic strength it is obvious that these lack democratic weight.

In pursuance of the 2004 Congress manifesto, on 10th March 2006, the Lok Sabha passed the National Commission for Minority Educational (Amendment) Bill according to which the provincial governments will have to give no objection certificate within 90 days of application for setting up an institution by religious minorities, or, else the government will have to specify reasons for refusal. The aggrieved party will have right to approach the Commission which, in turn, will take a final decision in consultation with the State. Composition of even this Commission is not representative to the total exclusion of Hindus and the wonder is that Hindus, howsoever secular or leftist, are debarred from being made even a member of this Commission by an Act of Parliament passed in November 2004.

However, if no reasons are given by a State government for not giving the NOC within 90 days, it would be deemed as the approval of the State.

The Act also provides for the right of minority institutions to seek affiliation to any university of their choice listed in this Act. The bill was supported by all UPA partners including the Left parties, Samajwadi Party of Shri Mulayam Singh and the Bahujan Samaj Party etc. It was criticised by the Bharatiya Janata Party and Shiv Sena. So, a Muslim institution in a far off place, say, Jhumari talaian in Bihar can demand affiliation to any named central university of its choice and its students will get degrees of that central university and, thus, will enjoy better marketability in the employment market whereas a Hindu student of the same region will have degree of a provincial university having less marketability in the employment market. Thus, with votes of Hindu parents, Shri Arjun Singh the then HRD Minister & the UPA Government placed Muslim and Christian students at higher and better pedestal in the employment market than Hindu students.

Bleak Future for Majority Students

Those Hindu parents in rural areas who voted for the Congress Party and its allies in the 2004 and 2009 elections have thus actually harmed the future of their own children.

[H] To reduce the percentage of Hindus and to increase the percentage of minorities in the government sector the UPA Government has ordered inclusion of minority members in all Selection Boards and Departmental Promotion Committees [DPCs]. The circular to induct religious minority members in Selection Boards was issued during Prime Ministership of Rajiv Gandhi vide OM No39016/6(s)/87-Estt(B) dated 10th June 1987, and, during the Prime Minsitership of Vishwanath Pratap Singh, another secular veteran vide OM 39016/6(S)89-Estt(B) dated 16th August 1990.

In January 2007 the Department of Personnel and Training, Govt of India, sent a note to all 'heads of departments, public sector banks and financial institutions, quasi-Government organisations, autonomous bodies etc. and all appointing authorities,' asking them to 'scrupulously observe' guidelines to make selection panels more representative. All selection panels recruiting ten or more vacancies must have one member belonging to a minority community. This circular instructs to give special considerations to minorities in all appointments, so danger bell is ringing loud and clear for all Hindu job seekers whether they are leftists or rightists, whether upper caste or lower castes that despite their better profiles they may not be selected.

At present Hindus constitute over 95% in all services and the Manmohan Singh Government with help of Hindu voters is trying to reduce the Hindu percentage in government and public sector undertakings to less than 85%.

Thus, it is clear that politicians have treacherously created such a system in which a minority is eligible to apply for each and every post paid by the State but not a Hindu. A minority student gets student loan and commercial loans at rates lower than a Hindu.

A minority student with more than 50% marks gets scholarship but not all Hindu students with more than 50% marks. In minority-run institutions a Hindu is given step- brotherly treatment in matters of admissions and employment but in government-run and Hindu-run institutions a minority candidate has to be treated at par with Hindus and to ensure that a minority is treated on par there are national and provincial minority commissions headed and dominated by minorities.

Hindu voters who do not want to harm the career prospects of their own or of their children and grandchildren must never cast their votes in favour of any Jaichandi Hindu politician or any Jaichandi party.

The writer served as Ambassador/High Commissioner to many countries and belongs to the 1971 batch of the Indian Foreign Service and retired in pay & rank of a Secretary to the Govt of India.

□

Nationalism in Politics

—R Balashankar

Arnold Toynbee in his book *A Study of History* wrote, "Growth takes place whenever a challenge evokes a successful response that in turn evokes further and different challenge. We have not found any intrinsic reason why this process should not repeat itself indefinitely even though a majority of civilisations have failed as a matter of historical fact." India is a rare exception. For generations we have grasped the dynamics of change and growth.

Issues in Nationalism

Most of the problems India confronts today have their origin in the country's independence. We have inherited them with our freedom on August 15, 1947. The freedom struggle against the British, which started in 1857, with the War of Independence was also an exercise in defining our nationhood. The partition of India was a tragedy. It was artificial. It was the success and culmination of the two-nation theory propounded by Muslim separatists, who were represented by the Muslim League, Aligarh Muslim University alumni, Deoband clergy and Mohammad Ali Jinnah.

The tragedy of partition could have been made into a golden opportunity to define our nationhood. If the composite culture of India, the Hindu heritage and the Bharatiya identity were declared the foundations of this nationhood, many problems of today would not have been there. It was convenient for the Congress rulers then to leave things vague. The British too played a role in keeping the burden of pestering sores alive.

Independent India could have identified and clearly laid down the frontiers of this Nation State. The Constitution is the basis of this Nation State. We have accepted the Tricolour as our national flag. We have a national anthem and a national song. We have a national language and a link language, we have an inviolable geographical boundary.

What is Nationalism?

Here Nationalism and Nation are used to reflect the meaning Patriotism and *Rashtra* respectively. In the last century nation, nationhood and nationalism have been defined extensively by political thinkers. But their interpretations differed on their ideological lineage. In India for instance, from spiritual renaissance pioneers like Swami Vivekananda and Maharishi Aurobindo to national leaders like Lokmanya Tilak, Veer Savarkar, Guruji Golwalkar, Mahatma Gandhi, Jawaharlal Nehru, Syama Prasad Mookerjee, Dr S Radhakrishnan and many other eminent personalities tried to define Indian nation and nationalism. Their political thinking differed vastly, but the essential approach to nationalism was rooted in the glorious past of this vast landmass which they worshipped as holy motherland. It is this unity of thought that became the inspiration of India's freedom struggle and its march to modern nationhood.

The stream of our cultural heritage became the eternal source of our understanding of nationalism. The basic concepts here are the uninterrupted flow of a cultural tradition, the idea of an inviolable geographical boundary, the belief in shared history, of common heroes and enemies, faith in a shared destiny and a common goal with a desire to be earnest proactive partners in building it, and willingness to even give up one's life and everything in this pursuit.

This dissertation is an attempt to understand the role of nationalism in Indian politics. Often these words are used in politics without understanding their full impact.

In our democratic republic, politics is the medium through which parties usurp power and no political party in its good sense would declare itself anti-national. Nationalism is the basic credo of all political formations in the country. However, there is a world of difference in their understanding of nationalism and our concept of nationalism. In the last six decades politics has seen to it that most of the basic features of this sovereign, socialist, secular, republic enshrined in the Constitution have been systematically undermined, rather wilfully, yet in politics, parties quarrel in the name of nationalism.

A whole lot of semantic misunderstanding has been created because of the difference in our idea of these concepts and the influence of foreign ideas. Nationalism in western thought is freedom from colonialism, self-determination and unity of some common material interest. At best it means a "self governing community for agreed common goals." In India, nationalism is always identified with patriotism and is often defined as cultural urge manifested in all beings on this land to treat everything this country has given to them as a blessing and a boon." (M M Sankhdher, *Patriotism A New Paradigm, Organiser Weekly*, December 29, 1991). Patriotism evokes a commitment to safeguard the interests of the country and preparedness to face all challenges.

The RSS Sarsanghachalak M S Golwalkar had studied the problem of Indian nationalism in depth and made original contribution to our understanding of this nationalism. He said that territorial nationalism was inadequate to define nationhood. Essentially, his thought was not different from that of other nationalist leaders mentioned earlier.

In comparison to the emergence of nation states in Europe which has a history of some five centuries, the existence of India as a *rashtra*, nation, has a history of several thousand years. There are views expressed by political scientists and Left historians that India is not one nation but a multinational subcontinent or that India as a nation was born on August 15, 1947. Another view is that India is a nation in the making. Guruji Golwalkar has stoutly refuted all these propositions and insisted that India is one nation, one people, one culture and all his speeches emphasised on the ancient nationhood and glorious past of the country. His ideas were in consonance with all the modern-day nationalist thinkers of India like Swami Vivekananda and Maharishi Aurobindo, Tilak and Gandhiji in this respect.

"Golwalkar asserted that to constitute a nation mere habitation of human species on a piece of land is not sufficient. Unless the bond of some kind of unity is established among the people, mere congregation of human beings will not constitute a nation. Human beings get collected even in railway platform or cinema theatre. But they do not constitute a nation. For a nation, he emphasised commonality in goal of life, ideas of life, values of life is a raison detre." (pg 17, *Political Ideas of M S Golwalkar* by Ritu Kohli.)

In politics this feeling gives expression at different stages in different ways. After independence, because we as a people have become masters of our destiny, the nationalism debate received a new impetus. Speaking in the Lok Sabha on a debate on the situation in Jammu and Kashmir, the Bharatiya Jana Sangh founder Syama Prasad Mookerjee on February 17, 1953 said, "It is not a question of mutual humiliation or gaining one point here or losing another point there. It is the question of settlement of a issue which is of national importance and which may create serious problems and destroy the peace and happiness of large parts of India, and I appeal to the Prime Minister to make a move before it is too late. We have been charged and branded as encouraging the movement. I repudiated it earlier on the floor of the House and repudiate it now. It is not our movement. The movement has spread and various classes of people have come into it. We have sympathised with it. We have supported it. We have extended our blessings to it. We have done that because it is not a struggle of Jammu, it is a struggle of the people of India. (pg no 674-75 *The Penguin Book of Modern Indian Speeches, 1877 to Present*). Dr. Mookerjee was referring to the Jammu agitation led by Prem Nath Dogra, for the full integration of Kashmir with rest of India and the discrimination against Jammu by Sheikh Abdullah.

The words he spoke there were an excellent expression of nationalism in politics. And they sound appropriate even today in the context of Shri Amarnath land struggle in Jammu. Fifty-five years have passed, but what Mookerjee felt then, the country is echoing today.

Political nationalism in the Indian context is being debated even today, because we have left many of the problems we inherited in 1947 unresolved. The political leadership has consciously avoided defining Indian nationhood to keep the term vague.

See what Dr. Mookerjee said on the language question. Speaking on the national language he said, "With regard to regional languages, I am now happy that the amendment proposes to include in the body of the Constitution itself a list of the principal regional languages of India. I hope we will include Sanskrit also. I shall speak here with frankness. Why is it that many people belonging to non-Hindi speaking provinces have become a bit nervous about Hindi? If the protagonists of Hindi will pardon me for saying so, had they not been so aggressive in their demands and enforcement of Hindi they would have got whatever they wanted, perhaps more than what they expected, by spontaneous and willing cooperation of the entire population of India. But unfortunately, a fear has been expressed, and in some areas that fear has been translated into action where people speaking other languages not inferior to Hindi by any means, have not been allowed the same facilities which even the much detested foreign regime did not dare to deprive them of." (Constituent Assembly Debates, Volume 9, No 33, on the National Language).

Take another example. After Pokhran II, then Prime Minister Atal Behari Vajpayee told the Lok Sabha, "At a global level, we see no evidence on the part of the nuclear weapons states to take decisive and irreversible steps in moving towards a nuclear weapons free world. Instead we have seen that the NPT has been extended indefinitely and unconditionally perpetuating the existence of nuclear weapons in the hands of five countries. Under such circumstances, the government was faced with difficult decision. The touchstone that has guided us in making the correct choice clear was national security…

"India is now a nuclear weapon state. This is a reality that cannot be denied. It is not a conferment that we seek; nor is it a status for others to grant. It is an endowment to the nation by our scientists and engineers. It is India's due, the right of one sixth of the human kind. Our strengthened capability adds to our sense of responsibility. We do not intend to use these weapons for aggression or for mounting threats against any country. These are weapons of self defence to ensure that India is not subjected to nuclear threats or coercion. We do not intend to engage in an arms race." *(Atal Behari Vajpayee, on Nuclear Test at Pokhran, Lok Sabha, May 27, 1998)*

These are instances of nationalism expressing itself in political discourse. Nationalism is what motivates political action. We as a people lost and suffered a lot in this long journey. The foreign invaders who ruled this land for nearly 800 years left deep wounds in our national psyche. We can pardon them, but cannot forget what they did to us. Because that legacy continues to visit and vitiate the atmosphere.

Who are We?

"In spite of the bewildering diversity of race, language, religion and political divisions of the people of India, a fundamental unity could be observed in their history; in the cultural homogeneity. It has been built up through ages. Indian empires have been of the hegemony type and the unity of India, till recently has not been political or administrative," says R. Sathianathaier, in his *History of India, Vol.1*. "The remarkable unity of India is mainly due to the outlook of her people on life and to their common heritage. We can speak of the people of India, but not of Europe in the same sense. Europe underwent many wars based on nation state conflicts. Through ages the Indians gradually evolved a common way of life." Sathianathaier quotes Sir Alfred Risely as saying, "Beneath the manifold diversity of physical and social type, language, custom and religion which strike an observer in India, there will still be a certain underlying uniformity of life from the Himalayas to the Cape Camorin."

Historian VA Smith, in *The Oxford History of India* points out that "India beyond all doubts, possesses a deep underlying fundamental unity, far more profound than produced either by geographical isolation or political suzerainty. That unity transcends innumerable diversities of blood, colour, language and dress manners and sect."

"The sense of unity of India was always present in the minds of Indian theologians, political philosophers and poets. The spread of Hinduism all over the country from ancient times helped the emergence of the spirit of unity. The Epics and the Vedas have been respected throughout the country. The respect for the cow, worship of common gods, places of pilgrimage etc also helped the development of a sense of unity", says Sathianathaier.

Indians were great chroniclers of history. A detailed study of the sources and chronology will enable us to understand the sense of history of the Indian of the distant past. The sources of Indian history are literary, (indigenous & foreign), epigraphy, numismatics and archaeology (monuments). Indian literary source consists of partly sacred and partly secular literature. There are the four *Vedas,* the *Brahmanas*, the *Aranyakas*, the *Upanishads*, the two great Epics—*Ramayana* and *Mahabharata*—the *Brahmasastras*, the *Puranas*, and Buddhist Jain literature and other literary works. Of the four *Vedas*—the *Rig, Sama, Yajur* and *Atharva* — the *Rig Veda* is the oldest and contains a lot of information about the history and political system of the people.

Some behave as if India's history began on August 15, 1947. This is the Marxian view. A few others think that the Hindu history terminated with the martyrdom of Rana Pratap or even earlier with Prithviraj Chauhan. True; for almost 800 years Hindu history writing took a pause. All these years the entire creative genius of India was geared on preservation and defence. So we have the great *Bhakti* literature. A great resistance movement that produced greatest of Indian heroes like Chhatrapati Shivaji and Guru Gobind Singh. And during this period India did not produce great works of history, art, architecture or science of the magnificence of the pre-Muslim period. But is that enough a justification to deny the Hindu his history?

As Arnold Toynbee notes, "The tension in Hindu souls must be extreme, and sooner or later it must find some means of discharging itself." He further noted, "The large hearted, broad minded religious spirit that was once almost worldwide survives in India almost alone. It is now laid upon India to preserve this spiritual heritage as a common treasure for mankind—a treasure of inestimable value." Where has this treasure come from? It is in the *Ramayana,* in the Hindu tradition. And that is why Toynbee said, "You have not made Hinduism the official religion of the Indian union. You have established a secular regime...Hinduism has refrained from insisting on being given a privileged status, and in this act of self denial it has, I should say, been strikingly true to its own spirit. The same care and tradition of toleration comes out in the attitude to Muslim and British architecture, some of which were ugly and even offensive". (*Faith of a Historian*)

What did the invaders do to us? And how did we respond? How could we survive? A western diplomat philosopher Pochammer narrated it passionately. "The first reaction of the Hindus to the occupation of north India by conquerors professing Islam was one of great horror in the face of their cruelties they had never before experienced. The immense and uncontrollable bloodbaths, the brutality with which civilian populations were massacred and the women and girls were dragged into harems which to the Hindus appeared as no better than brothels, the introduction of a slave trade in which thousands of people including children were sold; all these generated a hatred for foreigners, the like of which had never been felt by Indians before. The hatred was increased by the shameless way in which the foreigners destroyed holy places after having first defiled them in the most senseless way. And finally, there came economic distress as a result of the plundering and exploitation of the people... What took place here was a struggle between a quite primitive people whose only spiritual possession was a recently accepted Islam whose inner worth even their leaders were not yet able to understand, and an old civilisation whose superiority they might have instinctively felt, but tried to compensate for their lack of understanding of it by showing an exaggerated contempt. (*India's Road to Nationhood* by Wilhelm von Pochammer)

A whole lot of issues which are today traumatising the nation could have been settled long before if the leaders at the time of Independence had shown the political will. Instead, they left it to the future generations of India to settle, enclosing them as "Directive Principles" in the Indian Constitution. The issues of Uniform Civil Code, ban on cow slaughter, equal wages for equal work, total prohibition and many others could have been settled with finality.

Having been divided on religious lines to create a Muslim Pakistan we had every reason to enact laws that were in keeping with our national interest, security, pride and culture. Directive Principles of State Policy are in Part IV of the Constitution. They are not justiciable, i.e. one cannot go to court over the rights mentioned in this chapter. These are the guidelines of the Constitution-makers for good governance and progressing towards a strong Nation State.

The cow is worshipped by Hindus. But in many parts of the country, cow is slaughtered and the revered animal is exported illegally for its meat. There have been several agitations in the country demanding a complete ban on cow and calf slaughter. These have been mainly spearheaded by saints and religious leaders. But the successive governments have largely ignored the issue. Some states and religious groups behave as if slaughtering a cow is a matter of faith and pride. This, in the land of *ahimsa*, Buddha and the Mahatma!

Total prohibition is a far cry now with the state governments (including the Delhi state) launching official vents. The revenue earned from liquor and the booty from the liquor contracts are too lucrative for the state to give up.

Women constitute more than half the workforce in the country. The early urban picture may have been slightly different. But in the labour-intensive agriculture, construction and other sectors women have been working equal if not more. But even today, women are paid less than men. This provision of equal wage for equal work has been enshrined in the Directive Principles, but is yet to be implemented.

Uniform Civil Code is an issue which the politicians avoid like a mine field. They circumvent it, sidestep it and never address it. A number of issues of serious concern like women's rights, equal justice, equal opportunity, ban on conversions by enticement, population policy, dowry and marriage and other civil laws are being subverted in the absence of a Uniform Civil Code. All unifying aspects of Nation State get ignored and diversity is emphasised from all possible platforms.

There is very little incentive to learn Sanskrit, the treasure house of our knowledge and heritage. But state-funded *madrasas* teach foreign languages, alien culture and Semitic adventurism. The people of India are divided along religious lines in the eye of the judiciary, law and the legal system. For thc same offence against women, a Muslim gets a different ruling and a Hindu gets a different ruling and so does a Christian. The recent spate of women abuse in the country has once again highlighted the need for a Uniform Civil Code.

Of the 19 Directive Principles, only the ones on village panchayat and right to education have been made into law. The others like participation of workers in management, separation of judiciary from executive, public health, free legal aid, universal humane working conditions, maternity relief and protection of environment and wildlife have remained just pious goals of the Constitution of India. These are all issues confronting the nation, challenging the concept of India as a secular Nation State.

The people who live in this country are expected to be loyal, worshipful, of the identities of our nationhood. And what are they? Has anyone attempted to define them? Have we even launched a national campaign to propagate and popularise, create wider awareness of these concepts? Except for the Rashtriya Swayamsevak Sangh and a few other nationalist organisations nobody bothers to campaign on these issues. The Constitution enjoins upon us to adhere to these principles, implement them and ensure respect for them in the conduct of the citizens. But day in and day out we see these are violated, defiled, even challenged by fissiparous elements. Politicians are always pussyfooting on issues of national honour. Divisive elements get a fillip whenever a government panders to divided loyalties.

Reservations based on religion have no constitutional sanction. People or organisations challenging the integrity of the nation, asking for special rights or autonomous status are drilling a hole in the heart of the Indian Nation State.

Concerns of a Nationalist

No matter how educated or how liberal or intellectual one might be, but at some level it hurts. People are from the same social background, steeped in identical social condition but some are preferred for special treatment because they have converted. They have said goodbye to their ancestral faith, and vowed their loyalty to the alien. Because they are not Hindu. In this land of the Hindus, being Hindu has become a handicap. You cannot grow in this country and remain impervious to what is happening around us, how systematically our icons are being demolished, how our pride as a nation is being cynically diluted. Every country has to define itself. It has to underline its core values and concerns. That is what every secular country does.

Anti-national Politics

Secularism, to begin with, was a positive, almost indulgent rhetoric under Jawaharlal Nehru; understandable in the aftermath of partition for which the Muslim League and its supporters in India were responsible. Under Indira Gandhi it became vote bank politics. Rajiv Gandhi and his successors made it appeasement. Under the UPA, secularism is interpreted as brazenly anti-Hindu to the extent of denigrating Hindu ideals becoming state policy.

In one of the most significant books written on minority problem in India, *Indian Muslims: Where Have They Gone Wrong?* Dr Rafiq Zakaria says, "The British got, naturally, worried and they did whatever they could to disrupt that (Hindu-Muslim) unity. They engineered riots, they played politics by giving separate electorate to the Muslims, they devised various methods both political and social—to keep the two communities apart. They dangled grants and concessions alternately to both the religious groups. Ultimately they saw to it that the country was divided, through the distrust that they had so assiduously built up between the two over the decades. To perpetuate their rule, they followed the Roman policy of 'Divide and Rule.' But as Maulana Mohammad Ali rightly put it: 'We divided and they ruled.' The blame rests as much on our joint leadership as on the British; however, in the last stage it was Jinnah's obduracy which struck the final blow to our unity."

The UPA under Sonia Gandhi is playing the role of the British, to divide and rule. The historic parallels are strikingly similar and ominous. On the Muslim strategy in India after partition, MA Karandikar has written a scholarly book. He gives scores of narratives to explain this mindset. Take this instance, "Before he opted for Pakistan, Muslim League leader (Shaheed) Suhrawardy had decided to stay in India and lead the Bengal Muslims in India. His letter to (Chaudhary) Khaliquzzaman on September 10, 1947, was eloquent and made interesting reading. He was faced with the dilemma that unless Muslims derived their strength on account of group solidarity they would not be respected by the Hindus. At the same time solidarity and strength would raise suspicion about their bona fides. Hence he suggested formation of strong Muslim pockets dotted all over the country. His other alternative that both India and Pakistan should strive to destroy the complex of superiority of their majority populations and they should accept their minorities as their own was a cry in the wilderness so far as Pakistan was concerned." (*Islam: In India's Transition to Modernity by MA Karandikar*). Nehru had a different approach. He was hopeful of developing unity in diversity by conscious political intervention.

Calling planning the first attempt in India to integrate agriculture, industrial, social, economic and other aspects of the country into a single framework of thinking in his speech on first draft Five-Year Plan, Nehru said, "It has made people think of this country as a whole. I think it is most essential that India, which is united politically and in many other ways, should, to the same extent, be united mentally and emotionally also. We often go off at a tangent on grounds of provincialism, communalism, religion or caste. We have no emotional awareness of the unity of the country. Planning will help us in having an emotional awareness of our problems as a whole. It will help us to see the isolated problems in villages or districts or even provinces in their larger context. Therefore, the mere act of planning, the mere act of having approached the question of progress in this way and of producing a report of this type is something on which we might, I think, congratulate ourselves."

Again, in a speech *Laying the Foundations (Broadcast from the Delhi Station of All India Radio, December 31, 1952)*, Nehru after a visit to Kanyakumari said, "From that southern tip of India, I pictured this great country spread out before me right up to the Himalayas in the north and thought of her long and chequered story. Ours is a wonderful inheritance but how shall we keep it? How shall we serve the country which has given us so much and make her great and strong?..." "We look at our own country and find both good and ill, powerful forces at work to build her and also forces, which would disrupt and disintegrate her. We cannot do much to affect the destiny of this world as a whole but surely we can make a brave attempt to mould the destiny of our 360 (then) million people... In India, the first essential is the maintenance of the unity of the country, not merely a political unity but a unity of the mind and the heart, which precludes the narrow urges that make for disunity and which breaks down the barriers raised in the name of religion or those between State and State or, for that matter, any other barrier. We must aim at a classless society," Nehru said. (*Speech in Parliament, New Delhi, December 15, 1952, Jawaharlal Nehru's Speeches: 1949-1953, published by The Publications Division, Ministry of Information and Broadcasting, Government of India)*

After globalisation, power is shifting from nation states. New players are emerging. Will the state wither away? Will WTO, World Bank and MNCs come to control our entire political thinking? Money-driven politics is replacing ideology-driven politics. Still India is debating.

In the biography of JF Kennedy, Theodore C. Sorensen, who was special counsel to the late President of America notes, when he was thinking of applying for a job with the new Senator he was informed by a friend, "...Joe Kennedy hasn't hired a non-Catholic in fifty years." At another place he recounts that though Kennedy was not an orthodox Catholic and did not prefer Catholics in his staff and was not even deeply religious, "he faithfully attended Mass each Sunday, even in the midst of fatiguing out-of-state travels when no voter would know whether he attended services or not." The writer was explaining how it was important for a politician in America to convincingly prove his religious identity to be successful. The situation is the same even today. It is only in India, in politics, that Hindu identity is sought to be made into a disadvantage.

The power of the vote bank is vastly exaggerated. Compared to the strength of the nationalist forces the anti-Hindus are in a minority. The tyranny of circumstances should not blind our vision.

Can True Nationalism Work?

Broadly speaking, it is seldom that Hindus vote as Hindus. Hindus vote as Jats, Yadavs, Dravidians, Dalits and even as Brahmins. But only the call of nationalism, the need for asserting territorial integrity of the country, makes Hindus react as a united whole and in this they are not swayed by political affiliations. Both the BJP and the Congress benefited from this Hindu sentiment. Till the mid-eighties Congress rode to decisive victories, cashing in on the Hindu aspiration to keep India one as in 1984. The emergence of casteist formations with their open and sectarian appeal to the minority vote coupled with the Congress overdrive to keep its traditional vote banks intact created a situation where Hindus lost their political worth. The politics of vote bank divided the social fabric and weakened national unity. The Congress under Rajiv Gandhi in 1986 cynically overturned the political balance, even over-ruled the Supreme Court wooing communal vote banks. This fast depleted the national mandate that gave him unprecedented victories.

Change is the only permanent facet of politics. In every act of Muslim fanatic assertion Indians are reminded of the tragic sequence of Partition. A weakened Hindu society, split on caste lines, falling prey to the whims of short-sighted and disparate political gamblers offer a frightening prospect for the Hindu. The majority community, the mosaic of the Unitarian federal structure is under siege from within. It was the revered His Holiness Swami Chinmayananda, the founder of Chinmaya Mission, who first envisaged the Hindu vote bank idea in the mid-eighties. It was the outcome of a deep-felt cultural angst, the fear of Hinduism being submerged by the onslaught of Semitic evangelism, Islamic fundamentalism and pusillanimous political paganism. At this stage discussions veered around the need for creating a Hindu vote bank or a strong Hindu lobby in the centres of power. Simply put, Hindus have to be made aware of their political strength. An osmosis of the religious Hindu into a political Hindu like his Muslim and Christian counterpart.

There is a strong Babri lobby, there is a stronger evangelical lobby. There is a Pak lobby, like a Chinese or US lobby, there is a pro-Afzal and anti-Narendra Modi lobby. Staines and Setalvads will get Padma Shri for Hindu-bashing. But in India there is no Hindu lobby! There is no Hindu issue on which parties across the board will sit and argue so that the majority sentiment is also taken note of. The Hindu vote bank will emerge more as a consequence of UPA misrule.

This coalition has presented the nation with a centre that cannot hold or rule. It indulgingly promotes crude chauvinism, terrible antagonism and deafening rhetoric of fissiparous elements weakening the country. The terrorists never had it so easy. Instead of working to unite the people, the UPA has an agenda to encourage social tension. It has a well-defined anti-Hindu plank. The Congress under Sonia Gandhi has lost its nationalist moorings and the will to cultivate patriotic feelings in its ranks. They have no respect for the Constitution, the Supreme Court or democracy.

Nationalism Linked to the Fate of the Hindu

In the end Hindu is powerless, penniless and landless. Even numbers are slowly being worked against him. It is time for a new politics. We witnessed it working in Punjab, Gujarat and Karnataka. Why not all over India? This is not about dividing. This is about reconciling to realities. At one level the rural India travels to the urban India in search of its dream, a job, a better living and a secure future. And at another level the urban India sets the trend for the rural India to follow. Simply put, people travel from villages to cities, ideas travel from cities to villages. Any political idea that loses the urban trust loses the India of tomorrow. That was what happened to the NDA in 2004. That is what is happening to the UPA today. The urban middle class is uncertain and insecure about the future of his children. The cream of urban Indian youth is migrating to the West, even to the Far East. India is witnessing the highest human talent exodus of modern history, thanks to the politics of quota and Sachar.

Is India becoming a place unsafe for the average educated Hindu? Why should the middle class Hindu children seek their dreams in the West? This is another worry confronting the Hindu. The deprivation of the real Hindu is not only political but also economic. His history is distorted, his religion is lampooned, his heroes are caricatured, his social fabric is destroyed. All this because of his immense capacity to tolerate and his self-denial of power. Hindus have to survive and dominate their land for humanitys sake. This is the only guarantee for peace, co-existence, freedom and democracy. Should India become like Pakistan, Bangladesh, China or the West, whose record in keeping peace is nothing to emulate, secularism and democracy will become unworkable.

Considering that India is Hindu majority, issues concerning the community should have found a place in the manifestos of political parties. Why should RamJanmabhoomi, cow-protection, Ram Setu, protection of Hindu temples, common civil code, writing a national history, subsidy to Hindu pilgrims, conversion by inducement or fight against terrorism be issues of partisan politics? Relatively these are more secular than most issues on which there should be a political consensus.

There should be no place for Article 370, for instance, in a free secular democracy. It was meant to be temporary. Indians, especially Hindus are a very tolerant lot. We take a lot of nonsense, violence and even intimidation in our stride. But this tolerance should not be mistaken for timidity.

A survey in *The Guardian* two years ago said every two out of three Muslims in Britain want to leave that country after the 7/7 serial blasts! This is the result of the social and administrative pressure and communal ostracisation on that religious group. The open discrimination against the citizens who are colour different. One instance of terrorist violence where 58 people were killed and 700 injured has changed the attitude of an entire nation to a recalcitrant minority. Compare this with the Indian response. For decades we have been facing Muslim terrorism, in which nearly 80,000 Indian lives have been lost. A religious minority in the North-East is encouraging militant insurgency. Yet, we have a political system that pampers minorityism in the name of vote bank. We allow millions of Bangladeshi infiltrators to destroy our social fabric, destabilise our border states and imposing a debilitating burden on the economy. Union Minster Ramvilas Paswan wants to give Bangla infiltrators citizenship. India once offered asylum for the tormented and persecuted. Now it is fast becoming a *dharmashala*.

If India has to exist as a nation, we have to insist and enforce that every individual living in this country has to unequivocally declare affinity, respect and commitment to the symbols of the Indian Nation State, the national flag, national song, the Constitution and geographic integrity. Our national heroes have to be recognised and respected. And national sentiments honoured.

(The author is Editor, Organiser Weekly.
He can be contacted at editor@organiserweekly.com)

Bibliography

1. The Penguin Book of Modern Indian Speeches, 1877 to Present
2. Political Ideas of M S Golwalkar by Ritu Kohli.
3. R. Balashankar, Organiser Weekly, Volumes: August 17, 2008, April 6, 2008, January 27, 2008, November 11, 2007, March 25, 2007, November 6, 2005, August 21, 2005,
4. MM Sankhdher, December 29, 1991
5. Constituent Assembly Debates, Volume 9, No 33, Lok Sabha papers
6. History of India, Vol.1R Sathianathaier
7. Faith of a Historian, by Arnold J Toynbee
8. A Study of History, by Arnold J Toynbee
9. Indias Road to Nationhood by Wilhelm von Pochammer
10. Bunch of Thoughts of M S Golwalkar
11. Complete works of Shri Guruji
12. Jawaharlal Nehru's Speeches: 1949-1953, the Publications Division
13. Indian Muslims: Where Have They Gone Wrong?, Dr Rafiq Zakaria
14. Islam: In India's Transition to Modernity by MA Karandikar
15. The Concept of Dharma in Valmiki Ramayana, Benjamin Khan
16. Hinduism by SK Kulkarni
17. Kennedy by Theodore C Sorensen
18. Politics of Minorities by Moin Shakir
19. Kautilya on Rajaniti by K P A Menon
20. Memoirs and Musings by K P S Menon
21. The Indian Middle Classes: Their Growth in Modern Times by B B Mishra
22. The Age of Uncertainty by John Kenneth Galbraith
23. The Oxford History of India by VA Smith

□

Dispute Over Conversions turns Violent

Paying the price for ignoring the sage counsel of the founding fathers and the Supreme Court

—A Surya Prakash

India continues to witness inter-religious turmoil with Hindus and Christians engaged in violent conflict over the issue of religious conversions. It is indeed tragic to see the discord over proselytisation spilling onto the streets and leading to the murder of a revered Hindu monk and desecration of places of worship in Orissa, Karnataka and some other states. The images of vandalised churches in these states is a matter of distress for the large majority of polytheistic Hindus who feel outraged at the desecration of any place of worship. Similarly, the murder of Swami Lakshmanananda in Orissa and the damage inflicted on Hindu temples in these trouble spots is a matter of anguish for most Christians who value peaceful co-existence and democratic methods to resolve disputes. Yet, neither the political class nor civil society seem to have an answer to the problem of religious conversions, which has now become a festering sore.

The problems posed by proselytisation, which Christians insist is an integral part of their faith, have been discussed right from the time of independence in several fora including the Constituent Assembly, the Niyogi Committee appointed by the Government of Madhya Pradesh and the Supreme Court. Yet, these conflicts persist because the opinions expressed by each of these institutions – that the right to propagate in not a right to proselytise and that the states are empowered to make law to prohibit religious conversions brought about by force, fraud or inducement – have not been given effect to. As a result, we are virtually re-visiting the very issues which we ought to have resolved in a peaceful and democratic manner at least 50 years ago.

A fair and objective reading of the debates in the Constituent Assembly will show that the wording of Article 25 (1) in the Constitution — which gave all persons the right to profess, practise and propagate religion— was agreed upon on the understanding that the states would make law to prohibit conversions brought about illegally or unethically.

If this understanding – of all states making law in this regard — had not been breached, there would have been no reason for the current bout of discord on this issue.

Similarly, if only the recommendations of the Niyogi Committee had been implemented and subsequently, the weighty opinion of the Supreme Court and the import of certain observations of the court in Rev Stanislaus v. Madhya Pradesh had been understood, specially by the State and by the Christian minority, we would not be finding ourselves in a situation several decades hence when the dispute over conversions would translate into such large-scale violence.

We need to honestly re-visit these discussions and events of the past and look for solutions if we are to prevent inter-religious conflict on this score. Meanwhile, those who run governments in the troubled states will have to ensure that the Constitutional guarantees given to religious and linguistic minorities are fully safeguarded. The State must assert itself and declare that these rights are non-negotiable, even as efforts are made to bring about a peaceful resolution of the dispute.

The issue of conversions was discussed by the Constituent Assembly when it considered the first draft of the report prepared by an Advisory Committee headed by Sardar Vallabhai Patel, on minority rights. This committee said that the Constitution must declare that all persons are equally entitled to freedom of conscience, and the right to freely profess, practice and propagate religion. This would be subject to public order, morality or health, and to the other provisions of the fundamental rights chapter. However, it said "conversion from one religion to another brought about by coercion or undue influence shall not be recognized by law".

When the Constituent Assembly discussed these clauses on May 1, 1947, the first clause granting every person the right to "profess, practise and propagate" religion was passed without much debate, but the second clause pertaining to conversions ran into trouble with several Christian members opposing this provision. They argued that propagation was central to Christianity and the prohibition of conversion, as proposed, militated against the Christian faith. Several senior members of the Congress Party, including Mr.K.M.Munshi however opposed the idea of giving citizens the fundamental right to religious propagation, or as the Christians demanded, the right to convert others. However, though Christians comprised just 1.5 per cent of India's population at that time, their representatives relentlessly argued that the right to propagate must be a "fundamental right".

Mr Munshi however was vehement in his opposition. He said the second clause pertaining to conversions should prohibit conversion of minors and apart from terms like "undue influence" and "coercion", the word "fraud" must also be added. In other words, the second clause should read as follows: "Any conversion from one religion to another of any person brought about by fraud, coercion or undue influence or of a minor under the age of 18 shall not be recognised by law". Several members of the Assembly welcomed Mr Munshi's proposal but the Christians strongly opposed the move to ban conversion of minors. For example Mr Frank Anthony spoke of how "passionate" Christians were on the right to propagate their religion. He thanked the Congress Party for having conceded the right to practice and propagate religion but said what was being given in one hand was sought to be taken away by the other. The right to convert, he claimed, was a principal fundamental right for Christians and any embargo on the conversion of a minors will amount to an embargo on conversion. Mr Anthony was supported by Reverend JJNichols-Roy, who said he had himself been converted to Christianity at the age of 15. Apart from Mr.Munshi, there were many others who were opposed to the demands being made on behalf of the Christian community. Among them were Mr Purushottam as Tandon and Mr Algu Rai Shastri. Mr Tandon said he was "greatly surprised" to hear his Christian brethren. He gave vent to his feelings as follows: "We Congressmen deem it very improper to convert from one religion to another or to take part in such activities and we are not in favour of this. In our opinion, it is absolutely futile to be keen on converting others to one's faith. But it is only at the request of some persons, whom we want to keep with us in our national endeavour that we accepted this. Now it is said that they have a right to convert young children to their faith. What is this? Sir, I am astonished at the manner in which some Christian friends have advanced the claim to convert minors. We have agreed to the right to conversion. Generally, we Congressmen do not think it at all right... that people should strenuously go about trying to convert peoples of other faith into their own, but we want to carry our Christian friends with us... and we have agreed on their insistence to retain this formula about 'propagation'. They know that we are opposed to it, yet we have agreed... I know that most Congressmen are opposed to the idea of 'propagation'. But we agreed to keep the word 'propagate' out of regard for our Christian friends. But now to ask us to agree to minors also being converted is, I think, Sir, going too far".

Mr Algu Rai Shastri said, 'whereever European or white races... have gone, they have as missionaries.' 'A study of 'Prosperous India' by Digby he said, 'showed that the Cross was followed by the sword, the missionary was followed by the batons, the swords and the guns. It was in this way that they employed coercion for spreading their religion and for extending their empire. The elders in a family are induced through prospects of financial gain to change their religion and also with them the children are taken over to the fold of the new religion. It appears as if some are taking the land physically in their possession and the helpless trees go with it to the new master". Mr. Jagat Narain Lal said that the Assembly had gone to the farthest limit possible to accommodate the views of the minorities. "I want to appeal to those who profess to speak for minorities not to press for too much... That would be taking undue advantage of the generosity of the majority. That will be very regrettable. I think that the amendment tabled by Mr Munshi becomes essential if the right to propagate is conceded. The House should therefore accept it".

Sardar Vallabhai Patel also felt that the issue of conversions was a major issue and a matter of concern in Indian society. He therefore wanted the House to consider the issue in all its aspects. However, despite the opinion of all these stalwarts that the Constitution must ban conversions brought about by coercion or undue influence, their efforts to incorporate it in the Constitution failed. They succumbed to Christian pressure and finally agreed that while this would not be explicitly stated in the Constitution, it would be the responsibility of every state to enact laws to outlaw such conversions. Dr BR Ambedkar said there were "drafting difficulties" if one tried to constitutionally ban conversions brought about by coercion and undue influence. Therefore, he felt that the best course would be for the states to enact laws to ban such conversions. This was the consensus in the Constituent Assembly and based on this consensus it was decided to incorporate the right to "propagate" religion in Article 25(1). Sadly, only a few states have enacted such laws and there are no laws to prohibit such conversions in most parts of India. Thus, while the first clause giving citizens the right to "propagate" religion was cleared by the Constituent Assembly without fuss, the second clause which sought to prohibit conversions brought about by coercion or undue influence fell through. This decision of the advisory committee came as a big disappointment to many members.

Mr. M Ananthasayanam Ayyangar said that the Constitution must explicitly declare that religious conversions will not be allowed. He appealed to the House to realise the dangerous consequences of not checking conversions and warned that "later it may attain enormous proportions". Mr. Lokanath Mishra described this Article as "the blackest part of the Draft Constitution". He declared that "it can only mean paving the way for the complete annihilation of Hindu Culture, the Hindu way of life and manners. Islam has declared its hostility to Hindu thought. Christianity has worked out the policy of peaceful penetration by the backdoor". Mr. L. Krishnaswami Bharati however drew the attention of the House to the misconception that right to "propagate" is intended only for the Christian community. "It is up to other communities to emulate them, if they so choose to" he said.

It has taken the Hindus a long time to realize the import of what Mr Bharati had said in the Constituent Assembly, but going by the accusations that Hindus are "re-converting" the converts, it appears as if it has finally sunk in that religious propagation and conversion is a game that can be played by persons of all faiths.

However, in the first flush of independence after the Constitution was ushered in, proselytisation was primarily a Christian activity. The country got the first glimpse of the extent of the problem of religious conversions when a committee appointed by the Madhya

Pradesh government to enquire into the activities of Christian missionaries in the state, submitted its report in 1956. This committee, which was headed by Mr MB Niyogi, former Chief Justice of the Nagpur High Court, made a number of recommendations to put an end to religious conversions brought about by force, fraud or allurement. A prominent recommendation was that the State should make law to stop such conversions. It said the Constitution should be amended to make it clear that the right to propagation, which is guaranteed under Article 25(1) is exercised only by Indian citizens, and secondly, that the right to "propagation" does not mean the right to bring about religious conversion through force, fraud or other illicit means.

The committee was appointed by the state government because of complaints that Christian missionaries were converting illiterate aboriginals and other backward people either forcefully or through fraud or temptations and that non-Christians were offended by this activity. The committee undertook a tour of 14 districts of the state and submitted its report after two years of relentless work. The committee recommended that the influx of foreign missionaries is undesirable and should be checked; the use of medical or other professional services as a direct means of making conversions should be prohibited by law; religious institutions should not be permitted to engage in occupations like recruitment of labour for tea gardens; and prohibition of foreign contribution to non-official agencies except through government channels.

These very issues and arguments vis-à-vis conversions came to be examined comprehensively by the Supreme Court, 27 years after the Constitution came into being, when the court pronounced its verdict in Rev Stanislaus v. State of Madhya Pradesh and Others. A five-judge Bench of the court headed by Chief Justice AN Ray considered this issue when the anti-conversion laws enacted by the Madhya Pradesh and Orissa governments was challenged before the court. These laws prohibited conversion of persons from one religion to another by force, allurement (or inducement) or fraud. The court had to decide whether the two Acts violated the fundamental rights guaranteed under Article 25(1) of the Constitution and whether the states were competent to enact them.

Article 25(1) is the constitutional provision that is at the centre of this controversy since 1950. It says, "subject to public order, morality and health and to other provisions in this Part", all persons are equally entitled to freedom of conscience and the right to "freely profess, practise and propagate religion". Rev. Stanislaus' counsel argued that the right to "propagate" one's religion means the right to convert a person to one's own religion. Further, consequent to this interpretation of the term "propagate", it was argued that the right to convert a person to one's own religion is "a fundamental right" guaranteed by Article 25(1). This argument was similar to the arguments advanced by Frank Anthony and Rev JJ Nichols-Roy in the Constituent Assembly. The court however rejected this argument. It said the right to "propagate" guaranteed in Article 25(1) " is not the right to convert another person to one's own religion", but to transmit or spread one's religion by an exposition of its tenets. The court said it must be remembered that the very same Article also promises "freedom of conscience" to every citizen, and not merely to the followers of one particular religion, "and that, in turn, postulates that there is no fundamental right to convert another person to one's own religion". The court's reasoning was that "if a person purposely undertakes the conversion of another person to his religion, as distinguished from his effort to transmit or spread the tenets of his religion, that would impinge on the freedom of conscience guaranteed to all the citizens of the country alike".

In the course of this historic judgement, the Supreme Court pointed out, on more than one occasion, that the freedom of religion enshrined in the Article is not guaranteed "in respect of one religion only", but covers all religions alike, and it can be properly enjoyed by a person if he exercises his right in a manner commensurate with the like freedom of persons following the other religions.

What is freedom for one, is freedom for the other, in equal measure, and there can therefore be "no such thing as a fundamental right to convert any person to one's own religion". As regards the ultravires of the two anti-conversion enactments of Madhya Pradesh and Orissa, the court said these laws, which prohibit forcible conversions, clearly provide for the maintenance of public order for, "if forcible conversion had not been prohibited, that would have created public disorder in the State". The court said the government had the power to impose restrictions on the religion-related rights guaranteed under Articles 25 and 26 in the interests of public order. Quoting an earlier judgement of the court, the Bench held that "if a thing disturbs the current of the life of the community", and does not merely affect an individual, it would amount to disturbance of the public order.

"Thus if an attempt is made to raise communal passions, e.g. on the ground that someone has been "forcibly" converted to another religion, it would, in all probability, give rise to an apprehension of a breach of the public order, affecting the community at large".

The current strife over religious conversions only shows that we have failed to act on the advice our founding fathers gave us in the Constituent Assembly or on the invaluable recommendations made by the Niyogi Committee in 1956. We have also failed to grasp the essence of the Supreme Court's judgement in RevStanislaus' case. Those who wish to end this conflict over religious conversions need to act on the advice of Mr Lal Krishna Advani, initiate an inter-faith dialogue to restore peace. Meanwhile, India's Christians, who constitute just 2.3 per cent of the nation's population, need to realise the futility in insisting that religious "propagation" remain a fundamental right at a time when the Hindus and other religious groups are gearing up to exercise these very constitutional rights. Considering recent developments in Indian society, I am sure that all those who wish to protect the special rights given to religious and linguistic minorities in the Constitution will join me in demanding that the word "propagate" be deleted from Article 25(1) of the Constitution.

(A Surya Prakash is an Author and Newspaper Columnist. He is the Author of 'What Ails Indian Parliament', published by Indus, an imprint of HarperCollins)

□

The Pain of Partition The Promises & the Let downs

—**Bimolangshu Roy**

Before 1947, Assam consisted of two valleys – Brahmaputra Valley and Surma Valley with the capital at Shillong. At the time of partition in 1947 a 'referendum' in India was held in Surma Valley on the basis of limited franchise and as the tea garden workers were deprived of casting their votes, verdict went in favour of Pakistan and almost entire Surma Valley including Sylhet District seceded from the State of Assam and merged with East Pakistan (now Bangladesh). So, when partition took place in 1947, Assam as well as Sylhet District got divided. Only five Police Stations of Sylhet now form part of Assam's Karimgunj District.

Because of communal riots in succession, large number of Hindu displaced persons took shelter in Assam and other parts of the country. At that time, our national leaders had committed themselves to protect the hapless Hindus. Pandit Nehru had then said: "There is no doubt, of course, that those displaced persons who have come to settle in India are bound to have their citizenship. If the law is inadequate in this respect, the law should be changed."

The nation's sentiments were echoed by Sardar Patel when he said: "We cannot fully enjoy freedom that we have got until and unless we can share it with the Hindus of North and East Bengal. How can one forget the sufferings and sacrifices which they have cheerfully endured for freeing our motherland from foreign domination – their future welfare must engage careful and serious attention of the Government and the people of Indian Union in the light of development that may take hereafter."

The Nehru-Liaquat Pact was then made on 8.4.1950 whereby the then National Government of India and Pakistan agreed to protect their respective minorities and, inter alia, give them 'full sense of security in respect of life, culture, property and personal honour'. But, Dr Syama Prasad Mookerjee could envision the grim fate of Hindu minorities —especially of East Bengal — in the coming days and immediately resigned from the National Government Ministry in protest on 18.4.1950. In his statement to the Parliament on his resignation, Dr. Mookerjee brought out his sense of pain,

"...the circumstances that have led to my resignation are primarily concerned with the treatment of minorities in Pakistan, especially in East Bengal.

...Let us not forget that the Hindus of East Bengal are entitled to the protection of India, not on humanitarian considerations alone, but by virtue of their sufferings and sacrifices, made cheerfully for generations, not for advancing their own parochial interests, but for laying the foundations of India's political freedom and intellectual progress.

...The establishment of 'a homogenous Islamic State' is Pakistan's creed and a planned extermination of Hindus and Sikhs and expropriation of their properties constitute its settled policy. As a result of this policy, life for the minorities in Pakistan has become 'nasty, brutish and short. '

That Dr Syama Prasad Mookerjee was prophetic and a statesman of outstanding calibre is borne out from the fact that when East Pakistan was formed in 1947, its Hindu population was 1,14,00,000 (One crore and fourteen lakhs) i.e. 29.71% of the total population. But now it has come down to 9.2% only. As per 2001 official census report of Bangladesh, Hindu population of Bangladesh (erstwhile East Pakistan) after 61 years still remained 1,13,00,000 (One crore thirteen lakhs) and the percentage of Hindu population has come down to 9.2% from 29.17%. As per normal annual growth rate of population at the rate of 2.5% only it ought to have been at least 4,41,00,000 (Four crore and forty one lakhs).

Recently, Bangladesh's Prof Abul Barkhat, Professor of Economics at the Dhaka University and also General Secretary of Bangladesh Economics Council, divulged in a seminar in Dhaka, that landed property measuring 2.2 million acres valued at approximately Taka

2,52,000 crores belonging to Hindus in Bangladesh have been grabbed under Enemy Property Act, 1965 and Vested Property Act, 1974 by Bangladesh Government. The grabbers of land are leading members of all major political parties of Bangladesh including Awami League. Prof Barkhat has further revealed this included the ancestral home and landed property of famous revolutionary Surya Sen popular as 'Master da' (1894-1934) and hero of the Chittagong Armoury Raid of 1930. The raid was most daring act of revolutionaries during country's freedom movement for which Master da went to the gallows at Chittagong Jail on 12.2.1934.

After Bangladesh's independence, the 'Indira-Mujib Pact' which presented Bangladesh with a Secular Constitution, could not last long and was replaced by a Theocratic Islamic Constitution in the year 1988 which reduced Hindus as second-class citizens of Bangladesh. The Constitution of Bangladesh commences with "BISMILLAH-AR-RAHIMAN-AR-RAHIM (In the name of Allah, the Beneficent, the Merciful)" and declares in Article 2A that "the State religion of the Republic is Islam." Continuous persecution, forcible conversion, loot, arson, murders and rape of Hindu women are the reasons attributed for the dwindling Hindu population in Bangladesh. Thus, the mission of 'a homogenous Islamic State' – which was the policy of its predecessor State of Pakistan continues to be pursued with same vigor by the present day Bangladesh's Regime. It is however pathetic that these hapless Hindus don't find any shelter in India also when hounded out from Bangladesh.

LEGAL HISTORY

In line with the commitment of our national leaders to rehabilitate those uprooted Hindu displaced persons taking shelter in Assam, the National Government enacted the Immigrants (Expulsion from Assam) Act, 1950 (Act 10 of 1950) [Henceforth '1950 Act'] which came into force on 1.3.1950. Section 2 thereof provided as under –

"2. Power to order expulsion of certain immigrants. If the Central Government is of opinion that any person or class of persons, having been ordinarily resident in any place outside India, has or have, whether before or after the commencement of this Act, come into Assam and that the stay of such person or class of persons in Assam is detrimental to the interests of the general public of India or of any section thereof or of any Schedule Tribe in Assam, the Central Government may by order –

(a) direct such person or class of persons to remove himself or themselves from India or Assam within such time and by such route as may be specified in the order; and

(b) give such further directions in regard to his or their removal from India or Assam as it may consider necessary or expedient:

Provided that nothing in this section shall apply to any person who on account of civil disturbances or the fear of such disturbances in any area now forming part of Pakistan has been displaced from or has left his place of residence in such area and who has been subsequently residing in Assam."

This Act in so many words makes a clear distinction between 'infiltrators' and 'victims of civil disturbances/displaced persons'. The proviso to Section 2 gives protection to persons displaced on account of civil disturbances or fear of such disturbances. With the formation of other States in North-East from Assam, this Act has been extended to the other North-Eastern States also.

However, when sinister designs were hatched by Pakistani Government to capture Assam through demographic invasion and large number of Muslims infiltrated into Assam, Foreigners Tribunals constituted in different districts under the Foreigners Act, 1946 and Foreigners Order, 1964 were effective in pushing back a large number of Muslim foreigners to the then East-Pakistan. This was also largely due to the fact that the Section 9 of the Foreigners Act / paragraph 3 of the Foreigners Order placed the 'burden of proof' that he is not a Foreigner — on the alleged Foreigner himself, which in most cases they could not discharge, thus exposing their illegal infiltration. Not a single Hindu displaced person was, however, pushed back as 1950 Act was applicable at that time.

The illegal Migrants (Determination by Tribunals) Act, 1983 (Act No. 39 of 1983) [henceforth IMDT Act] was passed as a result of the movement against the foreigners. The said Act, engineered by the then Congress- led State government, primarily at the behest of then Law Minister of the State, Shri Abdul Muhib Majumdar. The IMDT Act sought to deport all foreigners who migrated into India after 25.3.1971 – the day of Bangladesh's independence. The Act treated all foreigners alike, irrespective of religious affiliation and, by the stroke of a pen, it did away with the distinction so long existing due to operation of the 1950 Act between 'Hindu displaced persons' and 'Muslim infiltrators'. The said Act, vide Section 4(1) thereof, gave 'overriding effect' to the Act, inter alia, over Foreigners Act, 1946 and Rules thereunder and the 1950 Act also. Section 4(2) of the Act specifically provided that the aforesaid proviso to Section 2 of 1950 Act shall not apply to illegal migrants i.e. persons coming to India after 25.3.1971. Thus, the IMDT Act gave de facto citizenship to Muslims from East-Pakistan (now Bangladesh) who came to India even post-independence. This, despite the fact that partition in 1947 was on communal lines and Muslims always wanted the creation of Pakistan for themselves.

The IMDT Act was so drafted, that contrary to its declared objectives, it made the detection and deportation of Muslim infiltrators almost impossible. It made a drastic departure from the Foreigners Act, 1946 by doing away with the 'burden of proof' that was so long cast upon the alleged foreigner and this meant that a heavy burden upon the State or the applicant to prove that the person alleged is a foreigner. Whereas, before the enactment of the IMDT Act, no case against the Hindu displaced persons were filed in Tribunal and all cases were against Muslim infiltrators, who were deported in large numbers. But as a result of operation of IMDT Act, the Muslim infiltrators enjoyed protection! The Hindu displaced persons, on the other hand, lost the protection they were so long having under the 1950 Act and as a result a large number of Hindus were proceeded against under the IMDT regime. The IMDT Act however failed to achieve its purpose and in more than two decades of its operation, only 1400 infiltrators were detected.

Ultimately, the Supreme Court has struck down the IMDT Act by holding the same to be unconstitutional and discriminatory in its application to the State of Assam. In so doing, the Supreme Court found the IMDT Act had wrongly cast a very heavy burden on the State authorities or the applicant to establish that a person is an illegal migrant and the provisions thereof were very stringent as compared to the provisions of Foreigners Act, 1946 or Foreigners (Tribunals) Order, 1964, which were far more effective in identification and deportation of illegal migrants. The Supreme Court revived the Tribunals constituted under the Foreigners Order, 1964 under procedure of Foreigners Act, 1946 and most importantly removed the cloud over the 1950 Act and, inter alia, directed that that the 1950 Act shall apply with full force in the State of Assam.

Subsequent to the aforesaid historic judgement, under the present political dispensation at the Centre had made another affront to revive IMDT Act and overcome the Supreme Court judgement by issuing notification for constituting the Foreigners (Tribunals for Assam) Order, 2006 exclusively for the State of Assam to follow the unconstitutional procedure of IMDT Act. The author was also one of those who had challenged the said notification in the Supreme Court and ultimately the Supreme Court had again struck down the said notification.

With the cloud over the 1950 Act being removed as result of the declaration of the IMDT Act as unconstitutional and simultaneously application of the whole of the 1950 Act, the protection available to 'displaced persons', which remained suspended so long the IMDT Act applied, becomes available again. As a result of this position prevailing at present, the 'displaced persons' would be entitled to protection of the 1950 Act and they cannot suffer expulsion!

However, there are strong reasons for the grant of citizenship to these displaced persons. Although the Citizenship Act, 1955, vide Section 6A thereof (which was incorporated in 1985 as a result of the Assam Accord) contains special provision for grant of citizenship to persons covered by the Assam Accord, the cut-off date 25th March, 1971 cannot be said to be a disability to restrict the benefits of protection to 'displaced persons' covered by the 1950 Act.

RECENT DEVELOPMENTS AND THE WAY FORWARD

In the context of the aforesaid, recent developments in law and amendments made to the Citizenship Rules sheds light on the way forward for Assam too. The NDA Government during the last year of its tenure in 2004 had amended the Citizenship Rules, 1956 whereby for the States of Gujarat and Rajasthan, minority Hindus from Pakistan who were 'displaced' as a consequence of the wars between India and Pakistan in 1965 and 1971 – their dependents married to Indian citizens or persons of Indian origin and also Hindus with Pakistan citizenship who migrated to India five years back were to be given citizenship. Initially the period of operation of this Rule was specified as one year but this period of one year was extended by two more years after the present UPA dispensation came to power at the Centre.

Thus, there appears to be an element of unanimity, as far as the political leadership of the country is concerned, that the Hindu citizens from Pakistan – displaced or migrated — needed to be protected and registered as Indian citizens. In the words of our present Prime Minister – who significantly represents Assam in Parliament:

"After partition of the country, the minorities living in Bangladesh have been subjected to various persecution and they were forced to take refuge in our country. While granting citizenship to these unfortunate people our attitude towards them should be more liberal and it is our moral responsibility."

[Statement made as Leader of Opposition in Rajya Sabha on 18.12.2003]

Yet history will bear witness that it is actually the displaced/ migrant Hindus from present Bangladesh who deserve such protection more appropriately and more urgently. The '71 war as a consequence of which Bangladesh was born — was fought mainly along the country's Eastern frontiers. It is well documented that the maximum casualties of the '71 war were Bengali-speaking Hindus of erstwhile East-Pakistan who were subjected to extreme ethnic cleansing at the hands of Urdu-speaking Muslim Pakistani forces. The census of Bangladesh bears testimony to the fact that the 'consequences' of the '71 war was most severe on Hindus in the Eastern Front. The *Time Magazine* in its 2nd August, 1971 edition reported:

"The Hindus, who account for three-fourths of the refugees and a majority of the dead, have borne the brunt of the Moslem military's hatred. Even now, Moslem soldiers in East Pakistan will snatch away a man's *lungi* (sarong) to see if he is circumcised, obligatory for Moslems; if he is not, it usually means death."

However, the atrocities on the minority Hindus in Bangladesh have continued with Bangladesh giving up a secular Constitution and adopting an Islamic Constitution and continuing with the policies of its predecessor State – of 'a homogenous Islamic Society'. Persecutions of Hindus in Bangladesh have been going on for communal and political reasons – Notable instances of mass genocide of Hindus begin in 1992 in the aftermath of Ram Janmabhoomi–Babri Masjid controversy and again in 2001 when the Fundamentalist Government lead by Khaleda Zia came to power in Bangladesh. These definitely qualify as 'civil disturbances' in Bangladesh within the meaning of

1950 Act. These atrocious incursions on the life and dignity of Hindus – especially Hindu women, have compelled teeming numbers of Hindus to flee to India, including Assam. They certainly qualify for India's protection as they come 'on account of civil disturbances or the fear of such disturbances'.

The steady decline of Hindu population in Bangladesh which continued unabated even after Bangladesh's independence in 1971 speaks for itself. In this regard, Bangladesh's population ratio between Hindus and Muslims (1901-2001) is selfdescriptive

While so, there is no denying the fact that the problem of illegal infiltration by Bangladeshi nationals is a serious threat to law and order and the unity and integrity of the nation generally, and Assam in particular.

But the reasons of migration are divergent in the case of Muslims and Hindus; while in the case of the former it may be anything ranging from better economic prospects to planned demographic invasion of Assam, but in the case of the latter, it is most definitely compelled in an endeavour to save their lives and dignity.

Illegal migration of vast number of Muslims from Bangladesh – have now posed an imminent threat to the demographic composition of Assam. As per the last population census of 2001, Muslim population in Assam has gone up from 28 % in 1991 to 30.92% in 2001 while during the same time the Hindu population (including Assamese, Bengali, Hindi speaking) have come down from 67% to 64.89%. This trend presents a grim forecast for the future and unless redressed immediately, Assam's majority faces the prospect of being converted to minorities! The recent blood-bath in the Districts of Darrang and Udalguri are only symptomatic of grimmer times. Thus, our commitment to deport illegal – migrants (not Hindu displaced persons) is and has to be unflinching. The most ominous signal in this disturbed zone has been the hoisting of Pakistani flag and raising of 'Pakistan Zindabad' slogans by illegal Muslim migrants which cannot but indicate the shape of things to emerge in near future.

The author's only endeavour here is to drive home the point that the mix of humanity, duty, history and the law mandates for a distinction between 'Hindu displaced persons' and 'Muslim illegal-infiltrators'. Both cannot be accorded the same yardstick as was done during the unconstitutional IMDT regime. That law is gone, and if one may say so, it has gone for good. The author's endeavour is not directed against bonafide and legitimate Muslim citizens of the country, particularly Assam. They are very much part of our society and their spontaneous cooperation is very much vital to the identification and deportation of illegal Muslim infiltrators in the larger interests of Assam and the whole country. However, the 'Hindu displaced persons' from Bangladesh definitely qualify for India's compassion and a helping hand!

(The author is former Assam State BJP President, former Leader of BJP Legislature Party, Assam (1996-2006), and comes from the Sylhet District of Bangladesh where his father Late Shri Sashi Bhushan Roy was an eminent freedom fighter.)

□

Impact of mining on Water quality

—Dr Umesh Kumar Singh
& Prof V Subramanian

WATER

"The ability to see, hear and speak is useless in the absence of adequate water. Water is the basis of life. Most life forms are born in water and live in it. "O" water stream come near me. You are the elixir of immortality".

Atharvaved, 3:13:6

Water is the most abundant substance on the Earth's surface. It is a prime natural resource, a basic human need and a precious national asset. The history of human civilisation reveals that the civilization and water are almost synonymous. Water is one of the most stable compounds as well as a universal solvents. It is required for most human activities like drinking, cooking, bathing, washing, agriculture, industry, recreation, navigation and fisheries etc. About 75% of the earth's surface area is covered with water. Out of which 97% of the earth's water is in the ocean, which is not fit for human use due to its high salt content. Remaining 2% is locked in the polar ice caps and only 1 % is available as fresh water in rivers, lakes, streams, reservoirs and groundwater, which is suitable for human consumption. As an essential component of life, it is also present in the bodies of all living organisms. India accounts for 2.2% of the global land and 6% of the world water resources, but has to support 16% of the world population.

Groundwater contains dissolved minerals from the soil layers through which it passes. It may also contain some harmful contaminants through the process of seepage from the surface water and biological activities. On the other hand the surface water contains a lot of organic matter, mineral nutrients and other contaminants brought by runoff from agricultural fields, contains fertilisers, pesticides, soil particles, waste chemicals from industries and sewage of cities and rural areas. These generate the secondary pollutants such as the feed algae and large bacteria populations. Bacteria, algae, fungi and microorganisms are the living catalysts for a number of chemical processes to occur in water. Algae are the primary producers of biological organic matter (bio-mass) in water, while the microorganisms lead to the formation of many sediment and mineral deposits. The water bodies are continuously subjected to a dynamic state of change with respect to lithological characteristics and geo-climatic condition. This dynamic balance in the aquatic system is upset by human activities, resulting in pollution. Mining is one of the major activities causing water pollution. Damage to quality and quantity of surface water and groundwater due to dumping of overburden (OB) and spoils (sometimes on the surface water body itself), or spreading of OB through rolling and washing may cause the chemical pollution. The OB dumping of mining creates mined out faces and dumps slopes that provide potential surface for erosion which if not properly protected will be washed by rain water and redistributed through surface runoff to result in "siltation." These cause reduction in infiltration rate and volume of surface water bodies. This invites flood hazard and turbidity of the water and may even cause drying up of surface water bodies or diversion of streams.

Groundwater

Groundwater is an essential part of the natural water cycle. It is present practically everywhere beneath our feet. It forms the largest available store of fresh water. However, it is hidden asset, out of sight and all too often out of mind. This store of groundwater comes mostly from rainfall that has filtered down through the ground. Providing it is not pumped directly out of the ground, for example for public water supply, groundwater eventually discharges into surface waters. Here it supports river flows, and maintains ecosystems. It is the primary source of water for rivers and lakes in summer or at times of drought.

Water-Pollution

Water becomes polluted when materials are added to natural

water so that it becomes less useful and desirable for humans. Water pollution is defined as "the addition of any substance in water or changing of water's physical and chemical characteristics in any way that interferes with its use for legitimate purposes." Normally water is never pure in a chemical sense. It contains impurities of various kinds – dissolved as well as suspended. These include dissolved gases (H_2S, CO_2, NH_3 and N_2), dissolved minerals (Ca, Mg, Na salts), suspended matter (clay, silt, sand) and even microbes. These are natural impurities derived from atmosphere, catchment areas and the soil. These are in very low amounts and normally do not pollute water and it is potable. Polluted waters, however, are turbid, unpleasant, bad smelling, unfit for drinking, bath, and washing or other purposes. They are harmful and spread many diseases such as cholera, dysentery, typhoid etc.

The wastes discharged into water bodies whether solid or liquid may be of three types, such as physical, chemical and biological. Biological wastes include sewage and human or animal washings. These contain many kinds of micro-organisms, which can cause illness and diseases. A large number of illnesses in India, especially in the rural areas, are that of water borne diseases. These include typhoid, cholera, infective hepatitis jaundice, diarrhoea, dysentery, paratyphoid, fever etc. About 25 million deaths occur in the world every year. Because of water borne diseases, about 6 million children under the age of five die from diarrhoea every year.

Chemical wastes from industrial processes contain toxic substances such as chlorine, ammonia, hydrogen sulphide, various acids and salts of metals like arsenic, copper, zinc, lead, nickel and mercury. When consumed either by drinking water or through eating fish, which have acquired it from the contaminated water, they can cause serious illnesses such as blindness, paralysis and major disorder of the circulatory system. About 500 million people suffer from water washed diseases like trachoma, skin diseases, scabies, leprosy, eye diseases, and conjunctivitis etc. Approximately 160 million people suffer from malaria — water insect related disease. About 20 million people suffer from schistosomiasis guinea worm, which grows to 80 cms long, emerging through skin causing severe pain. The contaminated water is regularly used for bathing and washing and because of these result skin diseases. When such water is used for irrigation, the pollutants can get transmitted through the crops to their consumers, resulting eventually in serious illness. No river in India is safe for fish. In India, 14 major rivers carry 85 per cent of the surface run-off; their drainage basins cover 73 per cent of the country, which has resulted in severe pollution of almost all the major rivers — Ganga, Yamuna, Narmada, Godavari, Krishna, and Cauvery. Around 60,000 carcasses of cattle, dogs and other animals are dumped into the Ganga every year. About 40,000 fully burned dead bodies and ashes and half-burned dead bodies are pushed into the Ganga every year. Physical pollution of water, because of particulate matter such as washings from quarries and mines, erosion of soil and other similar phenomena is relatively less hazardous. But it affects the use of water through turbidity and colouration.

Many metals occur in natural waters in different physico-chemical forms. Among them simple hydrated metal ions are considered to be the most toxic, while strong complexes and species associated with colloidal particles are usually assumed to be less toxic. Qrganometallic compounds of tin, mercury and lead (particularly simple methylated species) are more toxic than the corresponding inorganic species. Organoarsenic compounds represent an exception in this series. The contamination of water due to heavy metals arising from mining operations, metal plating, textile industries, tannery, etc. is a major environmental problem. The heavy metals are of great concern because of their extreme toxicity even at low concentration and the tendency to accumulate in the food chain.

The group of non-essential trace elements called heavy metals has toxic effects, because they interfere with the biochemical reactions and form part of the insoluble compounds that are bioaccumulated in the food chain. Intervention of man in soil may disrupt the balance of physical, chemical and biological processes altering the trace element equilibrium in the ecosystem. The relative mobility of trace elements in soils is of major importance with regard to their plant availability and their potential for leaching down soil profiles to the groundwater. Excess amounts of both essential trace elements and elements with no known essential function can have major toxic effects on living organisms and so their relative mobility is of major importance with regard to plant, animal and human toxicology.

Additional problems can occur in soils contaminated by heavy metals associated with mining activities, if the contaminants reach levels, which prevent growth of a protective layer of vegetation. This in turn may lead to erosion of the soil and dispersion of the contaminants to adjacent aquifers and other areas.

The topographic features of the area and its lithology may be responsible for the deposition of arsenic and toxic metals in the water and soil samples of the study area. Almost all the hillocks are steeping towards the sampling sites and these hillocks may be serving as a catchment for the existing water bodies and the ultimate deposition of the toxic metals and arsenic in the soil of the valley or the plain area.

The rain pattern, fractures and others tectonic features are highly responsible for the weathering and erosion in the mountainous region and the derivation of the toxic metals and arsenic from the parent source rock to the depositional sites of the study area.

Some of the major findings, which came out of this study that are based on the analysis of water and soil samples brought from the copper mining areas of Jharkhand and adjoining alluvial belt of West Bengal during both the pre-monsoon (April, 2005) and post-monsoon (October, 2004) seasons.

Case study-(1) Mining areas of Jharkhand

The pH of the water (ground and surface) lies within the normal range 6.0 to 8.5-8.9 of the global water in both the seasons. The electrical conductivity is generally high. Rain has had impacts on pH and electrical conductivity; pH increased during the post monsoon season while EC decreased. The electrical conductivity was largely due to the presence of major cations and anions. Among the major cations, sodium, potassium, and calcium ions dominate the cations concentrations in the water while bicarbonate and chloride ions dominate the anionic part of the water during both the pre-monsoon and post-monsoon seasons. Sulphide mines in and around sampling regions have added these ions to significant level and are responsible for abnormally high concentration of these ions. At all the sampling locations during both the pre-monsoon and post-monsoon seasons the concentrations of cadmium, chromium, lead and nickel in the water exceed the permissible limit for respective heavy metals prescribed by WHO. Cobalt and mercury metals were below detection limits in the water of the sampling region. The high concentrations of iron and manganese at certain places and of cadmium, chromium, lead and nickel at all the places may be attributed to the mining activities of copper situated nearby. The concentration of arsenic is below the permissible limit prescribed by WHO in both the seasons at all the sampling locations in the water of study area (around Rakha and Mosabani mines). Presence of high kaolinite indicates that the weathering of silicate minerals had influence on both cations and anions chemistry of the water system. pH, EC, bicarbonate, calcium, cadmium chromium, lead, and chloride constituted one factor which explained maximum variance of the data set and thus explains that the weathering of silicate and contributions from the anthropogenic sources largely determine the distributions of major ions and other heavy metals in the region.

The soil of Jharkhand is slightly acidic to slightly alkaline in nature. As per the average values of heavy metal's concentrations in the soil samples,the relative abundance of the various heavy metals is in the following order: Fe>Cu>Mn>Cr>Ni>Zn>Co>Cd>Pb>As>Hg. Soils around Rakha and Mosabani mines showed very high enrichment factor for cadmium suggesting their enrichment due to copper mines in the vicinity. Soils around Mosabani mines showed high enrichment factor for copper suggesting their enrichment due to copper mines in the region. Soils of Jharkhand were contained with arsenic suggesting sulphide mines at Rakha and Mosabani as the source of arsenic. The higher values of CIA at Rakha in both the seasons and at Mosabani in post-monsoon season indicate the extensive weathering resulting in the leaching of calcium, sodium and potassium in the area. The CIA value showed that there is not much variation in the weathering pattern due to season change.

Case study-(2) Alluvial belt of West Bengal

The high concentrations of cadmium, lead, iron and zinc above the permissible limits recommended by WHO, at certain places especially in the district of North 24 Parganas suggest anthropogenic inputs from the industries related to electroplating, batteries and metal painting etc. Some of the water samples from the districts of Hooghly, Kolkata,and North 24 Paragnas exceed the permissible limit for the arsenic concentration of 10μg/l for drinking purposes as recommended by WHO during both the pre-monsoon and post-monsoon seasons. Among the heavy metals studied, it has been found that iron has positive correlations with arsenic during both the seasons that indicates about the common origin of these two metals. Seasonal variations were observed for cations, anions, heavy metals and arsenic contents of water (ground and surface). During the post-monsoon season, the low levels of their concentration suggest the diluting effects of rain.

The soils of West Bengal were acidic to alkaline in nature. The relative abundance of the heavy metals in the soils of West Bengal was in the following order: Fe>Mn>Cr>Zn>Pb>Ni>Cu>Co>As>Cd>Hg. The enrichment factors for heavy Zn, Cr, Cu, Pb, Ni, Co and Cd were generally one suggesting their natural origin in the environment. However, enrichment factors for these metals were found to be more than one at certain places suggested anthropogenic input from the vicinity. Soils of the West Bengal showed high enrichment factor for cadmium and moderate enrichment factor for lead suggesting their enrichment due to their anthropogenic source.

The higher values of CIA at Midnapore and Kharagpur in both the seasons and at Ghatal in post-monsoon season indicate the extensive weathering resulting in the leaching of calcium, sodium and potassium in the area. Surface area of the soil particles had seminal impacts on the concentrations of heavy metals in the soil. The heavy metal content in the finer size fractions was found to be higher than in the bulk.

Dr Umesh Singh is Assistant Professor, ISERC Viswa Bharati University, Santiniketan, West Bengal

Prof V Subramanaian teaches at School of Environmental Sciences, JNU, New Delhi.

□

Evaluating Reservation

—**Ramesh Patange**

Historical Background

The issue of reservation has remained complex in Indian politics and society as ever before.

As and when the issue of reservation is raised, the society gets divided into two. One group belongs to pro-reservationists and the other of anti-reservationists. All those who speak reasonably on different issues start giving bizarre arguments on the issue of reservation. Among them are also included those who subscribe to the Hindutva ideology.

Some people due to ignorance give Dr Babasaheb Bhimrao Ambedkar credit for reservation. The issue of reservation in the government jobs was under discussion even before Dr. Babsaheb Bhimrao Ambedkar joined the public life. The root of reservation may be traced to the declaration by Swami Vivekanand. In a letter written in 1895, he writes, "If there is inequality in Nature then all should get equal opportunity. If someone is supposed to get more opportunity over the others then weaker should get more opportunity than the strong. In other words it may be said that a *chandal* needs education more then the Brahmins. If a son of a Brahmin needs one teacher then a son of a *chandal* needs ten teachers because Nature has refused to bestow upon him refined knowledge. Such people should get more help."

In 1902, Chhatrapati Shahuji Maharaj of Kolhapur declared 50% reservation to non-Brahmin castes in government jobs through an ordinance. In 1894 when Shahu Maharaja ascended the throne, there were a total of 71 staff among whom 60 were Brahmin. In 1922, there were 95 staff among whom 36 were Brahmins and 59 belonged to non-Brahmin castes. In the personal service of Shahuji Maharaj in 1894, there were 53 posts available among which 46 were occupied by Brahmins and seven by non-Brahmins. In 1922, among the 152 such posts, 43 were occupied by Brahmins and 109 by the non-Brahmins.

In Karnataka state Maharaja Woddeyyar of Mysore had declared 24% reservation for backward class through an ordinance in 1916. In 1918, the Maharaja of Mysore constituted Leslie Miller Commission which recommended the means and ways to give representation to different classes in administration. In North India, the issue of reservation did not come up before independence. The condition of South India along with Maharashtra is different from North India.

In the Indian Constitution, the provision for reservation for Scheduled Castes and Tribes was made for ten years. After the ten years were completed, it was made compulsory to extend it for another ten years through a resolution in the Lok Sabha. If such a step not been taken, reservation would come to an end automatically. Dr. Baba'saheb had not made a long term or unending provision for reservation that should be understood

The other issue related with reservation is that of political reservation. In all the electoral constituencies (Lok Sabha, Vidhan Sabha, Corporations, Municipalities, Gram Panchayats etc.) certain seats are reserved for Scheduled Castes and classes. Its roots are traced to Poona Pact of 1939 between Mahatma Gandhi and Dr. Babasaheb Bhimrao Ambedkar. The British government announced the Communal Award after the Round Table Conference. Under this, a separate electorate was decided for the untouchable classes. Mahatma Gandhi opposed it and started a hunger strike in Poona. Baba saheb had to give up the demand for separate electorate and accepted the elections for reserved seats. According to the Communal Award, untouchables were supposed to get 78 seats but as per Poona Pact they got 151 seats. The reservation in elections has started since then.

Reservation in Principle

The society in which inequality exists for hundreds of years, there is need for special provision for the weaker section of that society so that they can walk along with others. There is caste based inequality in the Hindu society. The higher caste people in the society get all kinds of rights by virtue of their birth. The untouchable class of the society is deprived of every right for hundreds of years. Between the upper castes and untouchables, there exist a large section of backward castes. All of them need to get equal and special opportunity for progress.

If one has to think in the context of nationalism then it is compulsory that every class participates in every activity. A nation cannot be built by having a system under which a section of the society enjoys every comforts and other sections reel under poverty and deprivation. Such a situation can be described in the words of Lincoln who had explained it as 'A house divided against itself'. The notion of oneness for each other comes to an end. There is a fable by Aesop – Calamity visits a village. People start running away. A washerman also starts to leave. He says to his ass, 'run away, calamity is coming'. Ass asks, "Why should I run away; the way you load me, the other would also load me in the same manner. I am bound to carry the load. There is no difference if the master gets changed."

Such kind of mindset develops in the oppressed class. A battle took place between the Britishers and the Peshwa near Poona in 1818. The British contingent was comprised of Mahar (untouchable) sepoys. They defeated the army of Peshwa. The Maratha state built by Shivaji came to an end. In the rule of the same Peshwa, the untouchables were extremely oppressed. How would they consider the Peshwa rule of their own? At the time of independence in Kashmir, only Bhatts or Pandits meaning Brahmins were left. Where had the other Hindus gone? All the Brahmins were mercilessly expelled from the Kashmir valley blood starts boiling on reading their plight. But why does a not common hindu react against such atrocities? Why do'nt Hindus belonging to all the castes stand up jointly? People are reluctant to give answers to these questions but I feel that a though Ram had embraced Nishad Raj or eaten the berry offered by Shabari, the sense of oneness has vanished from society.

If we want to make the country strong then there is no way out but to increase the participation of all the sections. There is administrative system in the country. In this all the sections should find representation. There are industries. All sections should be seen participating in the industrial sector. All sections of the society should get opportunities for education from primary level to higher level.

There is a story from Devi Ahalyabai's life. While she was a child, she was playing on the bank of a river. The Army had camped nearby. Some horses started running helter skelter, out of control. The child Ahalyabai was playing with a Shivlinga made of sand. Army men started shouting loudly a, 'run..run..'. But Ahalya continued to protect the shivalinga. Later Bajirao Peshwa arrived. He scolded the child for not running away. The child replied, "My mother has taught me to protect whatever you make". Later she became the wife of Sardar Holkar and protected the Holkar principality. The sections who participate in building the society even sacrifice their castes when protecting the same. If such a condition does not prevail then whatever it be Arab, Turk, Mughal or English rule, appears same to the common man.

Reservation guarantees the availability of opportunity. It is very easy to say that everyone should get equal opportunity without reservation. Equality may be preached among those equal in strength and power. There cannot be a race between a lame and a strong individual. Race is possible between the lames and between the strong. A person question Rajrshi Shahuji Maharaj, "By following the policy of reservation you are leaving the element of equality in opportunity". Rajarshi Shahu Maharaj led that person to the stable. He asked the stable incharge to free all the horses for their food. All the horses ran but the stronger ones grabbed all the food leaving the weaker ones behind. Shahu Maharaj said that the attitude of the stronger section of the society is like that of the stronger horses. They will never allow the weaker ones to take advantage of the opportunities.

The Politics of Reservation

Reservation essentially says, "The sections which experienced deprivation for hundreds of years should be compensated. It is a kind of historical compensation. Untouchability and Deprivation are the sin committed by our forefathers. The coming generations would have to pay for it. If Veda, Ayurveda and ancient sciences are ours then all the evils are also ours. We cannot run away from this and we should not."

Instead of this context, reservation has been made a tool for cheap politics. Vote bank politics has been encouraged due to parliamentary politics. To garner vote banks caste is used and for that reservation is used. It was started by VP Singh. He played the Mandal card to retain power at the Centre. He laid the foundation of casteism in Indian politics. He prepared a ground for bringing one caste in opposition to an other.

What do we see today? Every caste in the society wants to bring itself within the ambit of reservation on of one pretext or the other. Gujjars agitated in Rajasthan and before that Jats agitated for it. Yadava consider themselves to be among the backward castes. In Maharashtra, Marathas want to be counted among the backward classes. There was a time when in the words of Srinivasan it was said, "There was upward mobility of caste, there was Sanskritisation of the caste". But the trend has reversed now. Now there is downward mobility in place of upward mobility. This a political game. There is no scope for social justice in it. Politically strong castes of the state want to grab the reservation. Those who should have got the benefit of reservation could not claim the fruits of reservation.

The issue of reservation that is in focus due to politics should be brought to an end. The issue of Scheduled Castes and Tribes is different. Those who are living below the poverty line, should get the benefit of reservation. Government fixes BPL on the basis of consumption index. Where is the starvation line in this index? BPL should be fixed on the basis of actual income. On the basis of today's prices, experts fix Rs. 6,500/- per month for a family of five. The people belonging to this section should get reservation in education and jobs. I feel that instead of caste, family income should be the basis of other backward classes.

Reservation that is earmarked for Scheduled Castes and Tribes is mostly grabbed by the strong. In Rajasthan, Meenas get the benefit of the reservation. In Maharashtra, Mahars mostly claim the benefit of reservation. Therefore, proper policy should be made so that reservation serves the lofty ideals for which it was conceptualised. Today, a fact finding commission is needed. Following facts should be found:

1. How many untouchable castes are present in the country?
2. How much benefit have all the untouchable castes received?
3. Has the society developed due to reservation?
4. How many Scheduled Castes and Classes are there? Who have got the benefit of reservation from among them?

5. What is the status of education in both the sections mentioned above?
6. What is the economic status?
7. Has social status changed?
8. Whether there has been an increase in social harmony?

Many issues like these may be added to it. The main goal of all these should be the same. The country will have to march ahead by ensuring participation of all, justice to all, everyone's contribution in the national wealth, guarantee of benefit to everyone in accordance with their capacity, proper opportunity to increase prosperity etc. The security and prosperity of our country can thus be ensured.

(The writer is the Chief Editor of Marathi weekly Vivek)

□

Economic Empowerment

—**Gopal K Agarwal**

We all want a strong, developed and proud India.

A country can become powerful in world only when its people are empowered. Empowering people requires focus on three important areas:

- Political empowerment
- Economic empowerment
- Institutional empowerment.

True political empowerment can take place when devolution of power is complete. We have yet to cover a long distance. At the time of freedom struggle, Shri Raja gopalachari observed: 'We all ought to know that *Swaraj* will not at once, or I think, even for a long time to come, be a better form of government or bring greater happiness for the people. Elections and their corruptions, injustices and the power and tyranny of wealth will make a hell of life as soon as freedom is given to us'.

Democracy, to be successful, requires establishment of many powerful institutions. India inherited the administrative legacy from the British. Therefore, most of our institutions including bureaucracy, fulfil the requirements of a colonial rule, and are not strong enough to strengthen true democratic values. We need to rethink on institutional empowerment.

In this article I will focus on economic empowerment. Economy has gained tremendous importance in all walks of life, whether it is International Relations, Domestic Politics or even Terrorist Activities. A country commands reverence only if it is an economic power. Major international decisions are taken on economic considerations.

International conflicts are largely based on controlling natural resources. India has tremendous potential to become an economic superpower. But are we working towards realising that potential?

Coordination of official agencies as a secure measure for economic development is a myth, except when it is achieved through democratically controlled elected representatives of the people. If this is not done, programme of development will tend to concentrate on a few, who, together with their counterparts in the administration as well as in the political system, will ride on the hunchback of the common people.

Economic Development

Economic development is what education allows. Integration means the conscious fusion of the all elements constituting the body politics. It refers to fusion of political, economic, administrative, social, cultural and emotional aspect of the people. Lack of such an integrated approach is one of the factors responsible for failure of our planning. Successful implementation and realistic formulation of planning depends on suitable institutional framework. In our country different mechanisms are working, there are various schemes of control and regulatory measures. We have contradictory monetary policies, different instruments to attain different targets, which are beyond the comprehension of common man. He is unaware of the lacuna from which the current institutional framework suffers.

At the formulation stage itself, the various socio-economic organisations should be associated with planning and different interest groups should be involved in the process. The associations of already organised interest-groups should be accorded their important place in the scheme, and efforts should also be made to expeditiously involve the unorganised interest groups, under the supervision of committees consisting of the representatives of the general public, industries, vocations, professions, trades etc. The first pre-requisite for this is constant, persistent national effort for mass education. In its absence, various interest-groups would pull in directions opposite to what is required for the national development.

In India, the foremost painful and perplexing phenomenon is that even after sixty-two years of freedom, our poverty has continued to grow, despite abundant resources and planning. India accounts for majority of the world's poor. The second important area of concern is the falling employment. This situation is quite glaring, even though at present there is no suitable methodology to assess the magnitude of involuntary, disguised, seasonal, structural and cyclical unemployment and under employment. The third important aspect is the disparity. Development so far has failed to bridge several gaps or rather it has contributed in widening the gap. The biggest challenge before us is bridging the divides, overcoming disparities of growth and including the excluded. There are several disparities of gender, unbalanced regional development, rural-urban divide, uplifting of SCs, STs etc.

Agriculture Sector in Bad Shape

Our Agriculture sector is in bad shape. A large portion of our population is still not able to access some of the basic services such as health, education and drinking water. The state of urban and rural infrastructure in the country has deteriorated to the extent that benefits of rapid economic growth can not be fully absorbed and has inflicted a severe hardship on people due to congested roads, poor public transport, inadequacy of availability of water and inadequate housing, forcing large population in some metropolis to live in slums, severely decreasing the quality of life of urban population.

We have not yet formulated National social policy. The data, the statistics required are also not available. No National socio-economic survey has so far been conducted about the number of the blind, the deaf, the dumb, the crippled, the handicapped, the disabled, the restitutes, the criminals and the beggars. Statistical database organisations have to be established.

We must understand the difference between 'economic growth' and 'economic development'. Whereas economic growth is only concerned with gross domestic product, real national income and per capita income, economic development means not only increase in per capita income but improvement in variety of indicators such as poverty rate, literacy rate and life expectancy. United Nations has also developed Human Development Index (HDI) as an alternative indicator of economic development of a country. HDI not only considers the income and productivity aspects but also takes into account how the income utilised for education, health and other related programmes has resulted into human development in that country.

At Crossroads

We are at crossroads now. With failure of Capitalism and current global financial crisis, we need to go in to the details of the pitfalls of Western Economic Model and how to disengage our economy from the current global crisis a few years back, globalisation was the buzzword around the world. It was assumed everywhere that with globalization, economic development will come automatically. All countries were looking towards means of integrating their domestic economy to the world economy, basically the US and European economies. Not to be left behind, we also assumed that the world economies have to be integrated. We have to globalise. With the fall of Communism the path became more imperative. There was no alternative. Although in hushed tones we did talk of alternative ways, but it was not defined. The path was not clear; it was only conceptually delved upon. We were all confused. We formed the opinion that the lofty ideals of Swaraj and Swadeshi had more of a social relevance than economic foundation.

Too much on "ism"

If we talk of Capitalism, Communism or Socialism, the experience shows that, too much emphasis on any "ism", ultimately does not lead to the desired result. The alternative is to work for the requirements of the people on the ground level. The principle of private ownership of assets based on capitalism provides a good incentive for the people to work hard but it has to be controlled by the state machinery. This can also be taken care of by the equitable distribution mechanism based on the principle of Socialism and state ownership of scarce resources of the country based on principles of communism. These three principles, together, help in creation of wealth and its equitable distribution without concentration not beyond a particular point. What is required is the balanced integrated approach based on welfare of humanity as a whole. This can be called integral humanism. India has been successful in balancing various aspects of human existence through ages. We have not been consumed by the outside world but have been able to assimilate and integrate the good things from the whole world. In this debate we need not lose our focus on the action.

Sustainable development is what we all aim for. This will mean a radical shift of emphasis in favour of agriculture, rural economy, infrastructure development, small and medium enterprises, informal sectors of the economy, affordable healthcare for all, meaningful education for all, transparent governance, improved productivity, energy efficiency and security, environmental protection, safety and better justice delivery. This will come through good governance, which means honest, corruption-free, citizen-friendly, and participative governance.

Initiatives required for sustainable and inclusive development:

Education

Emphasis on education, health and other basic facilities is a must for inclusive development. The government has a constitutional obligation to provide free and compulsory education of good quality to all children up to the age of fourteen. Reduction in drop-out rates, using Mid-Day Meal Scheme to improve attendance and children's nutritional status, provision of well lit class rooms, improvement in teaching skills of teachers involved in the Programme are some of the issues which have to be addressed. Empowering *panchayats* and citizens' education committees in this can be fruitful.

Employable skills are required in the present educational setup. Most people are seeking white callar jobs and not going for vocational training, which is causing trouble. There is shortage of skilled manpower. Education and awareness empowers in the people true sense. Democracy can flourish only when its people are well informed and educated. Fruits of development will be shared by all automatically when people are well informed and can stand up for their rights and responsibilities.

Agriculture

There are a number of factors for the present crisis in agriculture but it is the growing indebtedness of the farmers that compels attention. His declining earnings force him to borrow largely from private sources. His inability to repay the debt leads the farmers to commit suicide. Hence, indebtedness of farmers has become a central issue.

Policy Initiatives Needed for Agriculture

As already stated, committee after committee appointed by the government have made their recommendations about reforming agriculture. Unfortunately, the UPA government's record is dismal in this regard. What is urgently required to be done is the following:

Introduction of proper tenancy legislation, preparation of land revenue records, and expediting the process of registration of mutation. Introduction of risk mitigation instruments such as the farmers' income insurance scheme. Judiciously using public expenditure for the development and maintenance of rural infrastructure and resources particularly water, power etc.

Linking of small farmers with high value agriculture by organising Self Help Groups is required. All kinds of linkages need to be developed. Proper chain of cold storage i.e. supply chain management, warehousing and transportation is required to connect farmers to the *mandi* and end user. Transparent price discovery across geographical regions and smooth mobility without artificial arbitrage is also required. All the intermediaries are to be regulated and controlled under a single and powerful regulator.

Expenditure in area of research, development and technological innovation for productivity enhancement is required, which is different for irrigated and rain-fed areas. Creation of off farm employment and promotion of all allied activities. All agricultural loans should carry a very low rate of interest and compounding should be abolished. Farmers against whom legal processes of recovery have been started should also be covered under the waiver scheme.

Irrigation and Interlinking of Rivers

Periodic droughts and floods are creating havoc to rural economy of the country. There is loss of valuable water resource of the country on one side and serious shortages on the other. Interlinking of rivers is one major solution to this problem. It will link various rivers of the country so that water is not wasted from overflowing rivers and is brought to areas and rivers, which have short water supply. It has the potential to give fillip to the economy of the country similar to that of national highway construction project of the NDA government.

HealthCare for All

In the ultimate analysis, any society will be judged by its ability to provide universal healthcare for its people. This does not merely entail its ability to treat diseases and ailments but also to prevent their onset by means of suitable systems and measures. After a good and clean environment comes the need for better nutrition, with necessary food supplements. Preventive healthcare systems inoculation, vaccination, immunisation, periodic health checks and medical treatment are the next steps. These should be made available and be affordable to all our countrymen.

Disease Prevention

Most communicable diseases can be prevented by suitable sanitation systems and by the immunisation programme carried out on a large scale. Paying adequate attention to nutrition and dietary supplements can control a number of diseases. There is absence of health education amongst the lower-income groups.

The current state of Primary Health Care (PHC) centres is very bad and they do not provide any tangible healthcare to people. The reason for this unwarranted state is: the irregular and limited supply of medicines, not enough doctors and paramedical staff, callous and apathetic attitude of these people, excessively bureaucratic operation of the system. It is true the public health services are under severe strain.

Sanitation

Proper drainage of dirty water, disposal of garbage, sewage and human and industrial wastes are crucial for a clean micro environment which is a prerequisite for preventive health care.

Employment

Employment is another area of concern for the Indian economy. The 'reforms' have accentuated rather than abated the problem of joblessness. The Economic Survey (2006-07) has observed: "According to the 61st round estimates (National Sample Survey Organisation) during 1999-2000 to 2004-05 the labour force grew even faster at an annual rate of 2.54 per cent compared to the annual employment growth of 2.48 per cent.

Overall, the 'reforms' undertaken after 1991 have failed to make employment-generation an integral part of the growth process. The adverse effects of this failure may aggravate, during the 11th Plan, when about 52 million more people are estimated to join the labour force. The additional labour force could be as high as 65 million if female participation rate mounts at the same pace as in the period 1999-2005. Already the backlog of unemployment on a typical day is 35 million persons.

Inadequate employment opportunities, low wages and increasing informalisation of labour market are going to pose one of the most formidable challenges to the Indian economy. The country's stability and integrity could face a serious threat. On the basis of Census (2001), it has been estimated that the population of Indian youth in the age group of 20-29 would increase from 174 million in 2001 to 238 million in 2016. It implies that 64 million jobs would have to be created in the next 15 years to absorb the youth seeking employment.

Infrastructure Development

A simple truth is that a modern developed economy cannot be built on a large number of people living just above the poverty line, producing agricultural products alone and cut off from the rest of the manufacturing and business centre. This means that every production centre in the country should have speedy economic connectivity with other parts of the country.

At every centre there has to be more and more value addition. Value addition is simply enhancement of the value of a material with processes attached. Such a continual value addition at each centre of economic activity can be achieved only when they are interconnected by road, rail, water and air. Such physical transportation systems are a part of the enabling infrastructure.

The fact that the development of infrastructure is integral to speedy economic growth, this is the only way our people can break out of centuries of poverty. Development requires increase in GDP. But without improving infrastructure GDP cannot grow. If a reasonable infrastructure were in place, our innovative people would find avenues to a better life. Money in the hands of our hundreds of million people constitutes a huge market.

India can launch itself into a developed status only when the economic machinery starts 'real movement' through the infrastructure. Once the machinery moves, the process of economic growth will create more money in about five to seven years. That money can be reinvested in further improvements.

Linkages

The world today has become connected in a much more complex way due to the technologies of transportation and telecommunication. Both domestic and global economic and physical connectivity depend vitally on telecommunication networking. Instant transfer of information is essential for any business today. Thus telecommunications and IT are two of the most critical elements of the modern economy. Virtual world created by IT has become as real as the real world in all activities: agriculture to health to education to manufacturing to security.

True development can take place through interlinkages between various sectors in addition to linkages of trade. Agriculture and agro-food processing will require some of the finest inputs from engineering industries, materials sectors and even sensors and electronics, in addition, of course, to the life sciences and biotechnology.

Small-scale-industries: The Backbone of Manufacturing

The small-scale industry of India (including the tiny industries, micro and small scale) has a long history of promoting economic growth that is employment-oriented and spatially widespread, and hence inclusive. At the beginning of the 10th Plan (2002-03), the segment provided gainful employment to 24.9 million people in the rural and urban areas of the country through 10.5 million units, engaged in manufacturing and providing a wide range of goods and services. Over the next four years (end 2005-06), they have grown to 12.3 million units providing employment to 29.5 million persons. If the units in the *khadi,* village and coir industries are also taken into account, the employment is well over 332 million. This is thus rightly called the segment, which provides employment next only to agriculture.

The contribution of this segment to the economic growth of the country is no less significant. Nearly 39 per cent of the gross manufacturing output and 34 per cent of the export of India arise from this enterprise.

Yet, the segment does not constitute a homogeneous universe and a large majority of the units faces several challenges. In order to assist them in fully harnessing their potential by availing of the increasing opportunities generated by trade liberalisation, it is necessary to build not only an enabling policy environment but also supplement the former with a specific set of measures to address the continuing challenges. A major initiative is required to give full support in the area of credit, technological upgradation, marketing and infrastructure.

Specifically, the following issues need to be addressed on priority basis:

Credit Support

Credit is an essential input for the smooth working of any industry. This is more so in the case of micro and small-scale industries. Because of obvious characteristics SSIs lack access to capital market, private lending or international borrowing. Consequently, they have to resort to commercial banks, State Finance Corporations and other state owned bodies for their fixed and working capital requirements by way of raising loans. But, despite a number of measures announced to improve credit delivery to the SSI sector, there has been no significant improvement in the adequate and timely availability of credit to micro and small-scale industries.

There is also a need to strengthen SIDBI, so that they can provide wider products and services including more banking operations, value added services, guarantees, working capital limits, venture capital, credit guarantee scheme, etc. Debit recovery tribunals should work towards rehabilitation of units, securitisation limit has to be expanded and the norms for NPA revised.

Fiscal Support

It is the prime responsibility of the government to ensure that policies are made specific to the requirement of the micro and small scale industry. The Excise Exemption limit needs upward revision and the limit of payment of excise duty to be increased. The definition of their units also needs to be changed at par with the development of the economy.

Infrastructure for the SSI

The SSI entrepreneur is mostly a 'one-man-show' and has to take care of all the aspects of his business. It is the duty of the government to ensure that his requirements are fulfilled in terms of availability of quality power, transport, water, roads, telecommunication, etc.

In addition, the law and the policies of the government require a major change. For this, the 'Inspector Raj' needs to be abolished completely, labour laws simplified, procedures made simple and any form of taxation to be made singlepoint.

Technology Upgradation

The SSI entrepreneur, with his limited resources, is unable to invest in technology upgradation which can be in the form of training, improvement of quality, product development, energy savvy measures, waste management etc. The government is taking some steps in the form of cluster development, setting of training institutes for specific sectors, subsidy for attaining quality certification, etc. However, these are grossly inadequate and further investment needs to be made in consultation with various SSI bodies and associations.

Marketing Development

SSI units require support in marketing their products both in domestic and international market. They also need assistance for development of entrepreneurship and management, knowledge of the IT techniques, availability of 'display centres', setting up of common product exchanges, etc. There is also need of legislation to ensure timely payment to the SSI sector by large consumers, both in private and public sector.

Management of Foreign Exchange

In normal circumstances, with the growth in the economy, appreciating currency and the consequent increase in reserves is a sign of a healthy economy. But at the present juncture some specific conditions prevailing in India point towards some serious concerns in the matter. These factors require immediate intervention and government attention.

Causes of Concerns

Normally trade deficit leads to depreciation in the currency thereby helping in balancing the international trade of the country by increasing the exports. However, despite the persistent trade deficit our currency is appreciating which is due to huge inflows of foreign exchange and therefore it is not leading to improvement in the balance of trade situation. Secondly, if this inflow was of good quality and not consisting of so-called hot money, which is primarily short term in nature, this would not have been that harmful. But this is not the case. Thirdly, if the foreign exchange reserves created out of this inflow had been properly deployed and invested in acquiring proper assets abroad and not in purchasing treasury bonds in the US, the adverse situation arising out of increasing reserves could have been avoided. Fourthly, this inflow and investment in real estate is leading to inflation in land prices, which is causing trouble for industries and housing sector. Finally, many of the PE funds are by way of replacement capital through mergers and acquisition and not as direct investments to create fresh assets and for new greenfield projects.

Maximum inflow has come when the Rupee was lying low during the last couple of years. Now that the Rupee has gained ground, any remittance out of the country will unduly enrich the foreigners, who may not sincerely be interested in the development of our country. Just parking of funds by overseas investors is giving good returns to them. India has given 48% return in one year in US $ terms. FII investment is creating extreme volatility in markets which is harmful to economy and spoiling investors' confidence.

If the government properly tackles these issues, our manufacturing sector will also be in a better position and inflated asset value syndrome could be avoided.

Tools of Exchange Management

- Deployment of reserves is not proper—China has taken the policy of investing in Natural Resources of the other countries, like, oil, iron ore, etc.
- RBI is investing in purchasing foreign government's treasury bonds, which can depreciate and is harmful.
- We should not keep our reserves only in Dollars but in other currencies as well.

- Arbitrage in interest rate is also leading to speculation, which again is distorting the currency rate. US interest rates are far lower than ours. We need to manage interest rates.
- Verify the source of foreign funds to check quality of inflows: compliance and data reporting under FEMA by the bankers and rigorous inspection of bankers is warranted.
- Redemption of high cost foreign debts.
- Attempt to stop under invoicing of imports.
- The government has announced the creation of a sovereign fund of US$ 5 billion; these steps should be expedited and should have been taken long back.
- Calls for Tobin Tax should be viewed seriously.

Knowledge Economy Initiative

Knowledge economy is the one in which knowledge plays the pivotal role in creation of wealth. It is about the more effective use and exploitation of knowledge in all facets of economic activity. The ability to use, analyze and share knowledge is becoming one of the key drivers of economic growth and wealth creation across all the advanced economies.

It is not to be confused with service sector. The knowledge economy is the way that new technologies have combined with intellectual and knowledge assets like research, design, development, creativity, education, brand equity and human capital to transform our economy. The most important aspect is to create a proliferation of materials and activities at all points and at all levels suggesting that every one shall reap the benefits.

Knowledge and innovation have played a crucial role in development from the beginning of human history. With globalisation and technological revolution in the past few decades, knowledge has clearly become the key driver of competitiveness and is now profoundly reshaping the patterns of the world's economic growth and activity, and as it is applied in entrepreneurship and innovation, research and development, software and product design, and in how people use their education and skills. For international competitiveness, countries must be able to participate effectively in the knowledge-driven supply chains and markets.

India has gradually been building a knowledge economy, having made great strides in pharmaceuticals, medical sciences, and information technology. This led to increased interest on the part of the government and private sector to look for ways to raise the country's growth rate.

Effective use of knowledge in any country requires appropriate policies, institutions, investments and coordination across various aspects.

E-governance

If a number of government agencies are to be involved in service delivery in an integrated manner, the need for common service standards is paramount. Implementing and adhering to specified service standards enables the seamless integration of various government agencies by ensuring dynamic and uniform information and process flows, as well as better customer journeys. This is not to be confused with mere digitisation of all records and online filing of documents. In true sense, e-governance is the concept of information sharing and end-to-end linkages of all information.

Major part of this initiative is the use of IT in governance, since it promotes transparency, accountability, efficiency, cost-effectiveness, innovation and participation of citizens and easy sharing of all information.

Major components of egovernance are:

E-Banking

All financial benefits accruing under government schemes to be transferred directly to the beneficiary's account. This will help prevent pilferages and reduce corruption.

E-Healthcare

Centralised health record of every citizen to be recorded and a basic health insurance scheme for every citizen. Promotion of Telemedicine involves linking hospitals and health centers in rural or remote areas with speciality hospitals in urban areas.

E-Records

- The official records of all ministries be digitised.
- All land and property records to be computerised.

The most crucial official document for any rural population is the one that validates information about his land holding; to obtain crop loans and concessions linked to the size of the land holding, in the manual system. Village accountants maintain these records. Since the records are not open to public scrutiny, there is considerable scope for manipulation.

- All citizens-related records (birth, marriage, death, etc) to be made available online.

These are some major areas, which can contribute to the overall economic empowerment of the people of our country. Although there can be many more areas but once the process of development is initiated in major fields, the momentum that is built will automatically create inertia for the rest of the economy to move further. What we need is a strong and collective will of the people of the country to make India a strong and powerful economic superpower in the coming century. This is a golden opportunity as the economic activity throughout the world is moving towards the eastern regions particularly to Asia.

(The writer is the National Convenor of BJPChartered Accountant Cell)

□

Common Man's Involvement Vital in Building India's Economy Strong

—**Dr Sharad Jain**

Do we need common man's involvement in buildingIndia's strong economy or else Government could make it stronger on its own, even without common man's involvement? If attempts are made to make economy stronger without citizen's involvement, its foundation will be like a house of cards. Experience shows that Governments in different countries do solicit people's support in their developmental programmes. "World Development Report", an annual feature of World Bank, throws sufficient light on this issue and describes non-uniformity in ways and means of soliciting public support in various developmental programmes by different Governments.

We in India, till now, have not been fully successful in obtaining people's support in implementing different governmental programmes. This is because of common practice of bureaucratic pre-dominance in formulation and implementation of various schemes. This has naturally led to spread of red tapism and corruption in them and people's participation has been restricted only on paper. Hence people's interest seems negligible in such programmes.

Building country's strong economy depends on three growth engines, viz

(i) Agricultural and rural development
(ii) Industry, and
(iii) Services sector

Following measures need to be adopted in attracting common man's involvement which has been negligible so far. This will not only help in strengthening our economy but would also make its foundation stronger.

Agricultural and rural development

Time is now ripe to gradually shift the pattern of formulation of agricultural and rural development programmes from government level to local levels. The budgetary support needed for their implementation should also be allocated to local bodies, viz *panchayats*, which in turn will transfer the entire sum to *Gram Sabha*, a body created for spending this sum as per set programmes. This procedure will check widespread corruption in such programmes at different channels of government agencies. As per new concept, all plans and programmes required for raising agricultural production and productivity including facilities needed for suitable marketing of crops and other products as well as all programmes related to raising of social and economic infrastructure should be developed and implemented through involvement of local people. To make these successful, respective State governments should allocate required funds provided in their budgets — a total of State's own fund and those received from Centre directly to *Gram Sabhas* through *panchayats* so that these institutions could utilize it with the assistance of available technical staff with them and implement the programmes in right time and with honesty.

Very often, it is reported that in the implementation of various schemes of agricultural and rural development, elected office bearers of *panchayat* bodies under the influence of government officials posted locally, get involved in corruption. This is also true for various centrally sponsored schemes, including rural employment guarantee scheme. To eradicate such illegal practices, three measures need to be adopted—

(i) Gradual eradication of contractual system in implementation of various developmental works, including construction works and its replacement through common responsibility of *Gram Sabhas*, which will carry out the above work through independent channels under their strict supervision.

(ii) A well thought out high powered civil services of senior citizens, social activists, NGO's, representatives of local religious as well as women's organisations, well recognised by government, should be formed in states to monitor progress of developmental works being implemented at local levels as also to undertake social audit.

(iii) Under a well thought out strategy, each and every citizen should be encouraged and firmed up to provide maximum support to the programmes being implemented at local levels.

The above system will create a new dimension for people's involvement in rural developmental programmes.

Industries

To strengthen public sector undertakings economic potential of existing industrial enterprises should be exploited in two ways—

(i) Special attention should be paid to those enterprises, where full capacity utilisation is not being achieved. All attempts should be made to achieve full capacity utilisation.

(ii) Those enterprises running into losses and having become a burden on Central and State's exchequer should be openly auctioned in free market. Up to 10 to 15 percent disinvestment should be made of those enterprises which are constantly running in profit.

The sum of money received from both should be set aside and fully invested in establishing small and medium scale industrial enterprise in the strategic partnership of common people so that lakhs of youngsters can get employment in the public sector undertakings. This will be a unique example of people's participation.

Services Sector

The contribution of service sector in our national income has reached to around 45 to 50 per cent. The maximum contribution comes from Information Technology (IT) sector, which employs a large section of young boys and girls, which forms a big section of our society and gives boost to the growth of this sector.

These days a sizeable number of youth, both boys and girls, including those from rural areas after completing their computer education, are freely going to foreign countries to work in IT sector there. Just ten years back no one could have imagined that IT sector will bring such a big revolution in the world economy including the Indian subcontinent. Hundreds of call centres have opened in big and small cities providing services to foreign companies. Thousand of youth who are employed in these call centre are supporting these in a big way.

In the past few years, Indian IT companies have opened shops in the US, UK, Germany, Canada and other countries. But nowadays a recessionary trend is being witnessed in the economy of these countries, which are influencing working of several of our companies, resulting in reduction of employment opportunities of Indian IT personnel.

This is the right time when Indian companies working in IT sector spread their business network to eastern countries including South Asia and Arabs, where IT development is in the infant stage at present. This strategy will boost employment potential among our educated youths and thereby their participation in the growth of this sector.

(The writer is former Chief Economist,
Asian Development Bank, Manila. Presently,
he is the Convener, Economic cell,
Madhya Pradesh BJP)

□

Ethnic Indians in India's Diaspora Policy

—**Dr Amit Singh**

The Indian Diaspora has emerged as one of the largest in today's globalised world. There are more than twenty million People of Indian Origin (PIOs) and some six million Non-Resident Indians (NRI) spread over 136 countries. The Indian Diaspora constitutes more than forty per cent of the population in Fiji, Mauritius, Trinidad, Guyana and Surinam. The Indian Diaspora ranks third after the British and the Chinese Diaspora. People of Indian Origin (PIOs) and Non-Resident Indians (NRIs) are present in all parts of the globe. While the history of the Indian Diaspora dates back to the pre-Christian era, large-scale emigration of Indians took place mainly in the 19th and 20th centuries, which may be divided into four phases. The colonial period witnessed unprecedented emigration of indentured and other labourers, traders, professionals and employees of the British government to the European (British, French and Dutch) colonies in Asia, Africa, Latin America and the Caribbean. However, it was only in the post-World War II period that the most far-reaching emigration of Indians took place, mainly of professionals, to the developed countries namely England, USA, Canada, Australia and New Zealand. The oil boom in the 1970s and 1980s saw millions of Indians migrating to the Gulf and West Asian countries. Overseas Indians in various sectors like IT, Medicine, and Trade are finding opportunities abroad, which also include a large number of students seeking admission in developed countries, thereby adding to the numbers of the Diaspora.

No other country in the world is characterised with such diversity as India, in terms of culture, language, region and other forms of social stratification. Emigration from India too has been widely varied in social characteristics, such as in levels of education, caste and class, place of origin, religious and linguistic affiliations. Indian Diaspora is highly differentiated especially in the case of the "old" and the "new" emigrants. Indian policy towards Indian Diaspora has also varied from the colonial times to the early years of independence and on to the present times. While it could be discernable that during colonial period, the British were only interested in replacing 'slavery' by recruiting 'indenture labour' from India, the policies it pursued were essentially to facilitate labour emigration rather than to mitigate their plight in the plantation barracks. Not only were they 'encouraged' to renew the period of their contract under the indenture system, the colonial rulers actively discouraged the labour from returning by charging heavy amounts of money for their return passage. This essentially served the interests of the British colonial masters rather than that of the exploited Indian plantation worker. Following the ban on indenture system, the British encouraged the indenture labour to settle down in their island colonies. The British left most of their colonies with the legacy of conflict between the indentured labourers and the ethnic population of the host country.

Indian nationalism played an integrating role in mobilising the Indian Diaspora around the world to gain India's independence. They were exhorted to identify with India's cause as 'only a free India could hope to protect and safeguard their interests'. Since most of them were taken under a coercive colonial rule, they were visualised by Mahatma Gandhi as a segment of emerging Indian independence where they would share the socio-cultural space within India. Therefore, it was a policy of identification and association but these trends limited to the colonial period only.

While discussing India's Diaspora policy one observes that after the independence, India followed the policy of disassociation with regard to its Diaspora. The basic principles of India's Foreign Policy were laid during the independence under the Prime Ministership of Jawaharlal Nehru. Subsequently, there was noticeable continuity and change which subsequent governments blindly followed Nehru's path. In 1977, when a non-Congress government led by the Janata Party assumed power, the first signs of an official rethink vis-à-vis the Diaspora appeared. That official policies strike a balance between safeguarding India's foreign policy interests and show legitimate concern about Indians overseas. Although the Janata government did not remain in power for very long, the debate on expatriate Asians had restarted within the Indian government.

The proactive Diaspora Policy or from 'active-disassociation' to 'active-association' started especially after 1991, when the Indian economy faced severe crisis arising from the bankruptcy of its foreign exchange reserves. The crisis triggered a process of economic reforms as India prepared itself to exploit the opportunities to counter the threats arising from globalisation and liberalisation. There was a realisation that India needed to restructure itself economically and needed investment for infrastructure restructuring. Neither the Indian state nor private sector had the capacity to counter the drastic situation. If India intended to develop economically and remain competitive in a swiftly globalised world, it had to aggressively pull Foreign Direct Investments (FDI) and the infusion of new technologies. In this context, the larger policy shifts appears in the re-engagement of India with its Diaspora in the 1990s because only affluent section of the overseas Indians i.e. Non-Residential Indians (NRI's) can become a safeguards for the Indian economy in the 1990s.

This was the same time when India also initiated its 'Look East Policy' under the P V Narasimha Rao's Congress Government. When India initiated its Look East Policy towards the Southeast Asian countries then the large presence of the ethnic Indians in the region were unquestionably in the minds of the foreign policy makers but unfortunately India could not explore its Diaspora aspects in the strengthening bilateral as well as multilateral relations with the ASEAN countries. India also missed the opportunity to constructively engage its Diaspora and gratifying its aspiration and inspiration of the Diasporic community. But the Congress government of India was cautious and slow towards this segment. Because of its historical position, it was over cautious in including PIOs under overt policy framework. When Bhartiya Janata Party (BJP) led NDA came to power Indian policy changed very fast for this segment. Historically Rashtriya Swayamsewak Sangh (RSS), Vishwa Hindu Parishad (VHP), and Antar Rashtriya Sahayog Parishad (ARSP) a support base for BJP, had maintained very close people-to-people contact through its branches among Hindu overseas settlers. In contrast to Nehru's policy of active dissociation of PIOs from Indian foreign policy objectives, BJP stood for active and overt association of PIOs for foreign policy objectives of India.

In 1998, the government led by the Bharatiya Janata Party, with Atal Bihari Vajpayee at its helm, announced the introduction of a 'PIO Card' for Indians settled in specified countries, promising visa-free travel and privileges in matters of investment and education. In 2000, the government set up a High Level Committee on Indian Diaspora chaired by LM Singhvi, a parliamentarian, jurist and former diplomat responsible for assessing the issues concerning Indians overseas, suggesting new policy and organisational frameworks, and recommending a country-specific agenda to intensify India's engagement with its Diaspora. On 19 December 2001, the Committee submitted its detailed Report, running into 576 pages, with its recommendations. In 2001, the Indian Prime Minister formally inaugurated the 6th Convention of the Global Organisation of People of Indian Origin (GOPIO) in New Delhi. On the recommendation of the Singhvi Committee, the government implemented numerous novel policy initiatives, including the decision to celebrate the Pravasi Bharatiya Divas and institute the Pravasi Bharatiya Samman. Perhaps the most significant initiative was the Indian government's announcement, at the inaugural Pravasi Bharatiya Divas held in January 2003, of sweeping changes to the country's 48-year-old Citizenship Act, granting Indians living in Britain, Canada, Australia, Finland, Ireland, Italy, the Netherlands and the US the privilege of claiming dual citizenship. The restriction of dual citizenship to only one constituency of the Diaspora the NRIs settled in affluent Western countries led to widespread criticism from other NRI segments, especially from the West Indies and countries such as Fiji, South Africa, Malaysia and Mauritius, where Indian communities are not well-endowed. In 2004, when a Congress-led coalition spearheaded by Manmohan Singh assumed power, it adopted two significant measures: it established a separate Ministry of Overseas Indian Affairs; and at the Pravasi Bharatiya Divas held in January 2005, it declared that dual citizenship would be extended to all Indians overseas who migrated after the inauguration of the Indian Union on 26 January 1950, subject to the laws prevailing in their home countries, thus eliminating the basis of criticism of the earlier policy. However, at that time the dual citizenship would be granted without voting rights but in the recent Pravasi Bharatiya Divas, the eighth one, which was held at New Delhi, the Indian Government also announced "Voting Right" to the overseas Indians community. In such changed scenario, the proactive interest of India in the 90s does not have any element of imperialist design or racist preference as was likely to be construed during Nehru period.

The presence of the "New Indian Diaspora", which consists of highly skilled people has enhanced India's image world over. The Government of India is taking great interest in the Indian Diaspora, which is evident from the Report of the High Level Committee. Increased growth in trade and investment between India and other countries has had a positive effect with a surge of skilled workers, professionals and business people to almost all the countries. There is a great demand and respect for these Indian professionals who are so different from the Indian immigrants who went abroad in the nineteenth century, especially under the indenture system. The Indians who came as indentured labourers were no better than slaves. There was no question of their having political rights: they were used as tools for the advancement of British commercial interests. They were loyal and industrious and gave no trouble as long as they were allowed to live as separate entities, maintaining their links with "Mother India".

India's Diaspora Policy is not static. It has evolved during various political phases in India's political history. The sensitivities of the nationalist struggle, the winning of independence, and the trauma of partition and the creation of the Republican constitution of the Indian Union, engendered important changes in India's relations with the Diaspora. A concern for the treatment of Indian migrant labourers during the nationalist phase was replaced by post-colonial disavowal after independence of any lingering responsibility for those who were now part of a separate nation 'overseas', and later, a tendency to view the skilled migrants who left India as a brain drain. However, by the last decade of the century, during the period of rapid economic liberalisation, the value of the Diaspora was rediscovered, and India adopted a constructive approach towards the Indian Diaspora.

As history speaks itself, the Indian leadership totally ignored Indian Diaspora but occasionally with their 'own-convenience', they addressed a few of the Diaspora issues. These trends also appear in the ongoing racial attacks on Indians especially towards Indian students in Australia, where the Government of India watched the whole episode just as a mute spectator and engaged themselves only in lip-service seeking to pressurise the Australian authority. Take another example of Malaysia's recent unrest, on November 25 2007, when HINDRAF internationalised the wretched condition of the ethnic Indians in Malaysia; the Government of India's initial response was tight-lipped till the then Opposition leaders like L K Advani and Rajnath Singh of Bharatiya Janata Party (BJP) expressed concern over the plight of ethnic Indians. The BJP has taken a serious note of the incidents and has urged for immediate diplomatic intervention from the UPA government on this issue. The government should register its protest with the Malaysian envoy in New Delhi and convey its displeasure on the developments in Malaysia. The BJP expressed its solidarity with the people of Indian origin (PIO) in Malaysia and hopes that their struggle against the injustice and inequality would reach to a logical conclusion. The BJP statement said, "the party believes that India had a moral obligation to take up the case of injustice and persecution of Malaysian Hindus and PIOs with the authorities in Kuala Lumpur. The UPA government cannot shirk from this responsibility either out of its commitment to anti-Hindu pseudo-secularism or under the pretext that this is an internal matter of Malaysia. An ally of the UPA, the DMK has expressed its concern over the plight of the Tamil Malaysians and demanded the Centre's intervention in the matter. In fact, the exodus of Tamils from Malaysia has united the parties across the spectrum in Tamil Nadu. The AIADMK leader J Jayalalithha and MDMK leader Vaiko have also asked the Centre to take up the matter with the Malaysian government. Hindu Rights Action Force, an apex body of 30 organisations, has approached all political parties pleading for support but Waytha Moorthy, only got the chance to meet the leader of the Opposition, L K Advani.

In the seventh Pravasi Bharatiya Divas (PBD), 7-9 January 2009 held at Chennai, the Hindu Rights Action Force (HINDRAF) circulated a fiery report on the plight of Malaysian Indians. They urged the Indian government to slap trade sanctions on Malaysia, including a boycott of the country's palm oil, until Malaysia's government stopped discriminating against the Indian minority, but again the same story has been repeated by the Indian government. Nothing could be done to ensure for the safety and security of the People of Indian Origin in Malaysia.

During the 9 March 2003 incident, when nearly 300 Indian citizens, mostly IT professionals in Kuala Lumpur, were 'maltreated' and 'interrogated' by the Malaysian authorities, the Indian government reacted sharply and warned that any repeat of such incidents would affect bilateral ties. The Government of India indicated that it would re-examine bilateral agreements and other trade related concessions given to Malaysia. Foreign Regional Registration offices (FRROs), including the one in, were ordered to verify the Bengaluru credentials of Malaysian nationals registered here. India also expressed its inability to host Malaysian Health Minister towards the end of March 2003. During the visit of the Malaysian Entrepreneur Development Minister, his talks with Indian Ministers were confined to the harassment of Indian IT professionals, instead of the proposed agenda. Similarly, the Ministry of Sports in consultation with the External Affairs Ministry ordered a last minute pull-out of the Indian hockey team from the prestigious Azlan Shah Cup hockey tournament that year.

If both the incidents of March 2003 and November 2007 are compared, in each case the Indian government acted as a mute spectator of the whole episode or just offered only lip-service as the recent protest (November 2007) involved PIOs and the pervious one (March 2003) was related to the affluent NRIs. The Indian Government's biasness and dissociation policy towards the PIOs was once again witnessed. The same issues also haunted the Indian Government especially in the Pravasi Bharatiya Divas.

The Indian community has divided views on the Indian Government's current policy of developing links with wealthy and successful overseas Indian communities and its celebration of Pravasi Bharatiya Divas. In 2003, MIC President Datuk Seri Samy Vellu was awarded the Indian Diaspora Award, but some Malaysian Indians feel that poorer overseas Indian communities have been neglected. Likewise, the Indian Government's dual citizenship policy for non-resident Indians is sometimes seen as restrictive and confined largely to Indians residing in affluent western countries. The economic and technological rise of India brings benefits to the Indian Diaspora, especially those who have been neglected for long. The rise of India has provided powerful linkages for selected groups of Indians situated outside India but it remains to be seen how this new global Diasporic exchange will benefit the whole Indian community.

From January 2003 onwards India hosted eight Pravasi Bharatiya Divas (PBD) but it seems to be merely a yearly ritual and annual jamboree of Diaspora. During the initial phase of PDB there were plenty of expectations from the Indian Government especially towards the plight of People of Indian Origin in the host countries, which the Indian Government did not address. Rather Indian Government was more investment-centric. Therefore, lesser participation of the overseas Indians is witnessed in the recent years. Consequently, the Indian media also has lost its interest and there is poor media coverage of the PBD. Now the Overseas Indian Community has realised that the event is more about 'Bharat' rather than 'Pravasi' and it is essential to look forward for something for the 'Pravasis' in the Pravasi Bharatiya Divas. The report of the Singhvi Committee is also an imperfect document on Indian Diaspora. The Indian Government's action and reaction related to the concerns of PIOs in the host countries is a great need of the hour. The time has changed; hence, a more pro-active Diaspora policy is required. India should address the concerns of the ethnic Indians anywhere in the world, without jeopardising the relations with the host countries. Only then,

Will the condition of PIOs as well as India improve globally, as PIOs constitutes more than 75 per cent of the Indian Diaspora.

(The writer is Research Associate, National Maritime Foundation, New Delhi)

□

Strengthen Civic Sense to strengthen the Nation

—Amba Charan Vashishtha

Civic sense, as is — and should — generally be understood, is a sense of belonging to the society, to the nation and to the environment one lives in. It inspires the citizen to do everything to make life civilised and worth living. Further, it is the "ability to think or act in a reasonable or sensible way", as per the meaning of word 'sense' in the Oxford Dictionary. It also includes the ability to make a "good judgement". It is an involuntary feeling. It lies more in performing one's duty as a citizen than in demanding one's rights. And it is here that the famous words of the late US President John F Kennedy resound appropriate: "Ask not what the country can do for you, but what you can do for the country."

Civic sense is a code of ethics, a lesson in morality and a commitment to one's duties. It is a voice of the soul and the inner self. It is a spirit nobler than rights. Performance of duties is ephemeral; the spirit born out of civic sense is enduring, eternal. A person with a civic sense is sanguine to his duties towards the society and the neighbourhood and is the least demanding on his rights. To a great extent, civic sense inspires people to work selflessly without expecting or demanding recognition, appreciation or rewards. It is an exercise in self-satisfaction derived at having performed one's duty. The glow the civic sense ignites at other's faces gets reflected, in a greater measure, on the face of the person displaying his civic sense.

Traditions & Morals

Civic sense has something to do with our up bringing, with our family traditions and morals and, above all, with the environment we live in and grow up. It has something to do with the inner voice, matter of the heart and mind. It is an inheritance from our ancestors and learnt from parents, elders, teachers and friends.

Showing respect to our elders, senior citizens, to ladies and teachers is a part of the civic sense we have. The more gentleman a person is , the more civilised he is and possesses a higher degree of civic sense. Non-performing of it generates a sense of shame and regret in a person who values the civic sense.

Civic sense is social ethics, the unspoken norms of society. It has a lot to do with a propensity to be law-abiding, respecting fellow beings and maintaining decorum in public places.

It would be no exaggeration to admit that the dawn of independence has slowly but steadily ushered in the dusk of the civic sense in the country. A decade or two after we won independence our society, to a great extent, remained self-disciplined trying to do everything and not to do anything that came in the way of a decent, healthy, hygienic, clean, orderly and honest social life. At that time, people entertained a greater sense of belonging to the society, their neighbourhood and environment than they do today. There was greater emphasis on our duty as a citizen, as a neighbour and a human being. These days we are as alive to our rights as oblivious we are of our duties. Our personal goals today override our civic sense and as an ethic it has been pushed down to a low priority.

Forget about what was the position in pre-Muslim era. Even under the domination of Muslim invaders and British rule, people continued to display a higher civic sense. They were not dependent on the government of the day for doing everything for their welfare and of the village and society. Even towns looked after their own wellbeing with a collective sense of vision and action. People themselves put their heads together to find solution to their common difficulties and problem. They depended upon their own self, their own resources, their own manpower and their own capability. That solved many of their problems.

People in the past possessed a greater sense of responsibility for the society. There still exist paths laid with stones, pucca roads, wells, baulies and stairs constructed for common use. These things persist even today after a century or so and continue to serve the people although these were raised by the people themselves who were illiterate and not engineers. If a stone got dug out or a pit got created because of rains, floods or other reasons, people collectively or individually, lost no time to repair it. They did not wait for days and months together for the rulers to do that small job.

People then jointly made efforts to solve their water problems. Every now and then the whole village or town would cooperatively cleanse these water sources. People had the civic sense to ensure that the water sources were not in any way polluted. If anybody did violate that sense, whoever noticed it either made him see reason with argument or some recalcitrant even got thrashing. Nobody objected why an individual or a group had taken the law into their own hands. The guilty too realised his mistake and accepted the punishment without a murmur. The stress, then, was more on voluntary labour and monetary donations. People took pride in making *gupt daan* in which the donor kept his name secret instead flaunting his name for having made so generous a donation.

Temples and other places of worship were raised by the people and civic amenities provided there. Some philanthropists even constructed rooms and provided other facilities and amenities for the pilgrims to stay there. Some even ran langars (community kitchens) to feed everybody who visited the place. But at that time there was no yearning for credit and personal publicity. People, though rarely, at times do spend money for providing such facilities these days too, but they are more eager to install plaques to show that it was they who did this favour for the society.

Makes Life Worth Living

Our civic sense inspired us to do everything to make the life of the society easy, smooth and worth living. They would do nothing that put hurdles in the life of the society. In olden times, people would sweep, of their own, paths and roads leading to their neighbourhood and the village or town. Keeping their own household, the area near their house and the village spick and span was considered to be the sacred duty of every inhabitant. People would individually and collectively take to cleaning of the drains, village baulies (water resources) and wells.

People had a sense of belonging to the society and anything of common use was considered to be as much belonging to the society as much to the individual himself. If anybody damaged any property of common use it pained an individual as much as it did when anybody harmed his own personal property. A person individually or collectively may himself punish the defaulter to spread out the message that the society cannot put up with such nuisance under any circumstances. This injected a sense of fear among the irresponsible and undisciplined individuals.

If a pedestrian noticed anything on the village path or road that could hurt a passerby, he would remove everything— a small branch of the tree, a stone, a piece of iron or glass—on his own. They considered it a pious duty towards the society.

People would not throw any waste, particularly left-over of vegetables and fruits, on the path or road lest anybody could slip on the way. The banana peel is the greatest culprit that has made people suffer multiple fractures when inadvertently they stepped on. But now seeing waste, eatables and banana and other fruit peels on the way is a common feature. People travelling in bus and car are the worst culprits in this manner.

In earlier times, if one noticed a person wreathing in pain, lying on the road or pavement, one would instantly tend to him ignoring the important job or assignment one may be having on hand. If necessary, one would take that person to the nearest hospital and get him treated. He would get the address or phone number of his nearest relation in the town and inform him of what has happened to that person. One would spend from his own pocket and would not wish to be reimbursed of his expenses if the relation of the person wanted to.

Timely Help

Many people would be seen lying on the road completely drunk, unconscious of themselves. Many contract injuries when their gait staggered and they fell down losing their consciousness. In scorching heat in summer and freezing temperatures in winter many such inebriated persons would die if they were not helped in time to be lifted to their homes. People who never drank themselves or hated drunkards would swoop into action to help these persons in need.

But not now. People would overlook such unfortunate persons in dire need of help and pass by with a deriding comment. They would not come to the aid of a person lying injured in a road accident. They would not even care to inform the police. Many such injured persons die unattended. Had they been taken to the nearest hospital or dispensary instantly, many would have survived their injuries. We are growing inhumanly callous in such instances.

Motorists use boulders at the time of repair of their vehicles, but drive away without caring to remove these stones from the road lest a motorist could stumble against, get injured and his vehicle damaged. A person with a civic sense would not leave the place without ensuring that nothing is left behind that should harm another motorist or a pedestrian. Such carelessness proves fatal at night.

People use the public tap and leave it flowing after use. Even passers-by would not for a moment halt to turn off the tap so that not a single drop of water goes waste. But when our taps at home go dry, we curse the administration and not ourselves for our failure to perform our civic duty not to let water go waste.

Not long ago, people in public parks or those occupying seats in trains and buses would leave their seats for the elderly, handicapped and ladies of their own. But not now. Even those who occupy seats reserved for senior citizens, ladies and handicapped persons in buses and metro trains would not, of their own, vacate the seats they have usurped for themselves. Even when women and elderly people look at them in the hope that the unauthorised occupants would be gentlemen enough to offer them seats reserved for them, they would try to look the other side.

With shoes on, people would soil the bus or train seats while taking out their luggage from the shelf above their seats knowing fully well that somebody is going to occupy it after they deboard. They would throw the waste, fruit peels, etc. under their seats. Not only does it make the bus or train dirty, it also puts to inconvenience the passengers. What to them? Such passengers leave behind a legacy of dirt and lack of cleanliness for others who follow.

Earlier, there was great community feeling. People would throng to the place of a person who was to solemnise his son or daughter's wedding; who was organising some public feasting; or some tragedy had befallen on him. People would go to his place of their own to help in whatever way they could. They derived pleasure in performing duties at such occasions. But this sense is gradually — and fast — dissipating.

The tale of public toilets on the bus stands and railway platforms as also in the trains is the all the more pitiable. Nobody has the civic sense to understand that the place is also to be visited by some gentleman after him. In urine pots they would spit paan, throw cigarette/bidi pieces which choke the pipes rendering it all the more dirty. Many people would not use the cistern after going to the toilet and it is left to the next person to observe how dirty the person who visited the toilet earlier was. They want the toilet to be perfectly clean for themselves but would take pride in leaving behind a trail of dirt for the passengers to follow. It is below their dignity to flush it after use or leave it clean.

Modern Generation

Actually, and unfortunately, the modern generation thrives in violating what we consider as civic sense. At a number of places we come across signboards: "No parking". Yet we see numerous vehicles parked over there. People trying to cross the busy roads not on zebra lines but wherever they like. They put not only their lives to risk but of others too.

As we move from a social life lacking civic sense, we are moving fast towards an uncivilised society. There are spit marks, urine, vulgar graffiti, random garbage and overflowing sewers at every nook and corner of India. No city in this country has managed to fight the menace. It is easy to pin everything on the government, but people must first question themselves and their own civic sense. Roads are dirty not because nobody cleaned these, but because somebody did not care to see that these do not get dirtied.

People would be seen urinating on roads in full view of the people. This is an obnoxious view. At the same time, the municipal authorities too are to be blamed. They fail to provide adequate public conveniences at suitable places.

Our present generation takes pride in not respecting the law and the civic sense, and in breaking it. Crossing at red lights is a daring feat for them. This is giving rise to rising number of road rage cases and violence and even murders and deaths.

We are getting more passive and permissive. *Sab chalta hai* (it is order of the day) and *'others too are doing'* it are the wrong excuses we offer for our failures to respect the civic sense.

Creates Harmony

Civic sense creates greater harmony and peace in the society. Violation of it generates strife and tension. If we display a sense of understanding towards each others, there can be no strain in society. Our greater commitment to civic sense could prevent the growth of the spirit of separatism, vandalism, intolerance and racism. Spirit of intolerance raises its head when an individual or a group loses civic sense. It transcends all cultures, backgrounds and diversities. Civic sense is a spirit of tolerance. Failure to display and observe it unnecessarily fans communal friction and racial tension. Life in cities, towns and villages is turning sour only because civic sense is becoming non-existent among the people. Its absence is only giving rise to more problems, turning the existing ones more complex and.has become a hindrance in finding their solution.

Civic sense generates great sense of camaraderie and understanding. It helps mixing of people with different origins and backgrounds. One's respect for civic sense equally resonates in the mind of the other. It leads to peace and obviates friction. Lack of civic sense only gives rise to tension between individuals and groups and ultimately leads to violence and crime.

A criminal has the right to breach the law to commit a heinous crime like murder or rape and, equally, he has the right to prove that he did not commit the crime and that he is an innocent deserving to be acquitted honourably of the charge. The civic sense has no force or rod of law behind it. It can be breached with impunity but cannot be enforced by law. The civic sense has the silent sanction of the populace but not the protection of law. If an individual or a group of people rebuke a person for grievously hurting the civic sense, or if the violator displays the audacity to defy the people and if in the heat of argument he is thrashed, it is not the violator of the civic sense who attracts punishment but the individual or the group who wanted the civic sense to prevail. Human rights of the breacher of civic sense are his greatest safeguard against punishment.

Democracy Dissipating Civic Sense

Democracy, by laying greater stress on the rights of its citizens to the utter disregard of their duties, to an extent, is also the culprit for having killed the civic sense and made the citizens bolder to violate it. Since civic sense is a silent, unwritten law of the citizens, by the citizens and for the citizens. Its observance does receive the vocal and symbolic appreciation of the people, but its breach does not fetch punishment to the violator. In the perception of many of our young minds, chivalry lies in violating the law and civic sense and to observe it is meekness. In an environment when people take pride in violating law than in observing it and law of the land is losing its sanctity, expecting people to adhere to the civic sense without the rod of law is like expecting a cat not to drink the milk that is lying in an open bowl with no one to dissuade it.

In democracy, unfortunately, the stress is only on rights and duties, which include the civic sense, are invariably overlooked. A child has rights against parents. A student has rights against school and teachers. A citizen has his rights against the society and the government. But children only with exception perform their duty towards parents to obey them and to look after them in their old age and during illness or infirmity. Students have no duty towards their teachers, to obey them and respect them. That is the tragedy of democracy and of the people. Parents are hauled up if they use the rod against their recalcitrant children. Teachers have been punished if they scolded their students, but how many students have been punished for showing disrespect to their teachers? If parents reprimand their children and if teachers say a few harsh words for not having done their home work or for not behaving properly in the school, is it a crime? Should parents and teachers overlook the faults of their children and students?

A citizen has the right to vote but not the duty to exercise his right to franchise. A citizen must sow the seeds by performing his duty to participate in the process of electing a representative of his free will to pave the way for formation of a government of the people, by the people and for the people. Only then can he reap the bumper harvest of his right in a democracy. If he fails to perform his duty, how does he expect to reap what he had not sown? It is ironical that people do not perform their duties but want their rights to be enforced, protected and respected religiously.

The United Kingdom does not have a written Constitution. Its government functions on the unwritten word of the Constitution, on the precedents and traditions set by their forefathers. There have never been constitutional crises and strife in the UK only because the people, the politicians and the administrators go by the sense of the unwritten Constitution which only has the interest of the nation supreme in their mind. All other things are secondary.

It's Universal

The same is true of the civic sense. It is universal. It favours none and it works against none. The UK has a monarchical democracy which has stood the test of time. In the same way if we all collectively vow to respect the civic sense, many of the problems facing the country will vanish and India will be a land much better worth living.

We need to teach everyone — the child, the adult, young and the old, men and women — the niceties of civic sense. That alone is the panacea for many of the ills facing the nation.

(The writer is the National Convener of Literature & Publication Cell of BJP. He is also on the Editorial Board of Kamal Sandesh)

□

Is Education in India really Indian?

—Dr Shiv Shakti Bakshi

The much talked of 'globalisation-liberalisation' era is apparently unfolding its impact in almost every sphere of life including education. The nation is now witness to a new kind of debate with certain amount of media hype built around a sense of 'reformist' zeal which was hitherto said to be missing among the policy makers. Intelligentsia is showing a sense of urgency in dealing with the issues related to "grade-semester" syndrome leaving aside the real issues that should have engaged the attention of our policy makers. While the entire government machinery remains busy in flaunting the literacy data, issues like commodification and commercialisation of education catering to the rich along with the inbuilt duality in the system are seldom discussed. Such tendencies only point to the lack of zeal and interest among the policy makers to treat education as a mean to emancipate the weaker and poorer sections of the society who need not only to be made literate but also provided with the opportunity to get quality education that may ultimately empower them. The phase when 'globalisation-liberalisation' has become *mantra,* the policy makers now seem to suffer from "grade-semester" syndrome which is more interested in 'resolving' inane issues having marginal impact on elite sections of the society while shifting the focus from those who are even out of the ambit of the current education system.

Progress Not Encouraging

So far progress in the field of education has not been encouraging. For most of the period after independence, India continued to languish behind taking little initiative to come out of the colonial educational arrangement excepting instituting a few commissions to look into the issues. It was during the NDA regime that some concrete measures, like refusing World Bank loan and taking bold initiative by starting "Sarva Shiksha Abhiyan" through self-funding were initiated in the education sector. The inherent objective of the policy was self-reliance. It liberated the nation from the yoke of toeing the dictated lines of World Bank in the education sector thereby loosening the hegemonic foreign grips. It has resulted in huge progress in terms of increasing primary education attendance rate and expanding literacy to approximately two-thirds of the population. However, odds against India continue to be too heavy to overcome by simply embarking on a handful of measures. Despite growing investment in education, 40% of the population is illiterate and only 15% of the students reach high school. As per 2008 estimates, India's post-secondary high schools offer seats enough only for 7% of India's college-age population, 25% of teaching positions nationwide are vacant and 57% of college professors lack either a master's or PhD degree.

China Pushes Us Behind

In 1947 we had many more institutes of higher education than those in China but now it has moved ahead of us. As per 2009 estimates, India has 20 central universities, 215 state universities, 100 deemed universities, 5 institutions established and functioning under the State Act, and 13 institutes which are of national importance. Other institutions include 16000 colleges, including 1800 exclusive women's colleges, functioning under these universities and institutions. However, these institutions face shortage of faculty and concerns have been raised over the quality of education. Only three Indian universities were listed in the *Times Higher Education* list of the world's top 200 universities – Indian Institutes of Technology, Indian Institutes of Management, and Jawaharlal Nehru University in 2005 and 2006.One study has indicated that only 10% of Indian graduates from non-professional institutions are employable because 90% have no skills which are marketable. It is not that the other 90 % remain unemployed, but they supplement what they have got in the colleges through vocational courses.

Education forms one of the core components of the programme of national reconstruction. The colonisation of India led to intrusion of western institution in the society, which furthered the creation of an intellectual ambience wherein the policy makers considered westernisation of the Indian society as a legitimate goal. The intellectual-structural arrangement under the colonial education system was to facilitate the project to colonise Indian minds. A demarcation of academic vs. un-academic discourse was constructed; 'non-modern' was un-academic and 'modern' was academic thereby initiating a process of rejection of the knowledge systems which were pre-colonial hence 'pre-modern'. The leaders of the national movement were never reluctant in their opposition to the imposition of colonial education system. They also debated and discussed the alternative framework of education that would have replaced the colonial imposition on gaining independence. Unfortunately, the end of colonial rule did not end the system but Marxism along with a kind of secularist discourse further supplemented it. The debate continues even today between those attempting to rescue education from the clutches of Macaulay-Marxist paradigm and a handful of pseudo intellectuals seeking to perpetuate it. The goal now is to secure the establishment of Indo-centric system of education.

The coming of UPA in power has seen regressive measure sought to be implemented in the field of education. Apart from the controversy over NCERT textbooks, trends of minorityism are reappearing under the pressure of vote-bank politics. Education now stands shamefully politicised. Sex education was sought to be imposed with obscene and vulgar contents, foreign universities and private enterprises under GATT's (GATT defines education as a marketable commodity) have been allowed in an unrestrained manner, leaving education at the mercy of market forces. The vision of a system of education that would have created a real independent India liberating the minds from the shackles of the colonialism remains shattered. Such goals remain abandoned by the politicians who today prefer to engage themselves blatantly in power politics with myopic vision. The UPA has so far not taken a single step towards the realisation of an Indo-centric education which could have helped in de-colonising the Indian mind.

Sometimes it is argued that Macaulay-Marxist paradigm has no alternative and Indian education could not have been systematised without the colonial intervention. The proponents of such argument dismiss the idea of an Indo-centric education and regale in aping the

West. They even dub the Indian civilisational knowledge system as obscurantist and retrogressive. Such a mindset is a product of Macaulayian vision of creating blockheaded Indians who can neither look back to their ancient roots for inspiration nor have a blueprint for a strong and vibrant future.

Education in Ancient India

Ancient India is known for many valuable and path breaking contributions in the field of education. Ayurveda is the earliest school of medicine known to the world and 'Charaka' is known as the father of Ayurveda. He developed this system some 2500 years back. Takshila was the first university of the world established in 700 B.C while Nalanda University, built in 4th century AD, was considered to be the honour of ancient Indian system of education as it was one of the best universities of its time in the world. Indian language Sanskrit is considered to be the mother of many modern languages of the world. Indians are credited for developing place value system in 100 BC and for inventing number system. Aryabhatta is the celebrated inventor of the digit zero. Trigonometry, algebra and calculus studies had also originated in India.

The Indian society had its own tradition of imparting education since ancient times. The education was imparted in *ashramas* (hermitage) where pupils went to seek knowledge. The *Gurukul* system of education was in vogue in ancient time wherein the pupils were supposed to go to the home of the teacher and live there as members of the family. The education was a man-making endeavour focussing each and every individual that came for instruction; it was an artistic and constructive process rather than a mechanical one. In the Indian tradition, life is divided into four stages viz. Brahmacharya, Grihastha, Vanprastha and Sanyas. The Brahmcharya stage was expected to be exclusively devoted to education of an individual. Such a conceptualization intended to make even higher education compulsory and universal through a well-established social system. Education was free and the students used to pay *Gurudakshina*, a voluntary contribution after completing their studies. At the *Gurukuls*, the teacher imparted knowledge of religion, scriptures, philosophy, literature, warfare, statecraft, medicine astrology and history ("*Itihaas*"). Education as imparted through oral tradition from teacher to pupil in an unbroken chain is often called *Guru-shishya parmpara*.

India was also famous for its seats of higher learning. The Universities of Takshashila, Nalanda, Ujjain and Vikramshila were such centres of learning where the students flocked from across the world particularly from Korea, Mongolia, Japan, China, Tibet and Sri Lanka. These were centres of postgraduate learning for advance study and research in humanities, religion and philosophy, law, astronomy arts and crafts including medicine. Takshashila specialised in the study of medicine, while Ujjain laid emphasis on astronomy. Nalanda, being the biggest centre, handled all branches of knowledge, and housed a large number of students. There were also affiliated colleges or *Viharas* to these universities. Nalanda was said to have around 8,500 students on its rolls who were instructed by 1,510 teachers daily in hundred of discourses. These Universities were also having big libraries and hostels for students; the foreign students had separate hostels. These universities were maintained on the endowments given by the kings. Nalanda is said to have a library, which was housed in three buildings, one of which was nine storeyed and named '*Ratnasagara*' meaning 'ocean of gem of learning'. It is said that Kautilya composed his famous treatise *Arthashastra* in Takshashila and the famous Ayurvedacharya Charak was also one of its products. The renowned philosophers and learned men Silbhadra, Nagarjuna, Arya Deva, Asanga, Vasubandhu and Dinnaga used to teach in Nalanda. The students were provided their all necessities such as food, clothing, accommodation, bed, and medicines together with religious needs through the endowments granted to these universities.

Besides these centres of higher learning and traditional *ashrama* and *Gurukul* system, villages had their own system of education through schools maintained by the customary contributions of the villages at harvest time. The small *tols* and *pathshalas* helped in universalising the education up to the village level.

Condition of education in 18th Century India

It was generally believed that eighteenth century was a 'Dark Age' for India and the decline of Mughal Empire had led to degeneration of society and culture as well. The myth of 'Dark Age' was sought to be perpetuated in a calculated manner so as to legitimise colonial intervention. It was more an attempt to justify the colonial rule and to project it as an 'emancipatory' and 'civilising' force. Recent researches have proved contrary to these long held opinions. These researches show that the eighteenth century India was filled with a kind of cultural and social dynamism that was brought about by newly emerging regional power centres.

British records show that education was widespread in the 18th century, with a school for every temple, mosque or village in most regions of the country. The subjects taught included reading, writing, arithmetic, theology, law, astronomy, metaphysics, ethics, medical science and religion. The schools were attended by students representative of all classes of society. Mahatma Gandhi is said to have described the traditional educational system as a beautiful tree that was destroyed during the British rule. But unfortunately, the traditional structures were not recognised by the British government leading to its decline and degeneration.Thomas Munro's report in 1822 for Madras Presidency, Mountstuart Elphinstone's report in 1823 for Bombay Presidency and William Adam's report in 1835-38 for Bengal Presidency testify the presence of wide ranging educational institutions, at various levels. Scholars and teachers were held in high esteem and the educated commanded a distinguished position in the society. Regional rulers took keen interest in education and provided endowments of various kind for the upkeep of education institutions, and even for scholarships of the students. Benaras, Ujjain, Tirhut, Nadia, Rajshahi, Tanjore and Trivandram were the major centres of Sanskrit learning. In 1818, Calcutta had 28 seminaries of Sanskrit learning with 173 scholars, in 1801, 24 Parganas had 190 seminaries and Nadia had 31 with 747 scholars, in 1834-35, in Rajshahi, there were 38 colleges of Sanskrit education, 19 of Hindu law, 13 of general literature, two of logic and four of Vedanta, tantric, Puranic and medical learning. Elaborating the extent of the indigenous education system, Adam reported the existence of 1,00,000 indigenous elementary schools in Bengal Presidency in the beginning of the eighteenth century against a population of 40,000,000, concluding that there was a village school for every 400 persons. He also calculated that there was on an average a village school for every 73 children of school-going age and one for every 30 or 32 boys.

Colonial intervention in Education

Colonial intervention in the field of education started through individual initiatives and debates on the nature, character and structure of education system. This debate is known as Anglicist-Orientalist-Evangelist controversy. The Orientalists wanted that the indigenous educational tradition should be maintained while Anglicists pleaded in favour of English education. Evangelists wanted Christian missionary education in India. In 1781,Warren Hastings set up the Calcutta *Madrasa* for the study of Persian and Arabic. In 1791, the efforts of Jonathan Duncan, the British Resident at Benaras, bore fruit and a Sanskrit College was opened at Benaras for the 'cultivation of laws, literature and religion of Hindus'.

These early attempts for the education of the Oriental languages met with little success. It was found that there were more teachers than students. The Christian missionaries decried the attempts to revive an 'outdated' system of education and advocated the teaching of western literature and Christian literature through the medium of English. The Srirampur missionaries, particular, were very enthusiastic for the spread of education. However it was not taken into account that a large number of traditional educational institutions were surviving without the colonial contributions.

In 1813, a humble beginning towards education was made by the Court of Directors when one lakh of rupees were provided for the annual expenditure on education, "for the revival and promotion of literature and the encouragement of the learned natives of India, and for the introduction and promotion of a knowledge of sciences among the inhabitants of the British territories". A section of Indian reformers and leaders also protested against the government's proposal to strengthen the Calcutta Madrasa, Benaras Sanskrit College and establishment of more Oriental colleges in Bengal. They wanted that the colonial Government introduce English education in India. The government agreed to encourage the study of English as well as Oriental languages. A grant was sanctioned for the Calcutta Hindu College set up in 1817 by enlightened Bengalis, which imparted instruction mainly in English language and emphasised the study of western humanities and science.

But the real controversy took shape in the General Committee of Public instruction, which consisted of 10 members. The Anglicist-Evangelist and Orientalists were equally divided and the dispute between them was finally referred to the Governor-General. Macaulay, member of the Executive Committee wrote the famous minutes on 2nd February 1835 showing great contempt for Indian customs and literatures saying, "a single shelf of the good European library was worth the whole native literature of India and Arabia". Macaulay aimed at creating a class of persons who should be "Indian in blood and colour, but English in tastes, in opinions, in morals and in intellect". In other words, he sought the production of "Brown Englishmen" to fill the lower cadres in the company's administration.

The government of Lord William Bentinck in the resolution of 7th March 1835 accepted the viewpoint of Macaulay that in future the object of the Company's government should be the promotion of European literature and sciences, through the medium of English language, and in future all funds were to be spent for that purpose. Thus the Anglicist-Evangelist and Orientalist controversy was settled in favour of the Anglicist- Evangelists. Macaulay's system was primarily aimed at educating the upper classes of the society. The masses were deprived of education and lack of governmental support led to the decline of village school system in India along with indigenous seminaries and colleges.

Current Scenario

Even after independence, education could not be rescued from the clutches of colonial mindset. The Macaulayian system is now reinforced by the Marxist ideas which resist the cultivation of Indo-centric approach under the garb of pseudo secular politics. Education has re-emerged as a controversial issue under the UPA government. The ongoing trends of de-Indianisation, commercialisation, communalisation and politicisation of education since colonial times have been reinforced with politics of minorityism by the UPA government. There is a kind of competitive minorityism between various state governments and different ministries among which HRD is one. Its decision to reserve fifty per cent seats for Muslims in Aligarh Muslim University is a result of such misguided politics. The politics of discrimination in education on the basis of religion has received impetus in instituting the Minority Education Commission. Even in the Central budget special provisions have been made for coaching Muslim aspirants for UPSC examination. The state governments have also become victim of the politics of minority appeasement. This has sunk so low that the Andhra Pradesh and Tamil Nadu governments had announced highly objectionable decision to reserve seats in government jobs for Muslims even in the face of adverse court verdicts in this context.

Education Not for All?

In the last decade, the process of commercialization and marketisation of education has been strengthened in the wider context of globalisation. In the last three and a half years, the present UPA government instead of accepting the challenges posed by commercialisation and marketisation, has surrendered before it. By remaining oblivious of its responsibilities, this government is thus extending an open invitation to private institutions to commercialise education. It thus remains insensitive by sacrificing the interests of the Dalits, OBCs, Scheduled Tribes and economically weaker sections of the society. The NDA government had introduced a fee-cut in the IIMs so that students from the weaker sections of society may be able to study in these institutes but it was highly unfortunate to note that the UPA government immediately after assuming power allowed a hefty fee-hike so that these institutes remain exclusive domain of a particular section of the society.

New challenges have emerged in the field of education with the opening of private institutions and coming up of foreign universities in recent years. The probability of multilinear changes in the educational environment due to these private-foreign institutions cannot be denied. These institutions, it is a matter of concern to note, are exploiting the students economically in the absence of governmental control, appropriate legislation and required standards. The quality and importance of the courses introduced by these institutions are also extremely doubtful.

Textbooks Demeaning Our Heroes

Instead of initiating constructive measures, the UPA government had no hesitation in re-introducing controversial NCERT text books which denigrate our national and spiritual heroes like Bhagwan Mahavir, Guru Gobind Singh ji and Shivaji. Jats have been described to be the plunderers in these books. Textbooks are being introduced in Delhi University and IGNOU which despise Hindu gods and goddesses and freedom fighters like Mahatma Gandhi and Sardar Patel.

The theme of national integration is replaced by the Marxist notion of class struggle. Nationalist poets and writers are relegated to the background and naxal poets are eulogised. The students are forced to read the biography of Maqbool Fida Hussain who has run away from the country in the face of cases pending against him in the courts for nude paintings of Hindu gods and goddesses. In contravention of the Supreme Court verdict, Sanskrit is being equated with Arabic and Persian under the category of classical languages. In place of Yoga and moral education, sex education was sought to be introduced.

The mindset of those who take decision on education is responsible for the plight of education in India. It is the same mindset that files affidavit in the court on Ram Setu claiming that there is no historical evidence of the existence of Bhagwan Ram. The Macaulay-Marxist paradigm continues to haunt the policy-making apparatus in education, which finds the pseudo secular politics a convenient ploy. Unless emphasis is given on Indo-centric education, the vision of realising a universal, non-commercialised, easily accessible and nationalist educational system would remain a distant dream.

Our system of education is not in tune with our historical past and culture. We are trying to find solutions to the problems in India's education by employing western, globalised and market vision in utter disregard of the Indian conditions and requirements. They wish us to inject a sense of inferiority, the like of which was done by the British rulers, that everything Indian is bad, crude and orthodox and everything western is the best, most modern and most suited to India. In our zeal to open up education, we are trying to ignore our own stark realities.

Our policy makers wish to make us disbelieve the reality of our hoary past and wish us to ape only the West. For India, only that system of education will suit which has its roots in the soil and looks up to fresh ideas and avenues good to the people from wherever they may be.

(The writer is on the Editorial Board of Kamal Sandesh and has recently been awarded Ph.D. degree by the Jawaharlal Nehru University)

□

Rising menace of Maoist terrorism UPA fails to act firmly

—**Ram Prasad Tripathy**

National security of India is under great threat mainly on two fronts: cross border terrorism and Naxalism. The country is facing the scourge of terrorism for the last three decades. In fact, no other country in the world has waged such a long, relentless struggle against terrorism as has India. The threat from within is more dangerous while that from cross border terrorism and aggression is no less. We do not seem to have learnt a lesson in dealing with such a menace and continue to make a mess with our confused and inconsistent approach. Scores of people, mostly poor and living in backward regions of the country, have fallen prey to this mindless violence. Still India is dithering to take firm action to restore law & order and peace in the country. This is evident from the statement of the former Home Minister of India Shri Shivraj Patil who had the audacity to say that Maoist violence was not the biggest security challenge to India.

The so-called Red terror unleashed by the Maoists and Naxalites has now spread its tentacles to around 231 districts of India across 13 states and poses the greatest challenge to country's security. The rapid geographical expansion in the area under Maoist influence in the past decade is also marked by inconsistency, indecision and lack of coordination and resolve on the part of the government to respond the way that is best suited to contain this security threat. It clearly betrays the fact that security and intelligence agencies as well as political leadership are not fighting the Naxalites with full force as they should. The security agencies and the government at the Centre and in the states are clueless and lack enough force and will power to tackle India's greatest enemy within.

Not a day passes without an incident of Left-wing extremism taking place in one corner or the other of the country. India wants to emerge as the next superpower and, at the same time, it is clueless about how to fight these internal elements which are virtually at war with the country, challenging the very sovereignty of India. The sacrifice by thousands of police personnel and paramilitary forces is not getting the recognition it should as they are fighting nothing less than a war with the ultra Left forces. Terrorist strikes of even small intensity do grab national headlines but the cases of hundreds of people and policemen falling victim to this Maoist terrorism does hardly raise similar concern in media and government. In fact the danger to national security has grown manifold in view of the reports that Maoist groups active in Nepal and other anti-Indian outfits from Pakistan, Bangladesh and some other neighbouring countries are working in tandem with the Maoists in India.

Government cannot wash off its hands now as it is also equally responsible for indecision and casual approach in recognising the enormity and magnitude of the challenge. We wasted almost a decade in finding the root cause of this problem and designing the suitable response to the Maoists who spread their tentacles to even the remotest corners of India virtually without any planned resistance from the police forces. Now we are facing an explosive situation where neither the root cause of underdevelopment is addressed nor the gun wielding guerillas have been reined in. With a huge population living in utter poverty and lack of development, regional backwardness and illiteracy remaining unaddressed for more than six decades after independence, the Maoists have a virtually unlimited supply of potential recruits. The regional backwardness and underdevelopment of vast stretches of India come handy for these violence mongers to justify their brutality.

There is no logic behind underestimating the Maoist mayhem as a mere law and order problem as this is in no way less dangerous than the threat posed by cross border terrorism. Even the magnitude of loss to life and property is much more on account of Maoist activities over the last decade than from anti-India terrorist activities sponsored from outside. The following data substantiate this fact.

Ministry of Home Affairs in its review report has stated that Naxal violence poses one of the gravest internal security threats before the country. The report says in the year 2009 the number of incidents of Naxal violence have been 2,016 in which 514 civilians and 304 personnel of security forces have been killed. Number of Naxalite Incidents, Casualties of Security Forces and Civilians in India from 2004 to 2009:

Notwithstanding thousands of deaths over the years, the unrealistic approach of UPA was evident on more than one occasion. Repealing of POTA; extension of olive branch to Maoists for illusive talks and even underestimating this challenge and failing to recognise this as the biggest internal security threat facing the country sent confusing signals on the sincerity of the government and bolstered the morale of Maoists. The Congress, led UPA's track record in fighting Left wing terror has been abysmal and is evident from the fact that the expenditure on internal security remains woefully inadequate. Further, the Indian State and Central government responses suffer from lack of coordination, are piecemeal and some States who took stringent action were discouraged by the human Rights-brigade and the issue was politicised. Killing of Swami Laxmanananda Saraswati and his associates in Orissa by the Christian bigots with active support from Naxalites has exposed the double standards of UPA government on this issue. The Chattisgarh Government which showed the courage to stand up to this challenge did not get enthusiastic response from the UPA Government which has exposed the lack of coordination between the Centre and States on this issue.

Naxalism in India

In the backdrop of organisational upheavals within the Indian Communist movement, an incident in a remote area called Naxalbari in West Bengal changed the character of Left-wing extremism in India. Tribal people with the support of ultra Left supporters of the area retaliated against the landlords and started forcefully recapturing their lands resulting in a rebellion. Within a short span of time the All India Coordination Committee of Communist Revolutionaries (AICCCR) was formed in May 1968. 'Allegiance to the armed struggle and non-participation in the elections' were the two cardinal principles that the AICCR adopted for its operations. In the late 1960s and early

1970s, the Naxalite movement spread into different parts of the country. But, over the years, as the principles diluted, Naxalite movement saw much of its membership waning away, and terror remaining the only weapon of the Maoists to further their nefarious agenda. The movement which started from Naxalbari in 1967 has now assumed very sinister proportions.

Naxalism has now become a nearly Rs 1500 crore organised extortion business in the form of 'levy'. The Naxal literature and documents seized by Central security agencies and state police forces during their operations have revealed intricate details of levy extorted by groups which run in to several hundred crores every year. The 'levy' is not only paid by the contractors working in the areas dominated by the Naxals but also by the industrial houses including some of the nationally reputed ones. Though, CPI (Maoist) still remains the prominent Naxal group, there are other splinter groups which too have now started imposing 'levy' besides indulging in kidnapping, looting and narcotics trade, which results in around Rs 300 crore as annual income from the state. If a conservative estimate is taken of the income generated from 'levy' in the seven most Naxal-infested states — Jharkhand, Chhattisgarh, Orissa, Andhra Pradesh, Bihar, West Bengal and Maharashtra — security agencies feel the collection from these areas, which are commonly referred to as 'Red Corridor', amount to nearly Rs 1,500 crore.

The Naxals have even come out with a card, recovered by forces, which clearly shows the exact amount of 'levy' to be paid by contractors, petrol pump owners and land owners. Besides the fixed levy, the Left-wing extremists groups also demand money from industrial units functioning in the areas "as and when they need" and even issue receipts for the same. Various state government and police sources involved in counter insurgency operations have revealed that the chiefs lead a luxurious life with all modern facilities. Though they forcibly recruit children in their cadre, their own kids study in good public schools.

The Naxals also encourage local villagers to undertake opium cultivation, just like insurgents in North-eastern states. Of the total 1.07 lakh kg of ganja or marijuana seized in the country in 2007, a large quantity of it was from Nagaland (15,489 kg), Madhya Pradesh (14,815 kg), Maharashtra (12,551 kg), Chhattisgarh (7,470 kg) and Andhra Pradesh (7,059 kg).

News sources also claim that CPI (Maoist) has joined ranks with ULFA and SIMI, and lesser known entities such as Hynniewtrep National Liberation Council of Meghalaya, Kanglei Yaol Kanba Lup of Manipur and Akhil Bharat Nepali Ekta Samaj, which though virtually unheard of, are considered deadly enough by the government to be designated as terrorist organisations.

The 'Red terror' spots have begun to pop up in India's capital and northern States' forest and hilly areas too. The Maoists seem interested in enlarging their area of influence outside the jungles of the 'Red Corridor' that run from the Nepal border down to Andhra Pradesh. Lately, they have begun targeting India's major cities by setting up urban bases with the object of penetrating and influencing policy makers, judiciary, media, civil liberty, human rights, cultural, Dalit, women and youth organisations. So far, the urban units are not indulging in violence. But who knows when they may start firing guns.

Documents seized from the CPI (Maoist) Politburo and Central Committee talk about the need to run a secret service and unleash psychological wars through effective networking of various friendly groups in the urban areas.

The 'Red Corridor' runs through the dense forest and tribal belt, from Nepal through Bihar, Jharkhand, Orissa, Chhattisgarh, Madhya Pradesh and all the way to Andhra Pradesh and to the upper reaches of Maharashtra, and some parts of Karnataka. Inside their corridor, the Naxalites run a parallel government and vow to continue their fight against the state a full-fledged war they call 'People's struggle'.

All the Left-wing militant organisations, including the Maoist Communist Centre (MCC) and the People's War Group (PWG), after their merger are now operating under the flagship rebel party—CPI (Maoist). The Central intelligence reports have also issued a warning that the Maoists are now in the process of identifying 'new operational areas' across the country. They are keenly looking at industrial belts, where big corporate houses are planning to set up the Special Economic Zones (SEZs), an easy target to launch violent agitation.

The Central Committee of the CPI (Maoist) has published a secret red book *Strategy and Tactics of the Indian Revolution*, which is said to be the Naxals' Bible. The book says: "The central task of the revolution is seizure of political power through protracted People's war." Talking about supporting sub-national movements in India, the book says: "Lakhs of enemy's armed troops have been deployed since long in J&K and the North-Eastern States. More and more nationalities may come into armed confrontation with the reactionary Indian State, so it will be difficult for the Indian ruling classes to mobilise all their armed forces against our revolutionary war." It further says the urban areas are one of the main sources which provide cadre and leadership having various types of capabilities essential for People's war.

UPA Response Lacks Resolve

The UPA government woke up too late to recognise the growing tentacles of red terror as a grave internal security challenge. But, effective action is still awaited as some UPA allies are still seen to be soft on this issue. The continuing inability of the government to counter effectively the spread of Maoists was once again demonstrated by the temporary control established by the CPI-Maoist and its front organisation in 17 villages spread across some 300 square kilometres in the Lalgarh area in West Bengal. What started as a protest movement against police excesses was transformed by the Maoists into a violent political movement.

Maoist-Missionary Alliance

It is India's long neglect to develop the tribal areas which has created large pockets of alienation against the government and these pockets have become the spawning ground of Maoist terrorism. The government has failed to take note of the genuine grievances of the tribals and deal with them in a sympathetic manner. A new dimension of Maoist-Missionary alliance was observed in Orissa that has added a religious angle to this problem. Also, Maoist terrorism cannot be effectively countered without ensuring development in the backward pockets of the country, but the government hasn't come out with any integrated and massive development package that will ensure speedy development of these regions and dissuade people from joining the ranks of Maoist insurgents. Strengthening rural policing is another issue where the government is totally silent leading to growing insecurity among the people. The failure to develop road and railway communication infrastructure in the backward areas has also allowed the spread of Maoist terrorism and government is just trying to tackle it as a law and order problem without going into the contributory factors.

Lopsided economic development, and urban-centric policies have further impoverished and marginalised the rural poor, a large number of whom are tribals and poor, whose lives revolve around the jungle and villages for livelihood. While mines were exploited in the mineral-rich backward states, the sons of the soil fueled the ranks of the poor in these regions. Poverty, illiteracy, unemployment, social backwardness prepared breeding grounds for Maoists who provided guns and armed the poor people and tribals with guns to fight the government and thereby execute their agenda.

Instead of working out an appropriate strategy which will address issues of lack of development, operational deficiencies and at the same time pay equal attention to the political handling of the problem, there has been an unwise tendency of inconsistency in government policy in dealing with this problem and aggressively pursuing a developmental agenda has not happened till now.

In May 2006, the Planning Commission appointed an expert committee headed by D Bandopadhyay, a retired IAS officer instrumental in dealing with the Naxalites in West Bengal in the 1970s. The expert committee has underscored the social, political, economic and cultural discrimination faced by the marginalised sections across the country as a key factor in drawing large number of discontented people towards the Naxalites. The Committee established the lack of empowerment of local communities as the main reason for the spread of the Naxal movement. The Committee in its report states that "We have two worlds of education, two worlds of health, two worlds of transport and two worlds of housing..." The expert committee delved deep into the new conflict zones of India, i.e. the mines and mineral rich areas, steel zones, as well as the SEZs. The report holds the faulty system of land acquisition and a non-existent R&R Policy largely responsible for the support enjoyed by the Naxalites. On the other hand, the committee makes a forceful plea for a policy and legal framework to enable small and marginal farmers to lease-in land with secure rights while landless poor occupying government land should not be treated as encroachers. Making a departure from the usual government position, the expert committee concludes that development paradigm pursued since independence has aggravated the prevailing discontent among large sections of society. For the first time in the history of the Naxal movement, a government-appointed committee has put the blame on the State for the growth of the movement.

Recently, the Home Minister of India said, "regrettably for many years we did not properly assess the threat posed by Left-wing extremism. We under-estimated the challenge and in the meanwhile they (Naxalites) extended their influence." This underscores the failure on the part of the government to read the challenge posed by the ultra Left forces leading to its proliferation. Alarmed by the apparent failure of the State machinery to tackle Naxalites, Union Home Minister P. Chidambaram admitted in the Parliament that the government had failed in curbing Naxal menace in the country. Speaking in Rajya Sabha, he said the government had failed in assessing the threat posed by the Maoists, adding it also failed to tackle them with the seriousness they deserved.

Regardless of these numerous failures, much can be done to solve the Naxalite problem, but is there the will? The 'will' not only in asking the police and military to fight the Naxalites and investing in security apparatus but also in perusing an aggressive development agenda to restore hope among the masses who have remained outside India's economic growth story and lead a Stone Age life. UPA Government's ambivalent approach towards dealing with Naxalism is likely to cost the country dear if the present drift in strategy continues. Dealing with Naxalism needs a holistic approach with development initiatives as an integral part of the government response.

(The writer is on the Editorial Board of Kamal Sandesh & Research Scholar at Delhi University)

□

Gou Gram Yatra
A move to save the cow

—A report by Vikash Anand

Keeping in view the importance of *Gou Mata* (cow) in our life in protecting the earth, Poojya Jagadguru Shankaracharya Shree Raghaveshwara Bharathi Swamiji of Shree Ramachandrapura Math launched *'Vishwa Mangala Gou Gram Yatra'* on 28th September 2009 which concluded on January 17, 2010. The Yatra has covered more than 5 lakhs villages, 80 metropolitan cities and approximately more than a thousand cities. The Yatra has attracted people from different walks of life like saints, scientists, politicians, film actors farmers, in large numbers. Making human life meaningful is the purpose of this movement.

Our nation is a country of villages. Life in villages is mainly based on agriculture. In turn, agriculture largely depends on the cow and bull. The bull is given a place of pride in our culture and national heritage. The holy *'Gou Mata'* is a source of both food and economy. She is the centre of ayurveda, environment, Indian economy, culture and agriculture.

Neglect of villages and cows has produced ill effects on earth, environment and health of living beings. Due to this, our culture, agriculture and economic condition suffer. Due to the failure of crops, farmers are committing suicide. Our religions, culture as well as constitution do not sanction the killing of cows and other animals. In fact, the cow protection issues provided a platform for the Indian freedom struggle. During that time, all freedom fighters assured that 'after getting freedom, there will be no more cow slaughter in the nation'. But even today, cow slaughter is going on unabated. To stop cow slaughter and make people aware about the importance of cow the 'Vishwa Mangala Gou Gram Yatra' was launched.

The following points reflect importance of Cow in our life

Environment and Cow

Being part of farming, food, medicine, and industry, cow also contributes to the health of environment :

- Ancient scriptures state that "*Suryaketu*" nerve on cow's back absorbs harmful radiation and cleanses atmosphere. Mere presence of cows is a great contribution to environment.
- India has approximately 30 crore cattle. Using their dung to produce bio-gas, we can save 6.0 crore ton of firewood every year. This would arrest deforestation to that extent.
- Cow dung has an important role in preserving the environment.
- When we burn cow dung, it balances atmospheric temperature and kills germs in the air.
- Cow dung has antiseptic, anti-radioactive and anti- thermal properties. When we coat the walls and clean the floors of house with cow dung, it protects the dwellers. In 1984, the gas leak in Bhopal killed more than 20,000 people. Those living in houses with cow dung coated walls were not affected. Atomic power centres in India and Russia even today use cow dung to shield radiation.
- African deserts were made fertile using cow dung.
- We can reduce acid content in water by treating it with cow dung.
- When we offer ghee in fire as part of ritualistic sacrifices, it strengthens the ozone layer and shields the earth from harmful radiations of Sun.
- A relationship between increasing number of butcher houses and earthquakes is being proven.

Agriculture and cow

Joys of Cow Based Farming

Indian agriculture has variety. There is no farm-product that we don't cultivate. Our land grows all kinds of grains, pulses, vegetables, fruits, flowers, cotton and silk.

About 70% of our population has embraced agriculture as profession. Majority of them are small farmers, owning one or two acres of land.

Our agricultural landscape is diverse and vivid — in land topology, soil type and quality, irrigation method and frequency of harvesting.

Cattle are an integral part of this huge canvas of agriculture. We use oxen to plough, to pick and move harvested crops, in irrigation; cow manure as fertiliser, and cow urine as insecticide.

Unique Role of Cow in Agriculture:

- In our country with small holdings and small scale farming, there is no better alternative to employing cattle in farming.
- While ploughing, the oxen stride with gentle gait, not harming the surface of the earth, unlike tractors.
- Even as they plough the land, the oxen defecate and urinate, fertilising the land.
- Cattle manure, organic manure, green leaf manure, earth-worms, and slurry manure with cattle manure bond with nature and make the land fertile. They do not create the challenge of chemical waste.
- 99% of the insects in nature are beneficial to the system. Insecticides prepared from cow urine or well fermented butter milk do not affect these helpful insects.
- Dung from one cow is adequate to fertilise 5 acres of land and its urine can protect 10 acres of crop from insects.
- Cow dung produced by one oxen can support a family for 4 years.
- Oxen do not pollute the atmosphere.

Food and Cow

A mother nursing her infant depends on cow's milk for her own nourishment. A mother feeds her child for a year or two; then cow is the lifelong refuge for us all. Cow feeds its own calf and spares plenty for us too.

Uses of cow products:

- Different popular beverages like coffee, tea, etc require milk as an important ingredient.

- Scores of sweet dishes are milk based.
- Curd, butter, and ghee are an essential part of Indian meal. Taste of items deep fried in ghee is unmatched.
- Butter milk quenches thirst in addition to being a base for many popular dishes in our cooking.

Medicine and Cow

World Health Organisation (WHO) defines health as a combination of physical, mental, spiritual and social wholeness. WHO has also predicted that bacteria will become immune to antibiotics by the year 2020. That does not scare us! We can depend on *Panchagavya* – milk, curd, ghee, cow urine and cow dung. These have excellent medical qualities individually as well as a concoction, without any adverse side-effect. In addition, if we are already under some other medication, consumption of *panchagavya* acts as a catalyst.

Ancient books on Ayurveda state that consumption of cow urine increases resistance to diseases.

Health from Panchagavya:

Milk: *Charaka Samhita* states, "Milk is the best life strengthener." While Casein protein in milk helps growth of infants; calcium and sulphur strengthen our bones. Milk is also rich in vitamins D and B-complex.

- Curd arrests diarrhoea, controls fat, and resists cancer.
- Ghee improves intelligence and beauty. It is used to treat eye diseases.
- Distilled cow urine is an effective in treatment of flu, arthritis, bacterial diseases, food poisoning, indigestion, oedema, and leprosy.

Panchagavya Mix: Various medical formulations like *Panchagavya Ghrita, Amritasara, Ghanavati, Ksharavati, Netrasara* etc are invaluable medicines in Ayurvedic system.

Industry and Cow

Milk and milk products from cow are used in preparing wholesome dishes and food products. Cow products are effective in treatment of cancer, hypertension, diabetes, heart diseases, neurological problems, psychological problems, skin diseases, ENT problems, fever, cold, hair loss, etc. They can also be used in cosmetic products like soap, shampoo and beauty aids. They help in farming and provide manure and insecticides. We can get cooking gas and electricity from cow dung.

Cow Industry is Practical

- India leads the world in milk production. In 1998-99, India produced 7.5 crore ton milk. 70% of this produce is from small farmers.
- South India has more than 75,000 gobar gas installations, achieved by the SKG Society of Kolar.
- A scientist named Bug Jones established Inland Energy Corporation in California. They collect 1500 ton cow dung a day from the neighbourhood and produce 50 MW of electricity.
- Gujarat State Government purchases cow urine at Rs. 3 per kg and cow dung at Rs. 2 per kg.

Battlefield and Cow

Apart from responding to our daily needs, cows have fought for us in battlefields!

Recorded Battles :

- When Hyder Ali was ruling the Mysore State, the Nizam of Hyderabad attacked Chitradurga Fort. Hyder Ali had a fleet of *Amrit Mahal* oxen in his army! He tied burning torches to the horns of 237 of these oxen and let them attack Nizam's army, resulting in the defeat of 3,000- strong attacking army.
- Captain Javinson had *Amrit Mahal* oxen in his brigade in Afghanistan. As recorded by him, when his troop travelled in narrow valleys of Teri hills in 1842, the oxen were cheerful even after pulling the carts for 16 continuous hours.
- Commanding Officer Wellesley credits the *Amrit Mahal* oxen for his victory over Napoleon in Peninsular War.
- *Amrit Mahal* oxen were part of the troop deployed in Mesopotamia in the First Word War (1914-1918). They surprised the people by walking faster than camels, crossing narrow valleys and bridges with tact, adapting to adverse weather conditions and fighting with even reduced feed.

Religious Rituals and Cow

Our culture has retained a strong relationship between cows and temples.

- Cow is accepted as divine.
- Day dawns with worship of cow.
- Worship and feeding of cow is part of daily rituals.
- Cow has precedence in festivals at home.
- There are several festivals where cow is prominent.
- Many temples have cow sheds at the entrance, enhancing the divine feelings.
- Traditionally we have used *Panchagavya* to cleanse and purify.
- God's idols are washed with milk, curd and ghee.
- For lighting holy lamp we use ghee. We also give offering of ghee to deities.
- Preparation of various offerings to God use ghee and milk.
- Butter is used in decorating deities.

The reduction in the number of cows is creating new problems for environment and is harming nature. It has now been established that cow's breath has power to destroy bacteria of dangerous diseases. The declining population of cows is only spreading the bacteria of diseases in the environment. If we want to save the earth, then we should protect the cow and multiply its progeny. It is in the interest of all, irrespective of caste and creed.

(The writer is on the Editorial Board of the Kamal Sandesh)

□

The song that rattled the British

—Brig Chitranjan Sawant, VSM

Vande Mataram had indeed worked like a *Ved mantra*. This is what the author and poet, Bankim Chandra Chattopadhyaya had prophesied in answer to the criticism that the words used in the song were too difficult to pronounce. He said to his critics "I may not live to see its popularity, but this song will be sung by every Indian like a *Ved mantra*". How true his words were. The history of the Indian freedom struggle bears a testimony to it. *Vande Mataram* has spontaneity and emotional appeal to arouse patriotism even in a slavish heart. The song has the capability to transcend barriers of caste, creed, region and religion. It was sung with gusto by patriotic Indians throughout the length and breadth of Bharat. When the song was sung, with the fading notes of the last stanza, the emotionally surcharged crowd of men and women would raise the slogan : *Bharat Mata Ki Jai*. The sound and the echo shook the mighty British Empire to its foundation.

Bankim babu wrote *Vande Mataram* in one sitting in his native village, Naihati, just a few miles away from the metropolis, Calcutta. It was *Akshay Naomi* which fell on a Sunday on 7th November 1875 and Bankim babu, a Deputy Collector of the British Raj was relaxing in his ancestral home. His mind and heart were in turmoil. The English masters were forcing their own national anthem, "God Save the Queen", down the throat of all Indians. Bankim Babu felt the divine inspiration and words came pouring out of his heart and on to his pen. An immortal song, *Vande Mataram,* stood composed. It was seven years later that *Vande Mataram* was incorporated in the famous novel of the author, *Anand Math*, dealing with the history of the Sanyasi uprising in Dacca, North Bengal and other places from 1763 to 1780. The *Dharm Yudh* was against the foreign domination. The English and their collaborators were targeted. The saints uprising has inspired the youth of Bengal ever since. Indeed, it was a never fading source of inspiration for the patriots all over Bharat.

No less a person than Gurudev Rabindra Nath Tagore lent his voice to *Vande Mataram* when he sang it in the session of the Indian National Congress in Calcutta in 1896. It was a stirring moment, although the tempo was rather slow compared to that of the rendering of *Vande Mataram* by Lata Mangeshkar in the movie, Anand Math. Nevertheless, *Vande Mataram* had come out of the rural landscape to play its all-important role on the national stage. Bengal loved the song and the rest of India was not far behind. *Vande Mataram* was sung in many tunes, in many languages by many men and women voluntarily. North, South, East and West of India were equally involved.

1905 was the high noon of the national fervour that *Vande Mataram* generated. Lord Curzon, the then Viceroy, passed a decree dividing Bengal into two parts, East and West. The British are at their best when they play the game called, Divide and Rule. However, it was rather unfortunate for the rulers that the *Bang Bhang* united India as a whole. Men and women of all faiths walked the streets of towns and talukas of Bengal singing *Vande Mataram* with religious fervour. It was a sight to be seen to be believed. The decree of Curzon was rescinded. But the British were back to their game of dividing the united people. They made some elements believe that singing *Vande Mataram* was a sign of Hindu domination. Their trick worked. The bogey of religion took its toll. The Muslim League was born. No one was happier than the British masters.

The Indian National Congress, at its Varanasi session, adopted *Vande Mataram* as the national song on 7th September 1905. The cohesive spirit that the song generated could not be lost sight of by the national leaders. The momentous decision was taken unanimously a century ago. Since then the national song is sung at all sessions not only of the Congress but also the Bharatiya Janata Party and some others. It is sung in the closing session of Parliament too. Truly national in word and deed.

Vande Mataram has all along been a song of patriotism and unification. Gandhi and Jinnah sang it together on the Congress platform till the latter quit the Congress as he was a non-believer in the principle of *Swaraj*. Of course, Maulana Abul Kalam Azad and Shri Purushottam Das Tandon, born rivals, were in the forefront in singing *Vande Mataram* at the beginning of the session everywhere. Rafi Ahmad Kidwai, out and out a nationalist, never had a second thought about singing *Vande Mataram*.

Nevertheless, the divisive forces were working overtime at the behest of their British masters to upset the applecart. How sad, the mischief mongers had their way! The rest is history. Is history repeating itself ? Time alone will tell.

Singing *Vande Mataram* the Indian people had waged the war of independence non-violently. The song was all along the National Anthem to the rank and file of freedom fighters. A committee comprising Nehru, Azad, Subhas Bose and Narendra Dev had said that the first two stanzas of the song had no reference to any religion and should be our anthem. It came as a rude shock when the controversial decision to make *Jana Gana Mana* the national anthem was announced on 24th January 1950.

However, the words of Dr Rajendra Prasad, President of the Constituent Assembly, came as a soothing balm. He said, "...the song *Vande Mataram*, which has played a historic part in the struggle for Indian freedom, shall be honoured equally with *Jana Gana Mana* and shall have equal status with it."

Taking a look at the English translation of *Vande Mataram*, done by Shri Aurobindo, one may safely surmise that the storm in a tea cup brewing at the behest of separatists will blow away and patriotism will prevail.

Indeed the original song in Bangla with a rich dose of Sanskrit words is soul stirring. Although the British government in India had banned the national song *Vande Mataram*, it surfaced and resurfaced. The British failed in suppressing the spirit of independence. The Indians won their freedom. Let us now all sing in unison the song of the People.

(The writer, a retd Army Officer,
has been electronic media commentator on
Republic Day parade and other
National events for 36 years)

□□□